IMAGES
of America

NORTH CONWAY

On the Cover: The North Conway train station has been the hub of North Conway village for over 100 years. The well-dressed excursion party in the foreground anticipates a major shift—from steam engine to automobile—in the methods tourists and visitors will use to enter and explore the region. (Henney History Room, Conway Public Library.)

IMAGES
of America

NORTH CONWAY

Bob Cottrell

ARCADIA
PUBLISHING

ISBN 978-0-7385-9263-3

Published by Arcadia Publishing
Charleston, South Carolina

Printed in the United States of America

Library of Congress Control Number: 2011946007

For all general information, please contact Arcadia Publishing:
Telephone 843-853-2070
Fax 843-853-0044
E-mail sales@arcadiapublishing.com
For customer service and orders:
Toll-Free 1-888-313-2665

Visit us on the Internet at www.arcadiapublishing.com

Dedicated to my wife, Debbie, for her love, patience, and understanding

Contents

ACKNOWLEDGMENTS

Numerous historical photographs have lost their original context, even the name of the photographer and the date taken. While we are not always able to connect a specific photographer or studio to a specific image, I would like to acknowledge as complete a list as possible of North Conway photographers: James M. Bray, L. Leslie Buck, Bob Duncan, Gordon Holland, James Hunting, Dr. Leo Kann (Duck's Head Studio), Bob Knapp, J. Lazarus, Harold Orne, Nathan W. Pease, Mike Roberts, Guy Shorey, Don Sieburg, Dick Smith, Richard G. Smith, Frank W. Swallow, Noel Wellman, Gabriella F. Eddy White, Thomas Edward Mulliken White, and H.C. Williams.

I would also like to acknowledge the many historians, collectors, curators, and librarians on whose foundation I have built this book, including Jim Arnold, Conway Historical Society; Roger E. Belson, the White Mountain Art website; Racheal Brown, the *Mountainear*; Jill Burrows, Memorial Hospital; Mark Butterfield; John Cannell and family; Ann Cullinan; Benjamin Durgin Eastman; David Eastman; Tom Eastman, the *Conway Daily Sun*; David Emerson; Amy Gardner; John J. Henderson; Keith and Nella Braddy Henney; Janet McAllister Hounsell; Ruth Burnham Davis Horne; Robert Kennett; David Lazar, the *New Hampshire Troubadour*; Jeff Leisch, the New England Ski Museum; Barbara S. Lucy; Margaret and Sut Marshall; Ellen McRoberts Mason; Andrea Masters, the North Conway Library; Georgia Drew Merrill; Olga Morrell; Helen Elizabeth Nute; Dan Noel; Betty Parker; Richard M. Plusch; Frances Woodard Richardson; Rick Russack, the White Mountain History website; Carol Saunders and family; Frances Shaine; and Ed Stevens. I would also like to thank the generous staff and volunteers at the American Antiquarian Society in Worcester, Massachusetts, the Mount Washington Valley Chamber of Commerce, and the New Hampshire Historical Society in Concord. I am indebted to Tara Thomas, director of the Conway Public Library, for bringing this project to my attention and encouraging me in the development of the book. Significant direct help was provided by volunteer scanners Lorena Hoyt, the principal of Relative Echoes Genealogy and Historical Research Consultants, as well as Doug Sommerville and Debbie Cottrell. Any errors or omissions are my own.

INTRODUCTION

How does one define a place? North Conway lies within the well-delineated boundaries of the town of Conway, granted in 1765. Many locals would list Bowling Alley Hill as the southern boundary of North Conway village; others would place it, as I do, at the Saco Valley Overlook. We all pretty much agree that the northern boundary is the town line of Bartlett at Hurricane Mountain Road, about five miles north of the Saco Valley Overlook.

North Conway runs east from the Moat Mountains through the valley of the Saco about two miles toward the Green Mountains. As he was entering the area in July 1858, Henry David Thoreau exclaimed, "The Scenery in Conway and onward to North Conway is surprisingly grand. You are steadily advancing into an amphitheatre of mountains." The artist Benjamin Champney, who coincidently was born in 1817, the same year as Thoreau, bought a house and added a studio in North Conway in 1853 and was central to the development of the so-called White Mountain School of Art. Over the years, Champney continued to paint that "amphitheatre of mountains."

This book is written in a geographical format so the reader can follow in the footsteps of artists, explorers, settlers, and tourists while exploring North Conway's history. Just an hour from Portland, Maine, and an easy two-hour drive from Boston, North Conway has attracted visitors for many years. Promoters have referred to the area as the Eastern Slope and the Mount Washington Valley. Whatever terms and bounds one uses, North Conway is a great place to live and has been home to several notable residents, including coach Ed Ashnault, actors Gordon Clapp and John Shea, and Julia Ruth Stevens, the daughter of Babe Ruth.

Nothing is constant but change, and North Conway has changed in many ways. Recently, it has experienced a renaissance of new activities and become a major center for rock and ice climbing. There are zip lines, canopy walks, and several new water parks. The three-dimensional stereoscope views of the Victorian Parlor have been replaced by the three-dimensional movie and television technology of today. While the year-round population is around 2,500, this small place has a big history.

One

The Heart of North Conway

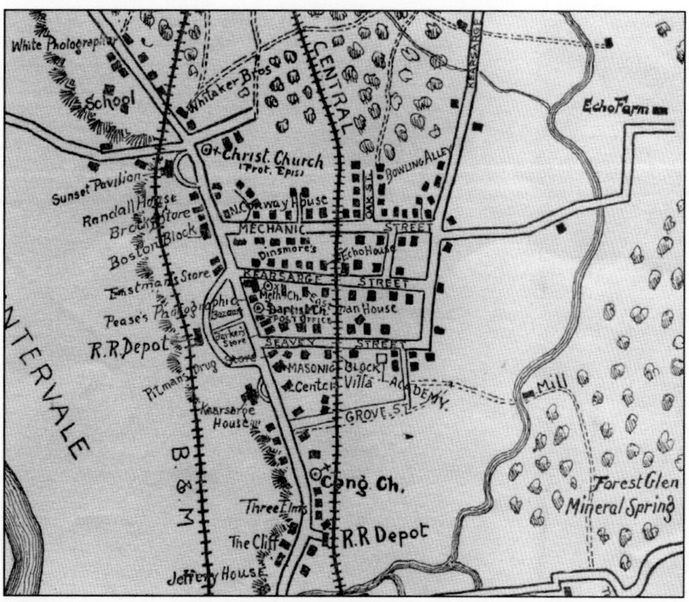

This c. 1900 map of downtown North Conway shows five east-to-west streets running about one-third of a mile at their widest. The two north-to-south streets run about a half mile. Two railroad lines served the town: the Boston & Maine (B&M) and Maine Central (Central). Key buildings have included the railroad depots, the post office, numerous hotels and stores, bowling alleys, churches, a school, and the Masonic Lodge. (Conway Historical Society.)

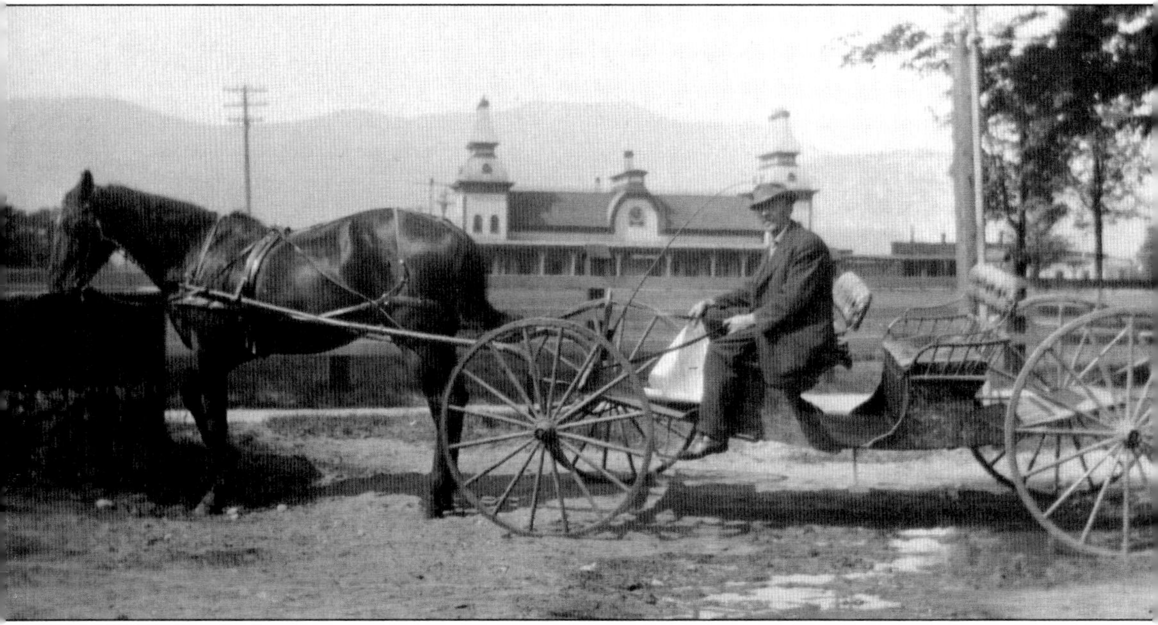

In this c. 1920 photograph, Levi Julian Ricker poses in front of the North Conway train station with the horse-and-buckboard wagon he used to carry the mail from the train to the post office. The horse stands near one of several watering troughs spread out through town. Ricker was the proprietor of the nearby Kearsarge Hall, not to be confused with the larger Kearsarge House Hotel. A variety of horse-drawn conveniences were available for guests to visit area attractions. A guidebook published by the Boston and Maine Railroad in 1887 reported, "Our first excursion was the regulation drive 'around the Ledges' in one of the trim black buckboards that go kiting over Conway's hills from May to October. There are single buggies and landaus, phaetons and waggonettes, carryals and gigs, Concord coaches and mountain wagons; but the buckboard has the most fresh air, exercise, and gayety to the mile in it—and we choose it every time." Buckboards also provided a form of comfort and suspension on the rutted dirt roads. (Conway Historical Society.)

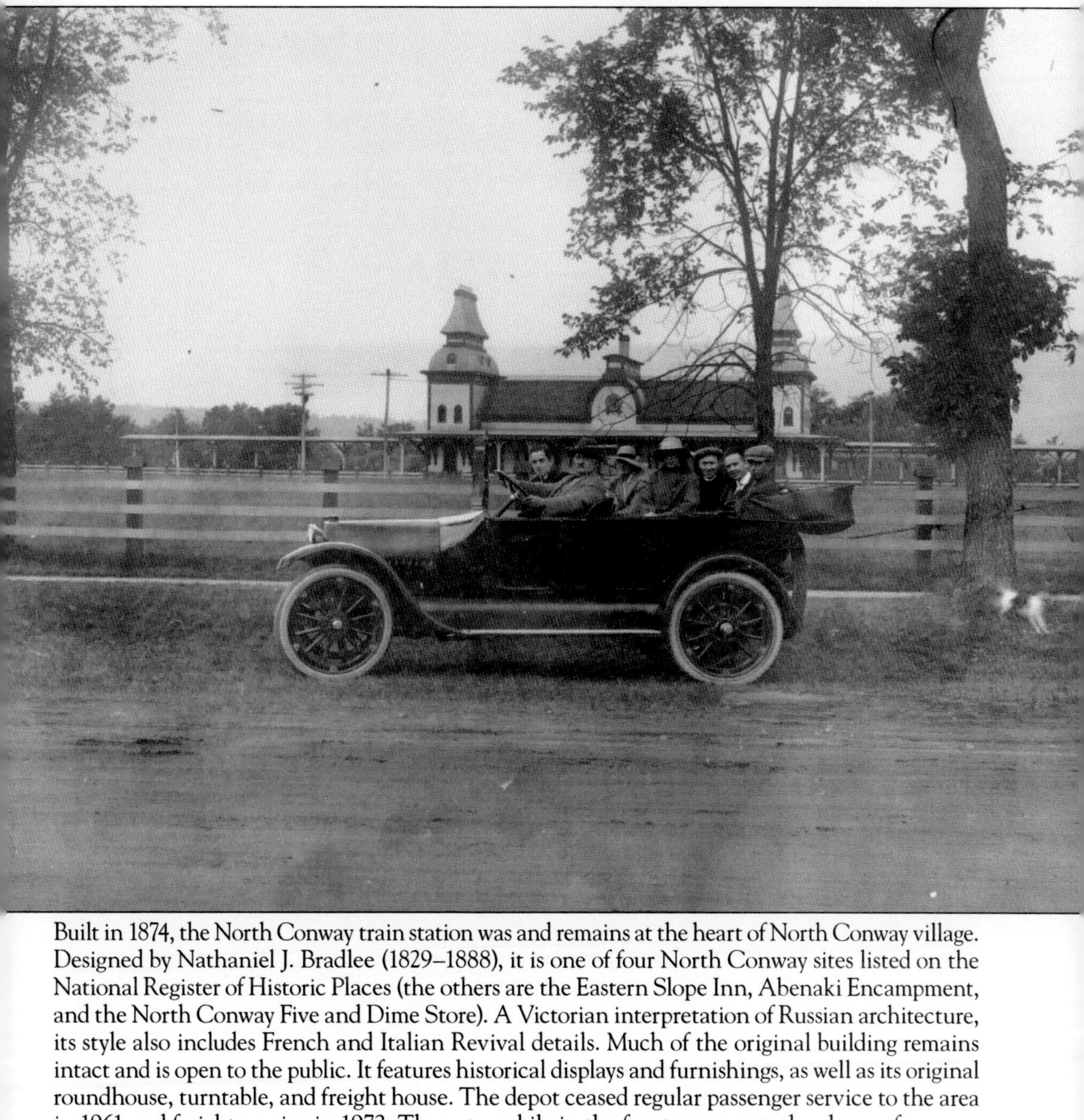

Built in 1874, the North Conway train station was and remains at the heart of North Conway village. Designed by Nathaniel J. Bradlee (1829–1888), it is one of four North Conway sites listed on the National Register of Historic Places (the others are the Eastern Slope Inn, Abenaki Encampment, and the North Conway Five and Dime Store). A Victorian interpretation of Russian architecture, its style also includes French and Italian Revival details. Much of the original building remains intact and is open to the public. It features historical displays and furnishings, as well as its original roundhouse, turntable, and freight house. The depot ceased regular passenger service to the area in 1961 and freight service in 1972. The automobile in the front represents the change from one transportation technology to another, from horse and wagon to steam train to diesel train to automobile. Over time, North Conway has embraced change while cherishing its traditions and history. The train station is now home to the Conway Scenic Railroad, which runs a number of excursions in the area and special events, such as the Polar Express (based on the book of the same title) and Day out with Thomas (based on the popular children's television show starring Thomas the Tank Engine). (Henney History Room, Conway Public Library.)

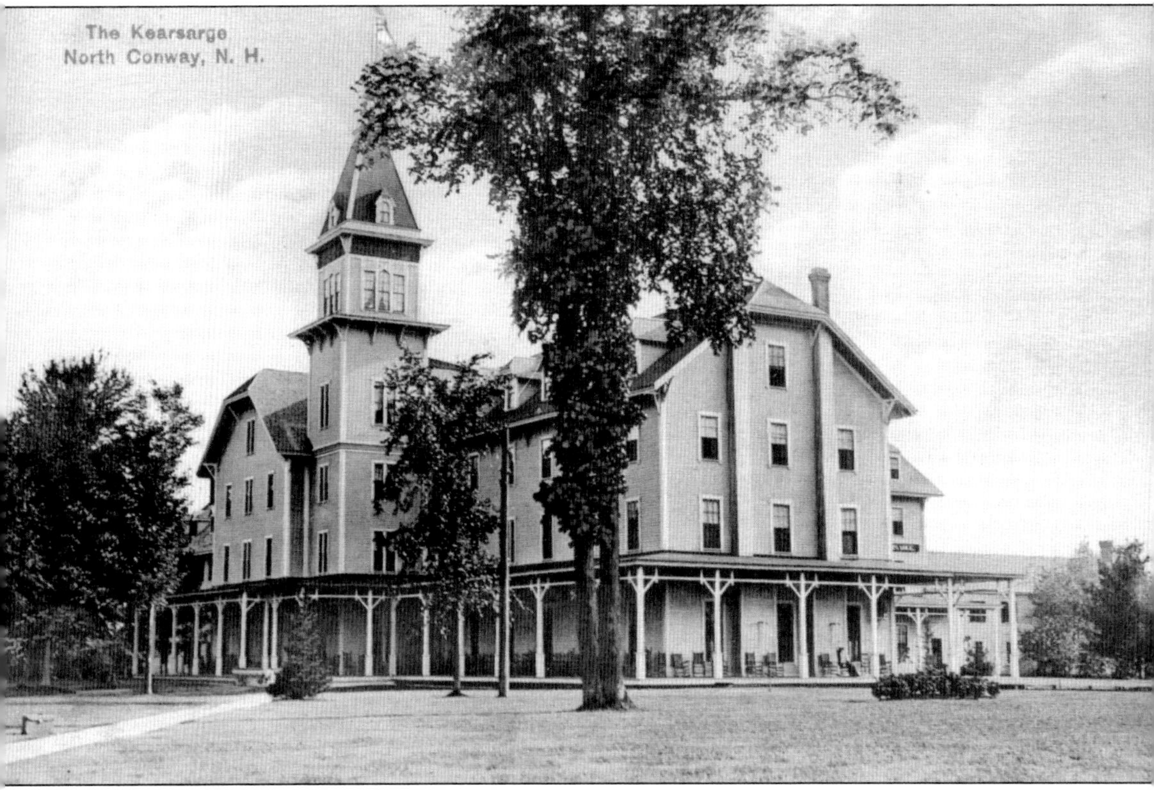

Situated just southeast of the train station, a farmhouse became the Kearsarge Tavern (then spelled "Kiarsarge") as early as 1860. It was expanded four times to become the largest downtown hotel, offering accommodations for 300 guests. Nearly encircled by a wide veranda furnished with rocking chairs, the hotel offered numerous places to see and be seen. One advertisement celebrated its location on a high ledge overlooking the wide floodplain of the Saco River as a spot with "positively no hay fever." Like many hotels of the era heated by wood and later coal, it burned down in 1917. The hotel was connected to the depot by a raised wooden boardwalk, which can be seen leading off on the right through a line of evenly spaced shade trees. The boardwalk made it easier for guests to walk to and fro and for baggage wagons to be rolled to the hotel. The Kearsarge was owned and managed early on by North Conway hotel men S.W. and S.D. Thompson. (Henney History Room, Conway Public Library.)

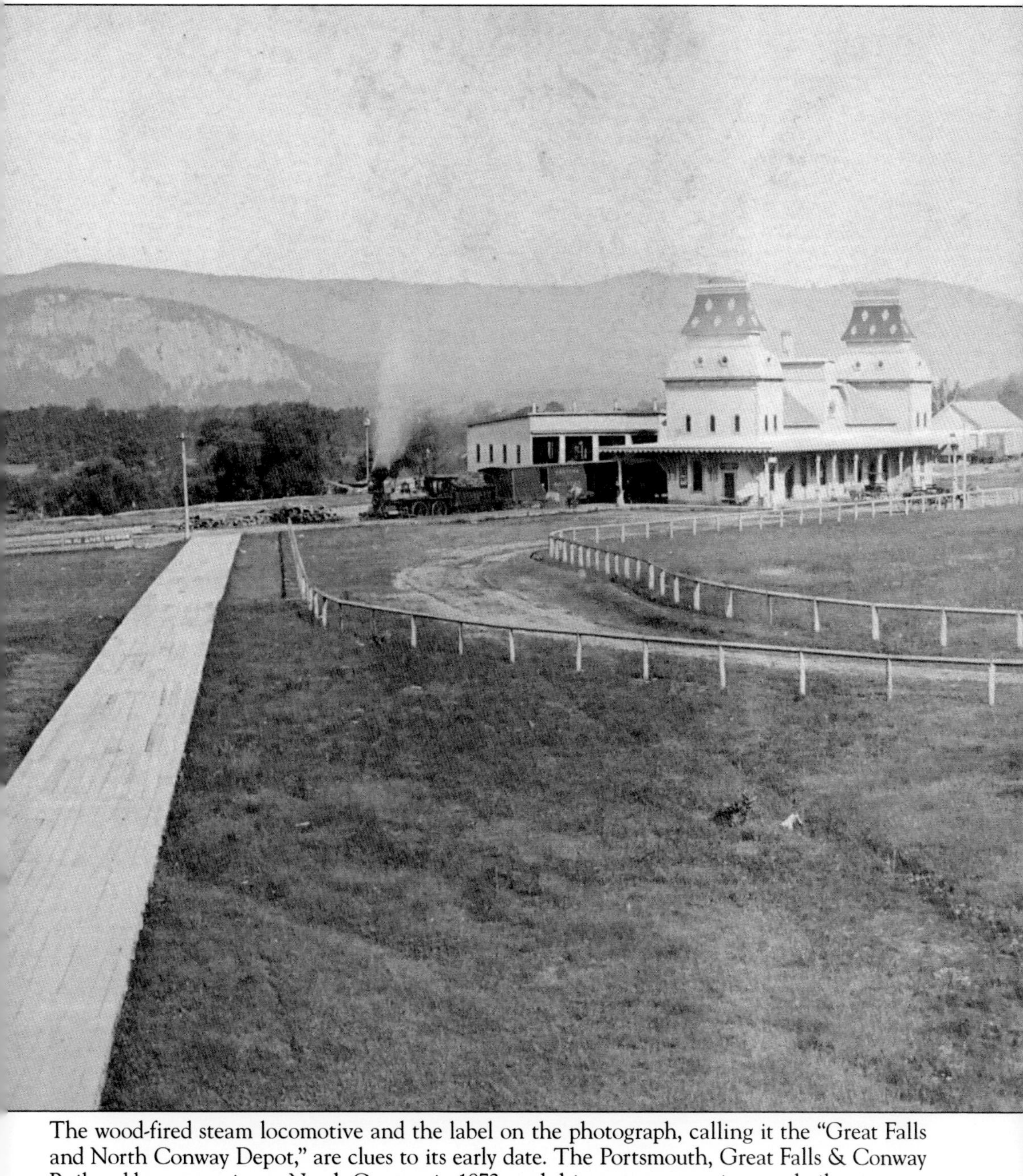

The wood-fired steam locomotive and the label on the photograph, calling it the "Great Falls and North Conway Depot," are clues to its early date. The Portsmouth, Great Falls & Conway Railroad began service to North Conway in 1872, and this passenger station was built two years later. Described in its Historic Landmark nomination form as "one of the best and rarest examples in the United States of its style and building type," the depot "is one of the most outstanding groups of early railroad service buildings surviving in New England. Little modified and still serving many of their original purposes, these buildings are rare documents of nineteenth-century American railroading." The 30-foot-by-100-foot station originally contained separate waiting rooms for men and women as propriety demanded at the time. (Conway Historical Society, photograph by Nathan W. Pease.)

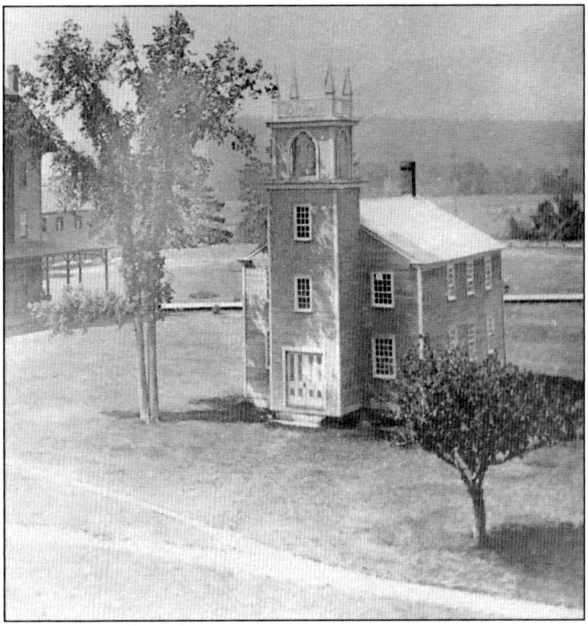

With its distinctive four-pronged tower, the old Academy building is useful in identifying North Conway in White Mountain art. Organized in 1828, the Academy continued until the building was torn down in either 1874 or, as some sources say, 1885. It is now the site of the community center. The newly planted trees along the boardwalk in the background have been traced in photographs through the years, and a few still remain. (Henney History Room, Conway Public Library.)

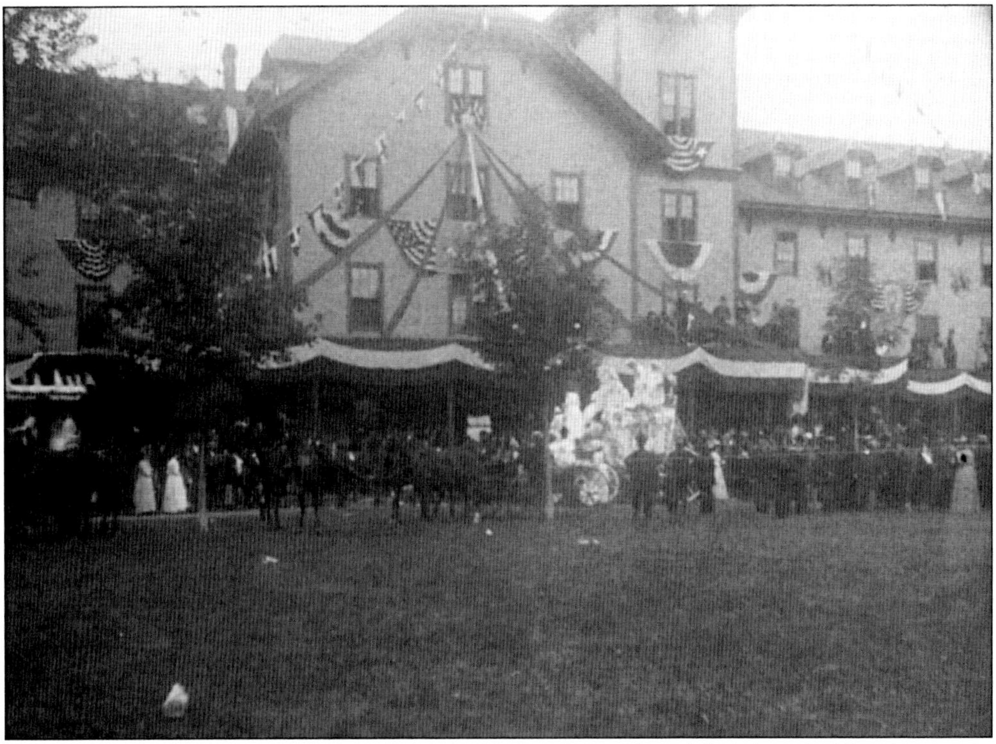

Coaching parades were a highlight of the tourist season, and each hotel worked hard to outdo the others in this annual competition. Flags, streamers, flowers, and ribbons were used to make creative interpretations of grand, or sometimes frivolous, themes. Accompanied by house bands and orchestras, the processions were cheered on by guests and residents alike. People climbed through their windows onto their roofs for a better view. (Henney History Room, Conway Public Library.)

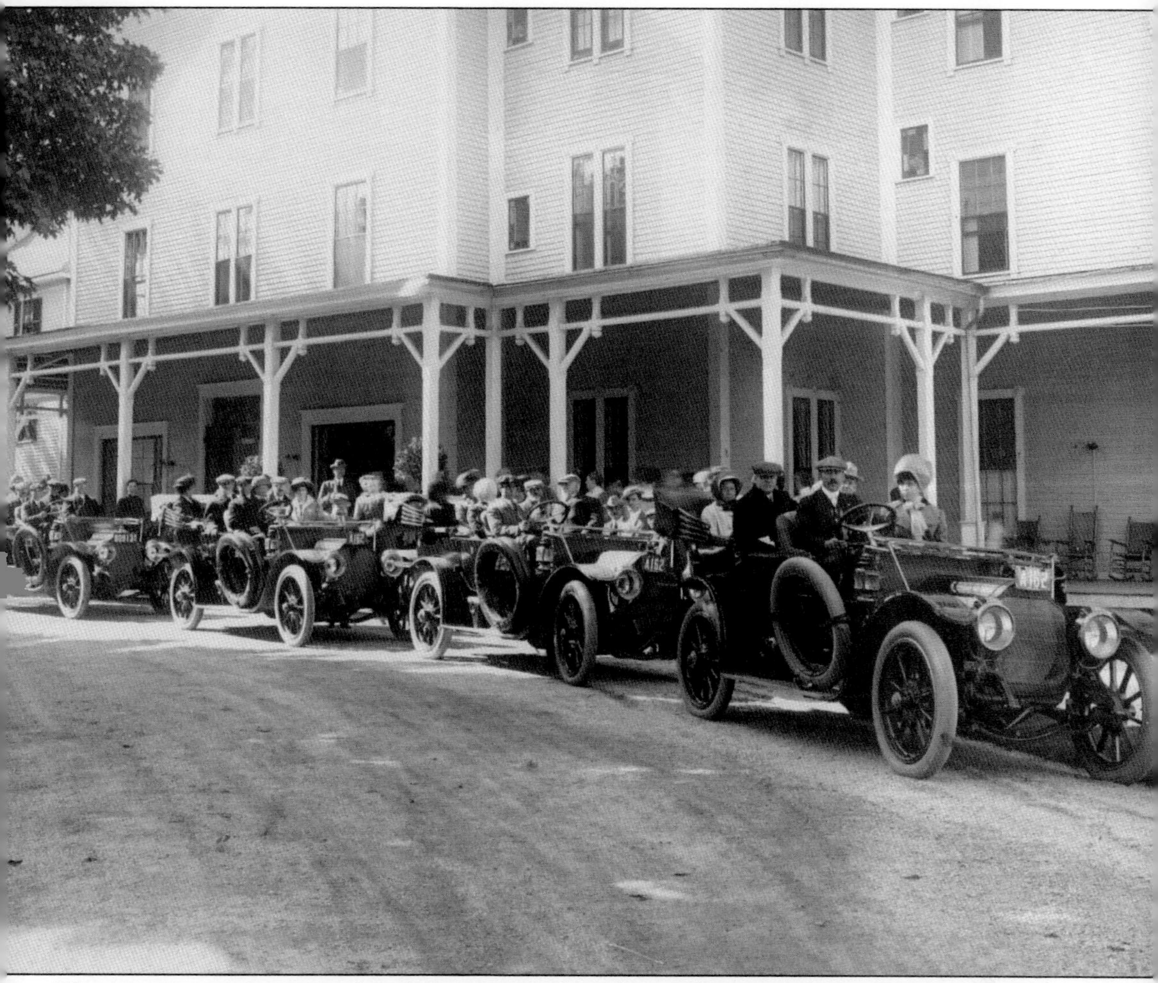

These open touring cars replaced the armies of coaches and wagons that transported earlier generations of visitors. Fashion and style were important components of these outings, as evidenced by the high polish of the cars, as well as the bonnets, caps, frocks, ribbons, bows, and high starched collars of the group. The rich automobile heritage of the early 20th century is carried on today by the ongoing Glidden Tour and reunions of Stanley Steamer drivers Model T Ford clubs, including their antique snowmobile variety, and Harley Davidson aficionados who converge frequently upon the Mount Washington Valley. (Henney History Room, Conway Public Library.)

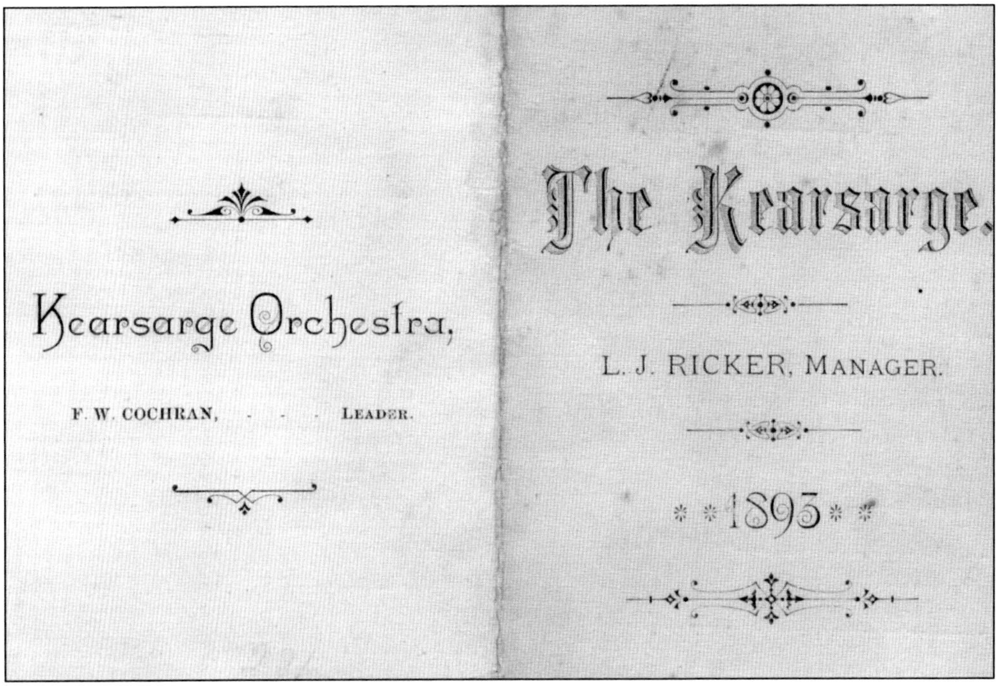

Kearsarge Orchestra,

F. W. COCHRAN, - - - LEADER.

The Kearsarge.

L. J. RICKER, MANAGER.

1893

In 1893, the Kearsarge Orchestra, led by F.W. Cochran, performed a series of 10 dances with the option for "extras." Dance cards were printed and issued to ladies for gentlemen to reserve their spot on the agenda. In this case, three gentlemen were awarded two dances each and one garnered the extra spot, leaving three dances for rest and refreshments depending on what the check mark on the Schottische refers to. These cards could be retained as romantic reminders of an evening's entertainment and are coveted today by collectors as mementos of a more gracious time. (Both, Henney History Room, Conway Public Library.)

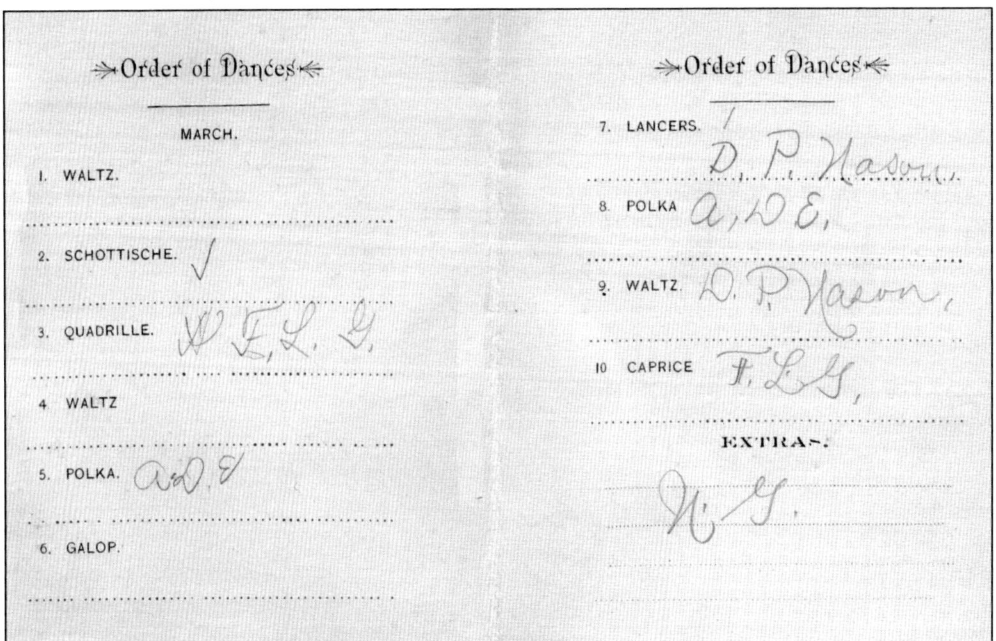

Order of Dances

MARCH.

1. WALTZ.

2. SCHOTTISCHE. √

3. QUADRILLE. W. F. L. G.

4. WALTZ

5. POLKA. A. D. E.

6. GALOP.

Order of Dances

7. LANCERS. D. P. Mason.

8. POLKA A. D. E.

9. WALTZ. D. P. Mason.

10 CAPRICE F. L. G.

EXTRAS.

W. G.

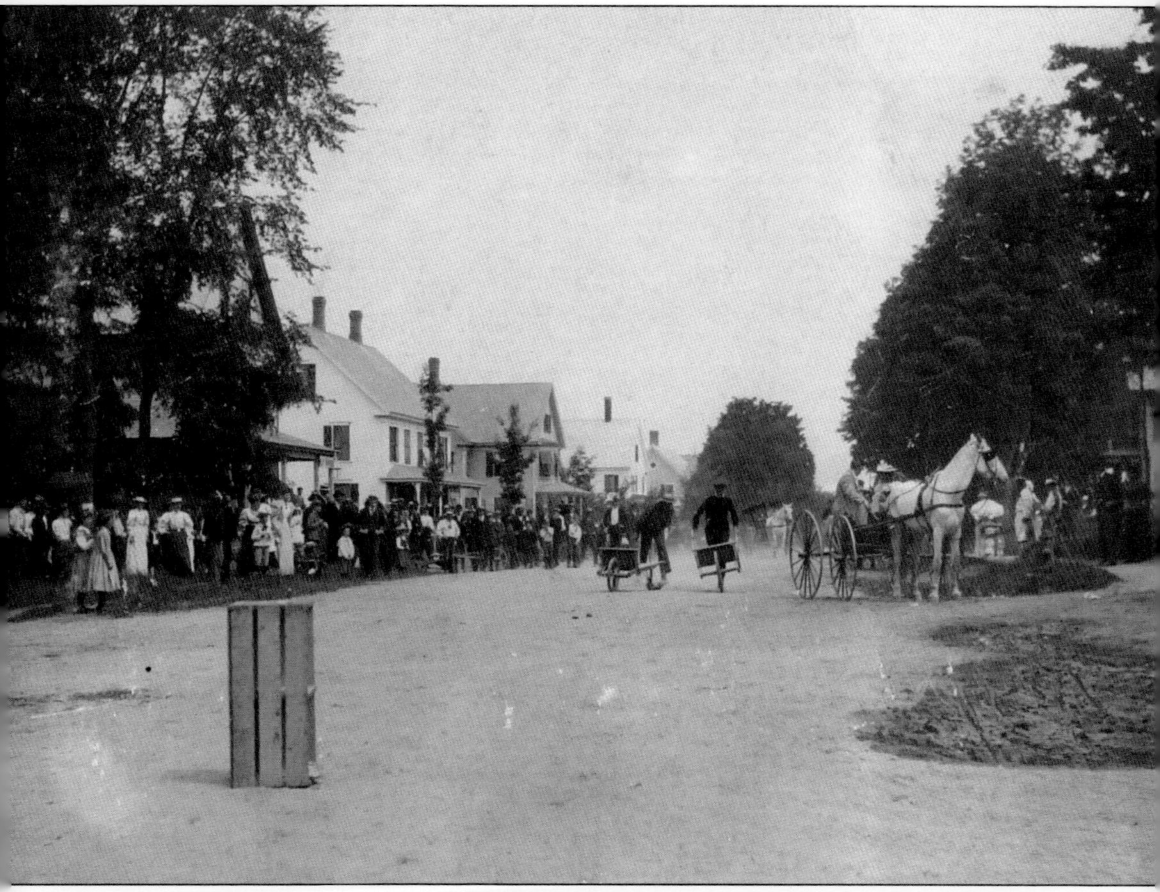

A more hardy style of recreation were wheelbarrow races, just one of many activities available to folks before the days of radio, television, and video games. All it took was a packing crate in the middle of the road and a few willing competitors with wheelbarrows. A sign on the building to the left reads, "Meat Market." Several other wheelbarrows and drivers to the right wait for their turn. On the opposite side of the road, a woman pushing a baby carriage can be seen under the horse's nose. (Henney History Room, Conway Public Library.)

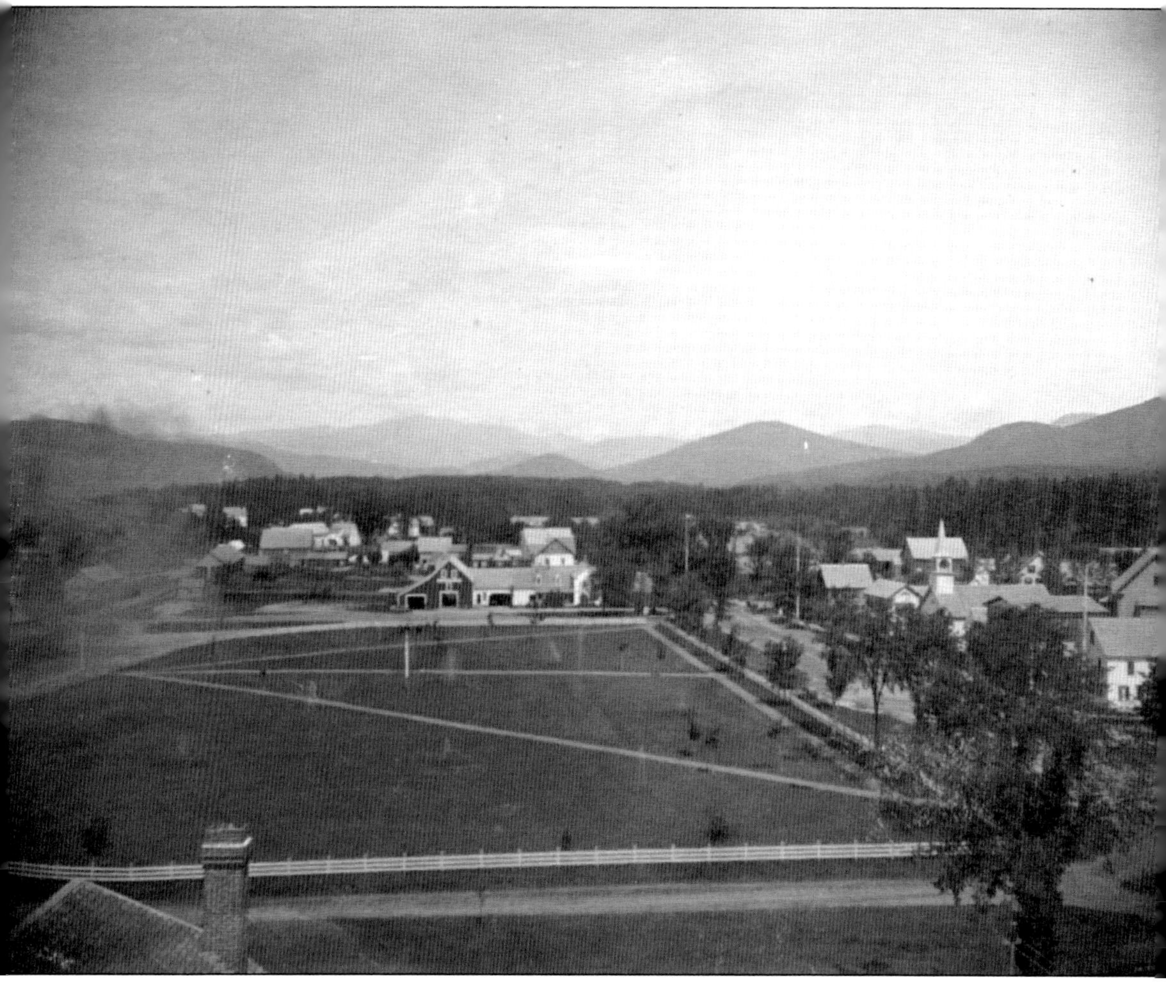

Railroad Park, now called Schouler Park, is seen here from the tower of the Kearsarge Hotel. On the right is the steeple of the First Baptist Church, which is still in the same location. Several other buildings also remain, allowing the village to keep its original look and charm. Beyond the village setting, the vast panorama of mountains to the north includes, from left to right, Humphrey's Ledge, Mount Washington, Pear Mountain, Thorn Hill, Thorn Mountain, and the foothills of Mount Kearsarge. The park was purchased by the town in 1924 and in 1961 was renamed Schouler (pronounced as "schooler") in honor of a local doctor, James Schouler. The space has been used for baseball, football, ice skating, concerts, art shows, and the annual Bark in the Park dog festival. (Henney History Room, Conway Public Library.)

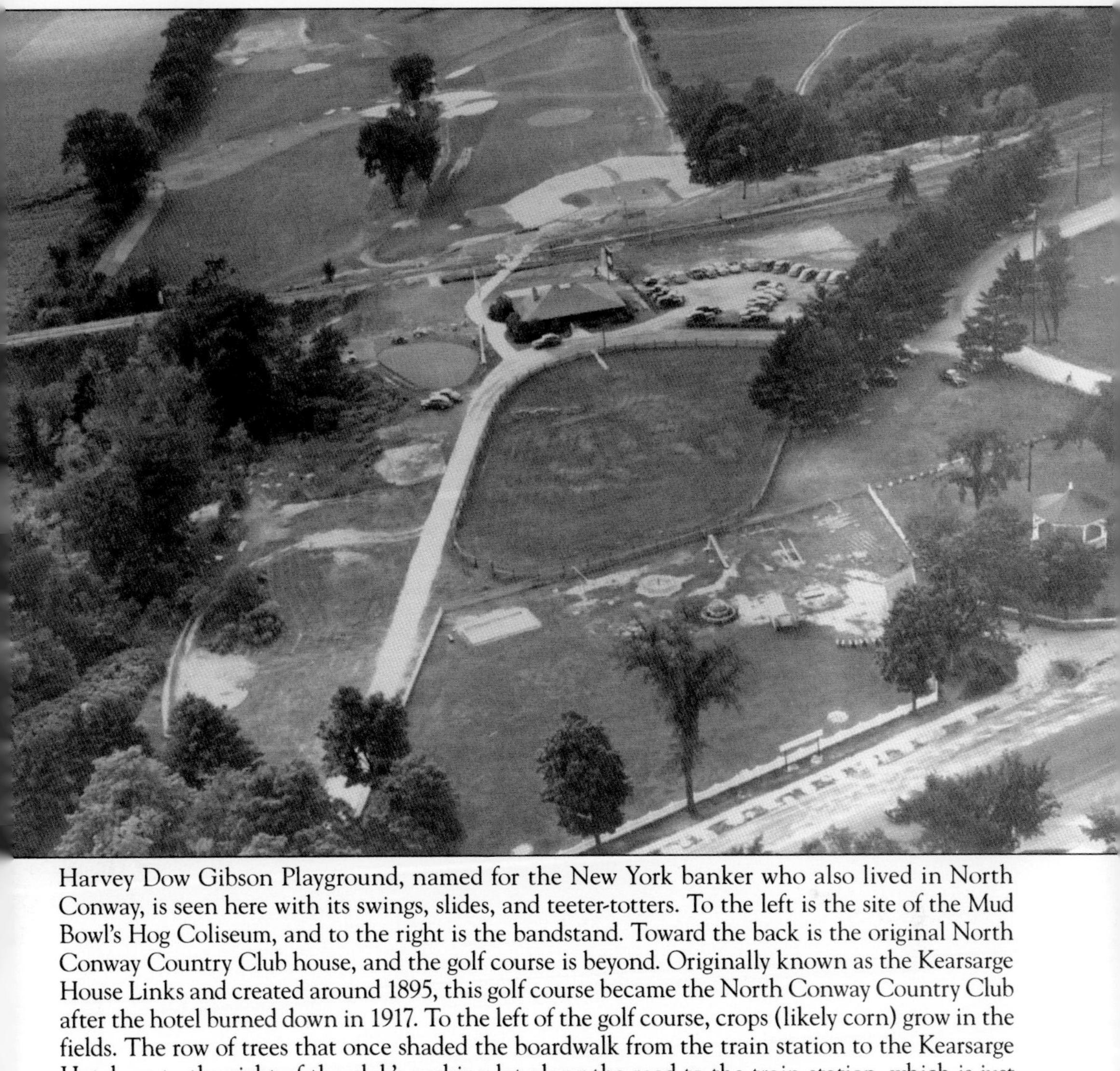

Harvey Dow Gibson Playground, named for the New York banker who also lived in North Conway, is seen here with its swings, slides, and teeter-totters. To the left is the site of the Mud Bowl's Hog Coliseum, and to the right is the bandstand. Toward the back is the original North Conway Country Club house, and the golf course is beyond. Originally known as the Kearsarge House Links and created around 1895, this golf course became the North Conway Country Club after the hotel burned down in 1917. To the left of the golf course, crops (likely corn) grow in the fields. The row of trees that once shaded the boardwalk from the train station to the Kearsarge Hotel are to the right of the club's parking lot along the road to the train station, which is just out of frame to the right. The fenced-in field between the country club and the playground was sometimes used for horse shows organized by Gibson himself. (Henney History Room, Conway Public Library.)

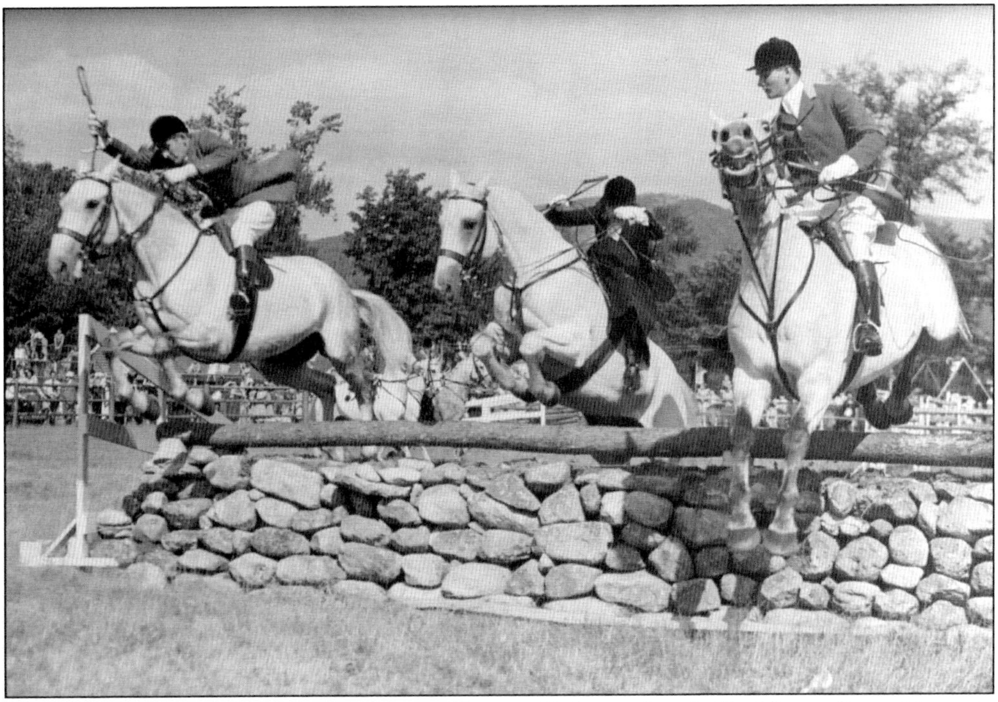

The Eastern Slope Horse Show, documented here in 1941, was founded by Harvey Dow Gibson in 1938. His wife, Helen Whitney Gibson, pictured atop a horse named Gray Star, clears the stone wall in the middle; she rides sidesaddle and is escorted by two traditionally attired gentlemen. In the background, spectators watch from the playground's swings and jungle gym. Gibson loved horses, as well as fox hunting, about which he cowrote a book. (North Conway Public Library, photograph by James M. Bray.)

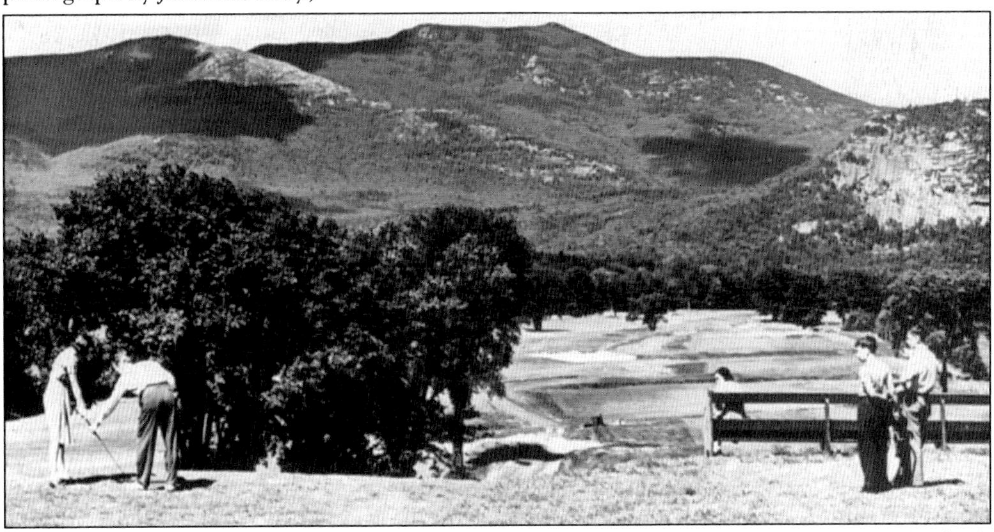

This view looks over the golf course toward the Moat Mountains to the west, showing the high ledge on which North Conway was built over the floodplain, or intervale, of the winding Saco River. In 1899, the newspaper *Among the Clouds* reported, "The golf craze is over-running the mountain resorts as none of its sportive predecessors has done." (Henney History Room, Conway Public Library.)

Through his connections and promotional activities, Harvey Dow Gibson brought many famous people to North Conway, including Babe Ruth, seen here playing a round with Gibson. In the background are the village playground's swing sets. (North Conway Public Library, photograph by James M. Bray.)

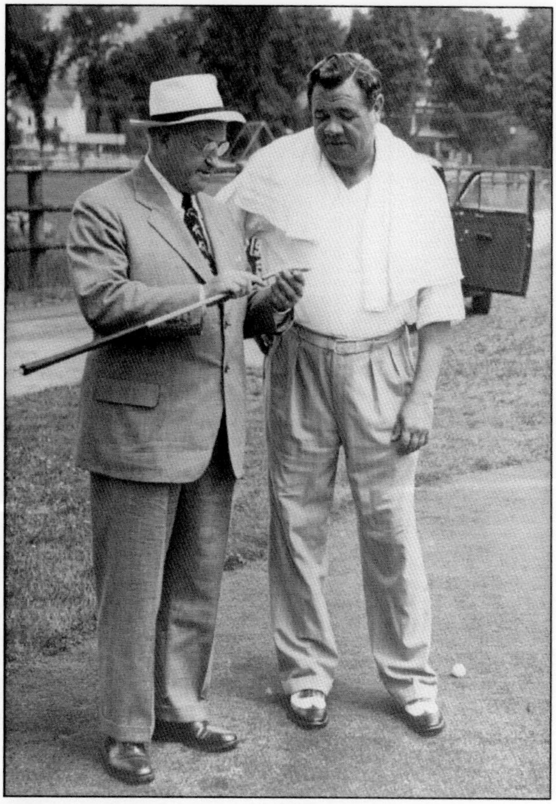

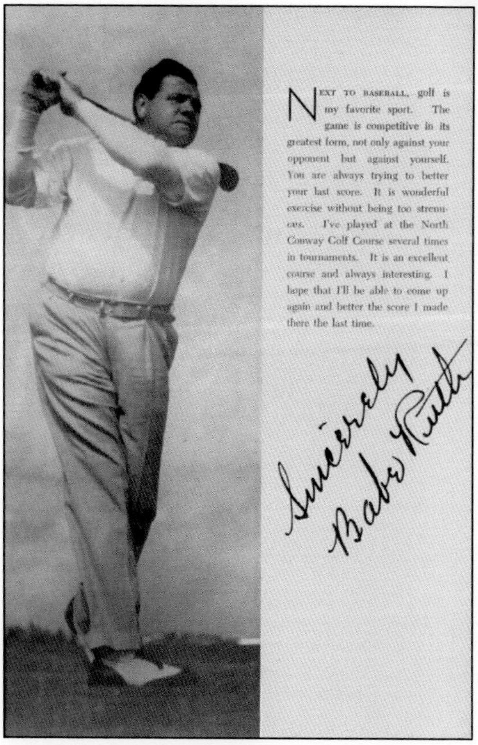

NEXT TO BASEBALL, golf is my favorite sport. The game is competitive in its greatest form, not only against your opponent but against yourself. You are always trying to better your last score. It is wonderful exercise without being too strenuous. I've played at the North Conway Golf Course several times in tournaments. It is an excellent course and always interesting. I hope that I'll be able to come up again and better the score I made there the last time.

Sincerely
Babe Ruth

Along with numerous other prominent people like filmmaker Otto Lang and travel commentator Lowell Thomas, Babe Ruth's praise for North Conway was published in local chamber of commerce publications such as the *Eastern Slope Regionnaire* magazine. (Henney History Room, Conway Public Library.)

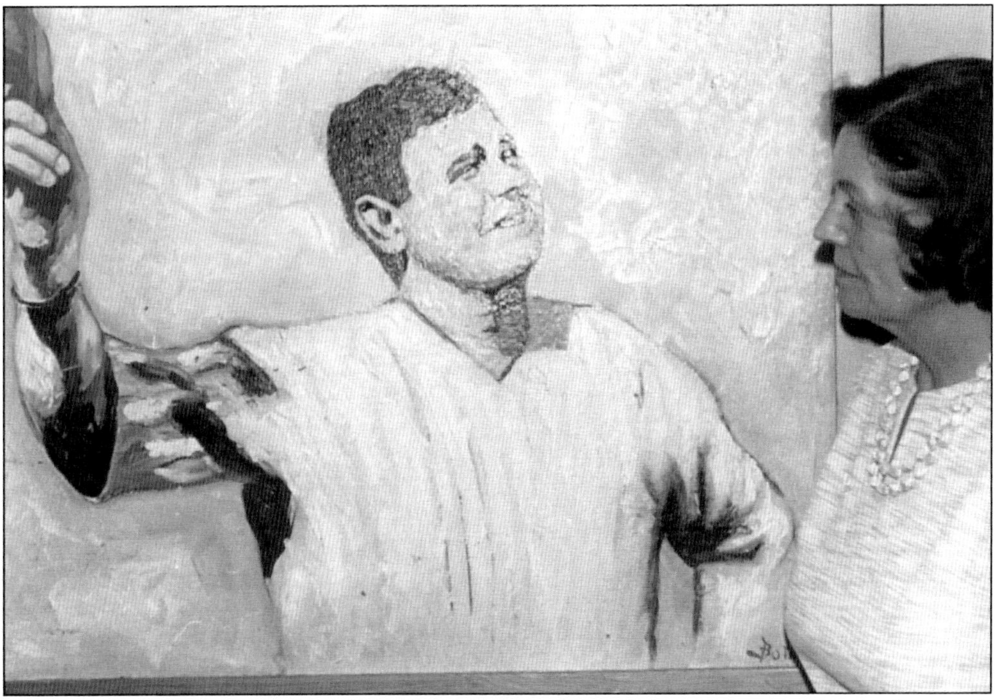

Babe Ruth's daughter Julia visited North Conway with her father and was active in the town's social and cultural scene. She gave programs on two of her books, *Major League Dad: A Daughter's Cherished Memories* and *Babe Ruth: A Daughter's Portrait*, at local bookstores. Proceeds from the book sales were donated to the local Babe Ruth League. (Henney History Room, Conway Public Library.)

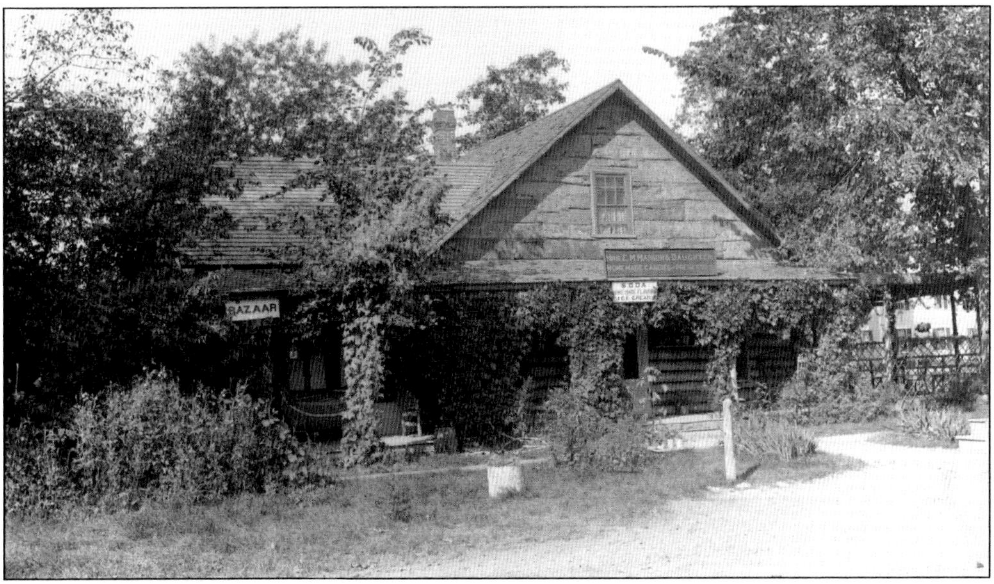

The sign over the porch in this photograph reads, "Mrs. E.M. Masson & Daughter. Homemade Candies and Preserves." Another reads, "Soda, home made flavors, ice cream." Reportedly, the structure was built as a gift shop and relocated here from near the Kearsarge Hotel. It now houses Richard M. Plusch Antiques. (Henney History Room, Conway Public Library.)

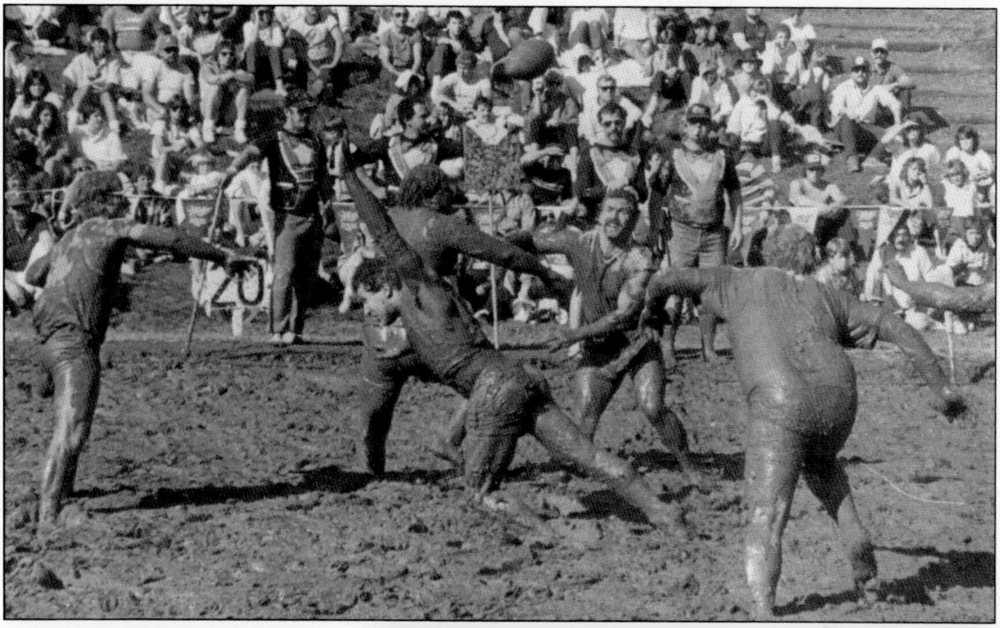

Just north of Plusch Antiques is the famous Hog Coliseum, current home of the annual Mud Bowl football competition, which has been held since 1975. The Mount Washington Valley Hogs was formed by a small group of bartenders and friends in the area. Teams had played before in muddy cornfields off West Side Road and Cranmore Mountain Resort. The Hog Coliseum was built in 1981. This unusual form of football helps raise money for local charities. The event includes a full weekend of events, including the Mud Bowl Parade. At right is the mascot for the Valley Rats at the Hog Coliseum, complete with rat tail. Teams who have played include the North Shore Mudsharks of Peabody, Massachusetts; the Nashua Mud Gumbys; the Mount Washington Valley Hogs; the Merrimack Mudcats of Franklin, New Hampshire; and the Cumberland Muckaneers of Cumberland, Rhode Island. (Both, Conway Historical Society.)

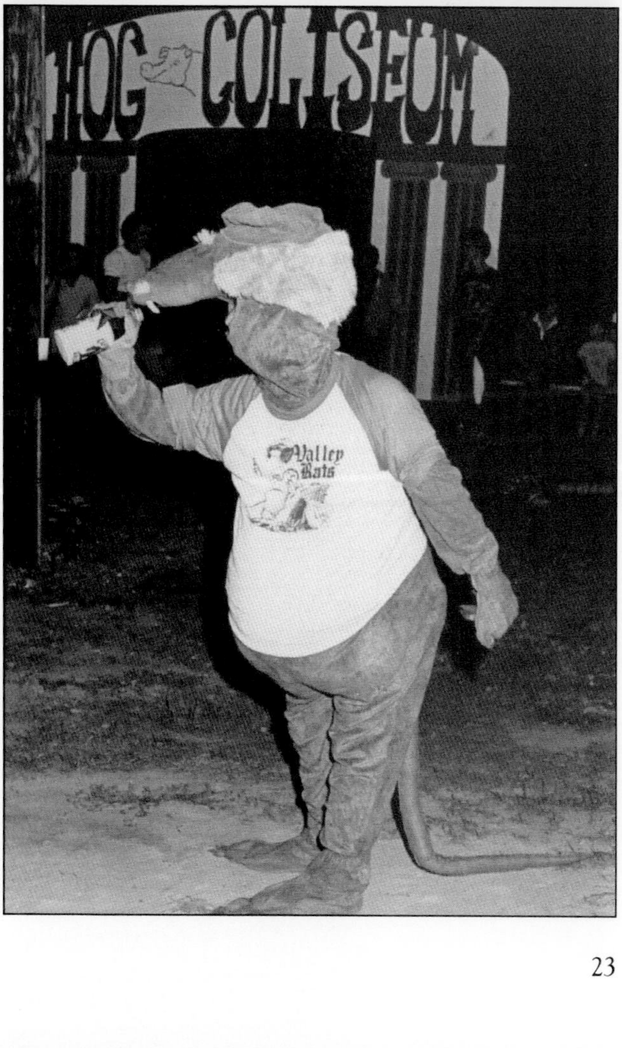

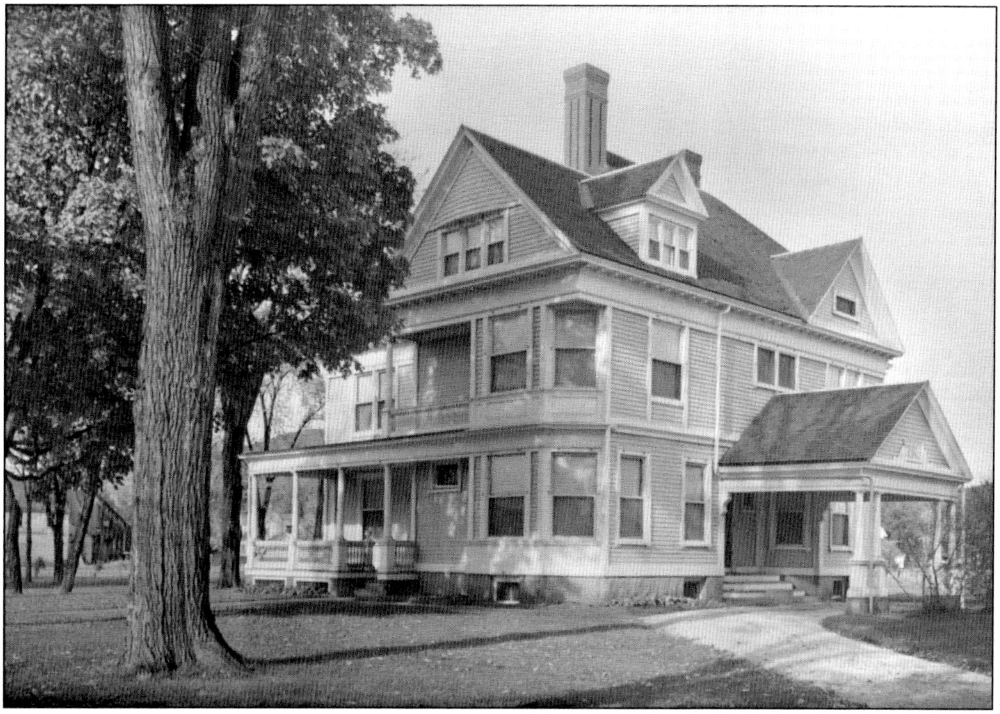

Harvey Dow Gibson and his wife, Helen, lived across the street from the golf course and park at their home, Moat View, which is now the Gibson Center for Senior Services. Gibson was at the center of much of North Conway's activities and organizations. Avid horseman, original owner of Cranmore Mountain Resort, successful businessman, and community leader are just a few roles he played during his life in North Conway. (North Conway Public Library.)

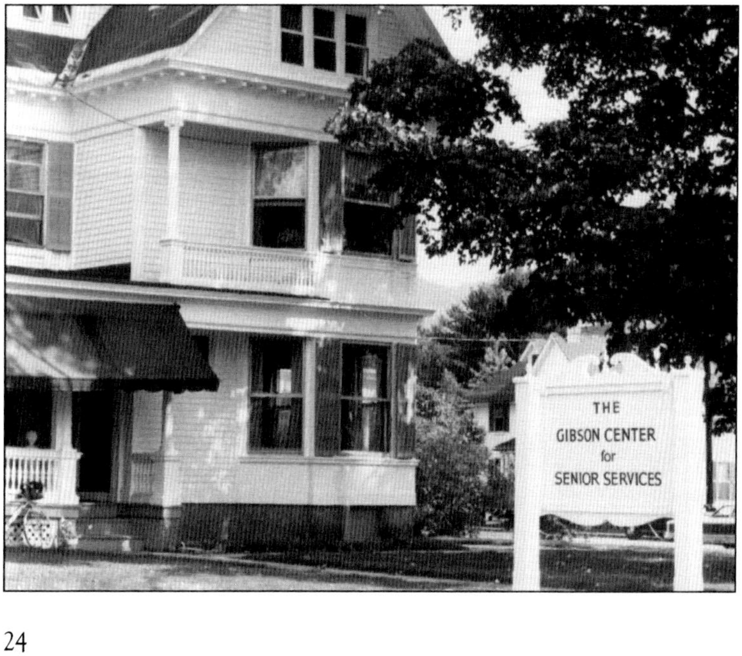

Pictured is the Gibson Center for Senior Services. In 1973, volunteers at the center began providing senior services. In 2000, the old Gibson House was purchased and added on to. The center offers a wide variety of programs, lectures, and bus trips to Boston. The original carriage house is now a thrift shop helping to support the center. (Conway Historical Society.)

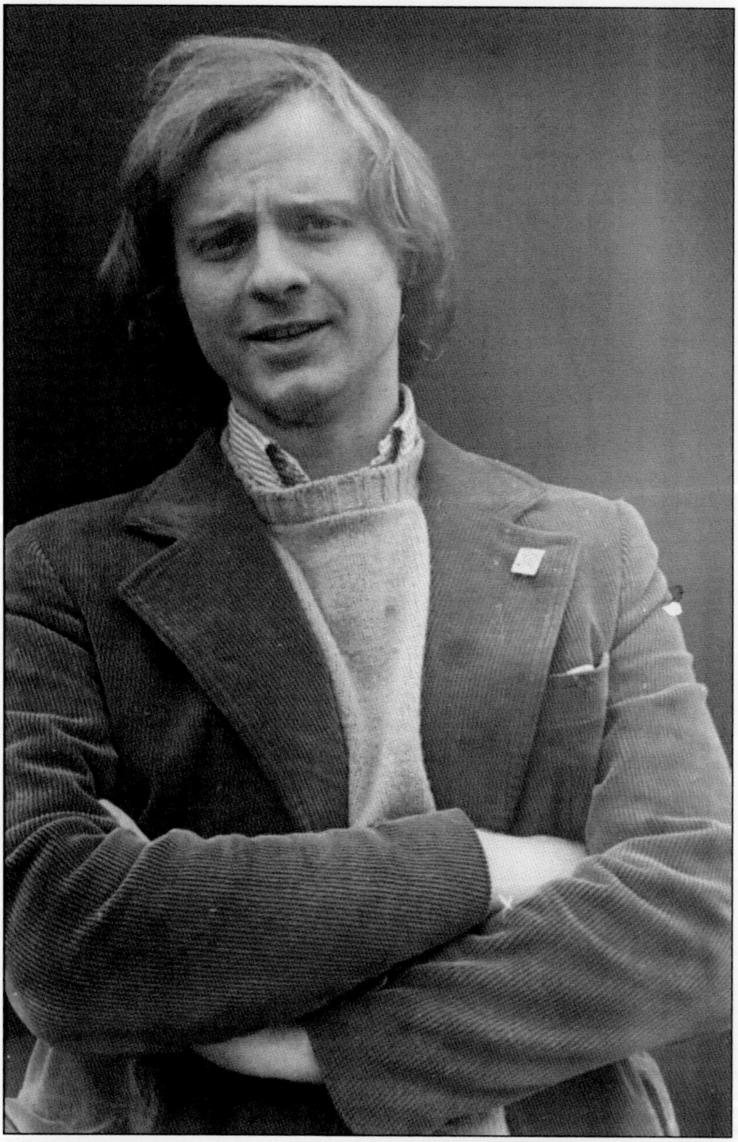

George Cleveland, the grandson of Pres. Grover Cleveland and the executive director of the Gibson Center for Senior Services, crosses his arms neatly in this outdoor photograph. He frequently dons the apparel of his grandfather and presents a living history program in the persona of his grandfather, most recently at a celebration at the Statue of Liberty in New York City. Known as the "Voice of the Valley" on Conway radio, he has conducted more than 3,500 interviews with news makers from all parts of the world. Cleveland has spoken with most major presidential candidates, a representative of an interplanetary confederation from the Unarius Academy of Science, and many noted authors and musicians. One of his more unusual fundraising endeavors was posing wearing only a hat in the 2003 "Tamworth Men In Hats" calendar, which raised more than $75,000 for local charities. Cleveland has been guiding tours throughout the White Mountains for more than 20 years. He is a well-known local guide, an avid collector of tales and legends, and has written frequently for local publications on people and places of interest, including one notable piece about a bird walk with David Allen Sibley. (Henney History Room, Conway Public Library.)

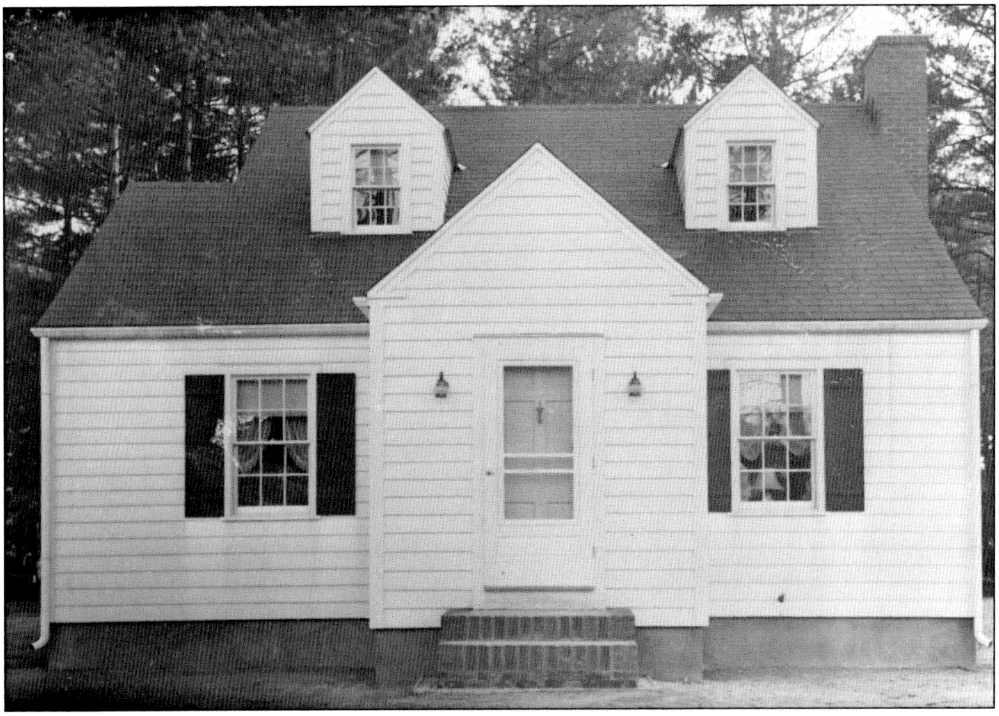

Harvey Dow Gibson was involved in many activities on the home front during World War II, including with the American Red Cross. He also served as finance committee chairman for the New York World's Fair from 1936 to 1941, which had the theme, "Building the World of Tomorrow with the Tools of Today." Gibson arranged for 10 World's Fair houses to be built in North Conway along the south side of Grove Street, all of which were designed to showcase modern techniques of prefabrication and standardized design in an effort to alleviate housing shortages during and after World War II. The variations between houses were subtle; notice the difference in the connection between the front gable and dormer. (Both, North Conway Public Library, photographs by James M. Bray.)

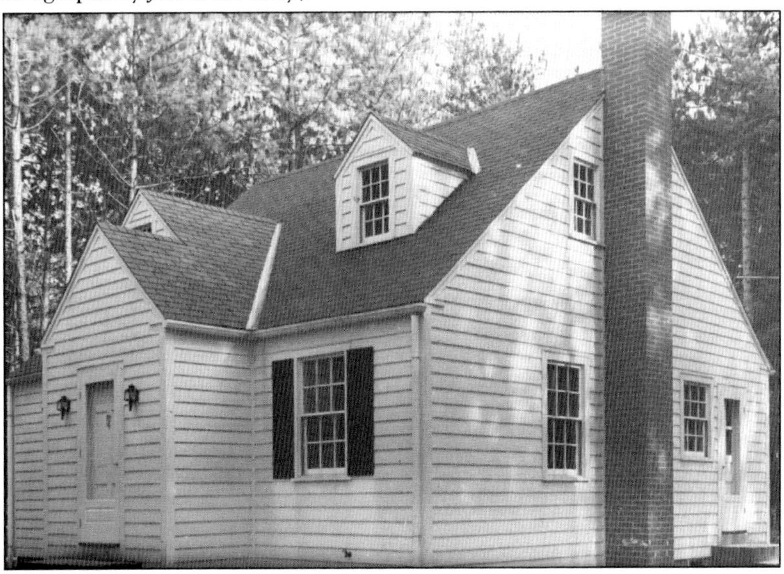

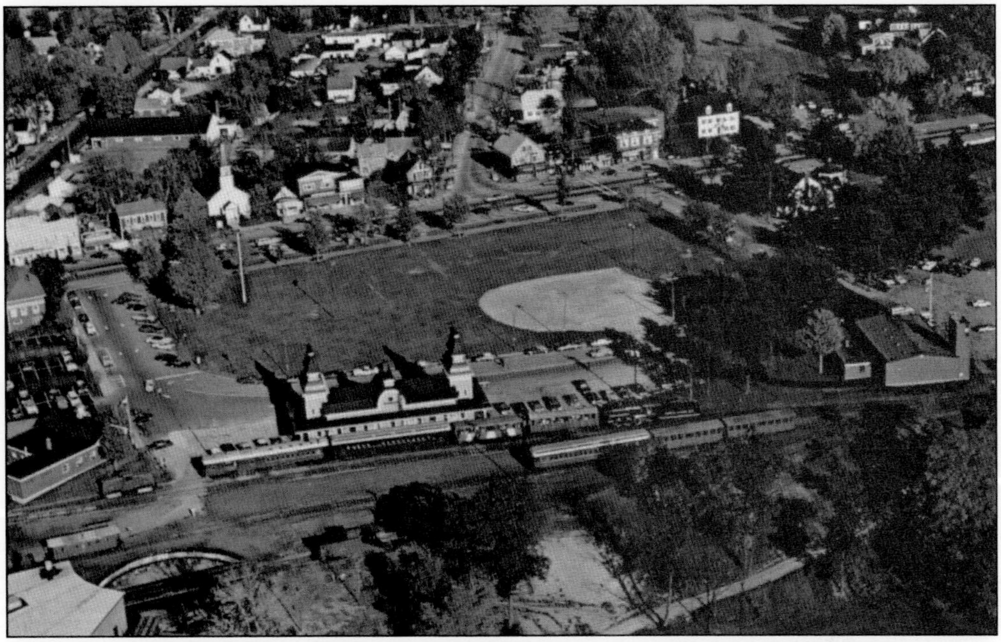

Moving counter-clockwise around Schouler Park from the train depot is the fire station with its tall tower, the community center and bandstand, the Masonic Lodge across the street, restaurants and stores on Main Street, the First Baptist Church, more stores, the old brick bank (now the Met Coffee House), a parking lot, another store, and in the bottom left corner the roundhouse and turntable for the trains. (Henney History Room, Conway Public Library.)

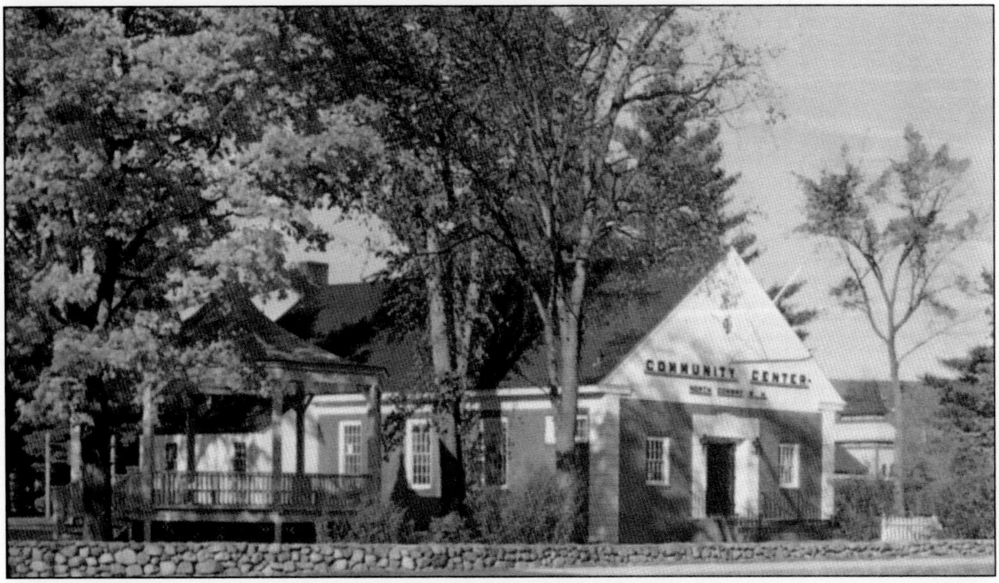

Built in 1950 on the site of the North Conway Academy through the generosity of Harvey Dow Gibson's daughter Whitney, the community center is a nonprofit organization established in the late 1940s in a Main Street storefront. The center provides a broad range of recreational opportunities for children and adults, including arts and crafts fairs, breakfast with Santa, intramural basketball, cheerleading, and garden club events. (Conway Historical Society, photograph by Don Sieburg.)

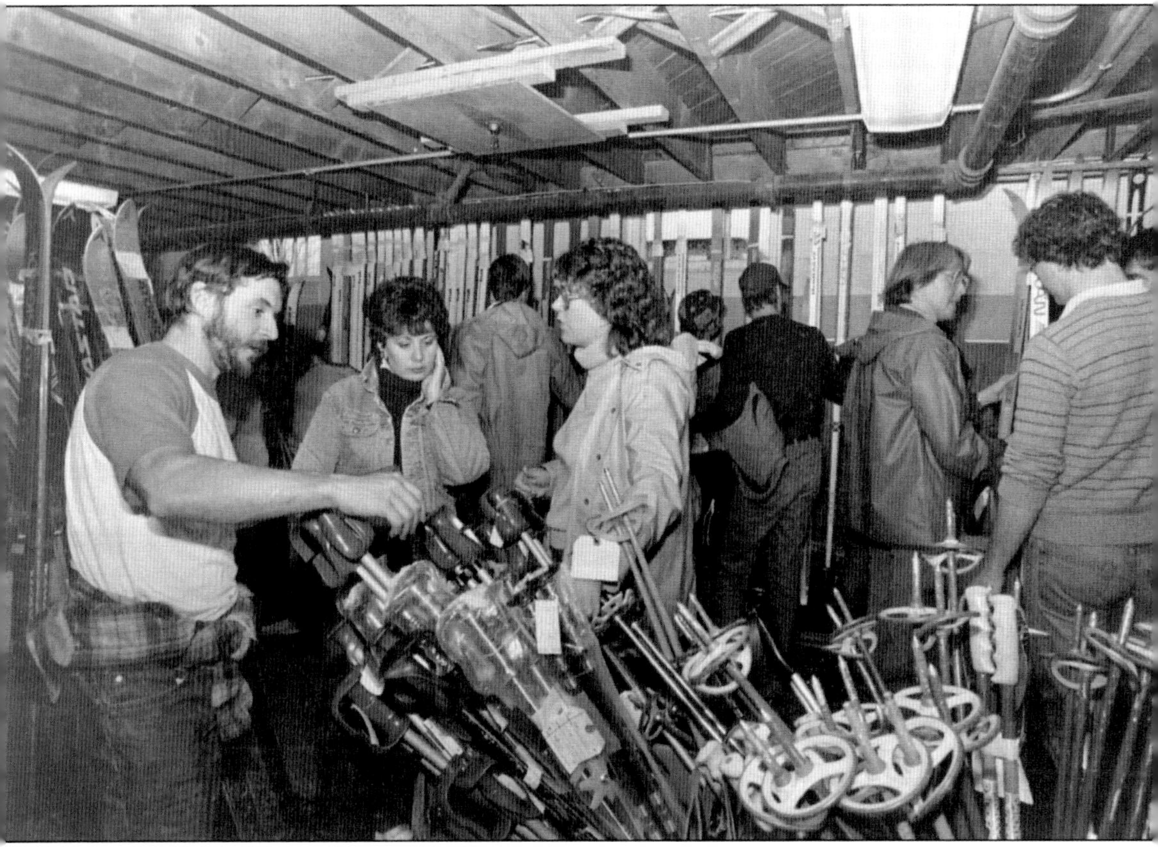

The annual used ski equipment sale is held in the cellar of the community center for the benefit of the Eastern Slope Ski School and its programs. Skiing has been a local passion and a major tourist industry in North Conway since the 1930s. Generations of skiers have passed on their equipment and expertise to students in area schools through sales, like this one, and weekly training programs. (Conway Historical Society.)

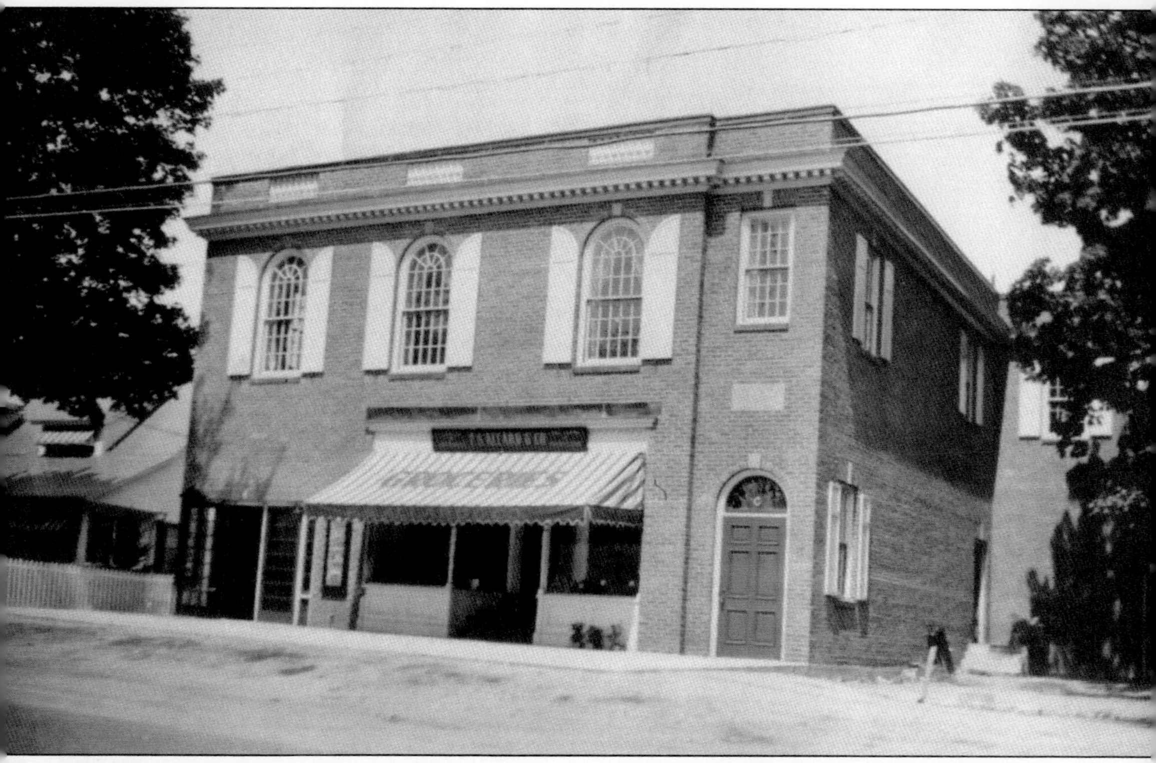

This Masonic Lodge was built in 1931 to replace an earlier wooden lodge destroyed by fire. The ground floor has housed several stores and a movie theater. The sign reads, "E.S. Allard & Co." and "Groceries" adorns the top of the awning. Wall murals dating from the 1930s explain the history and principles of freemasonry. The Masons host regular charity breakfasts, which support a variety of nonprofits. (Henney History Room, Conway Public Library.)

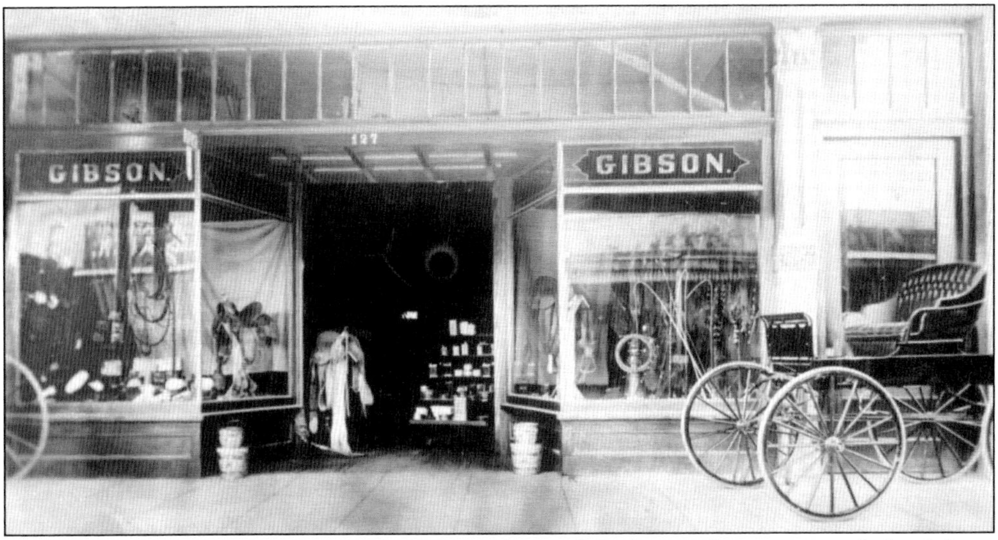

Saddles and tack were essential to the horse culture of the late 19th century, and the Gibson Store provided a central location to provision North Conway. The large plate-glass windows and artfully arranged displays captured the attention of potential shoppers, and the angled entrance guided them into the store. (Conway Historical Society.)

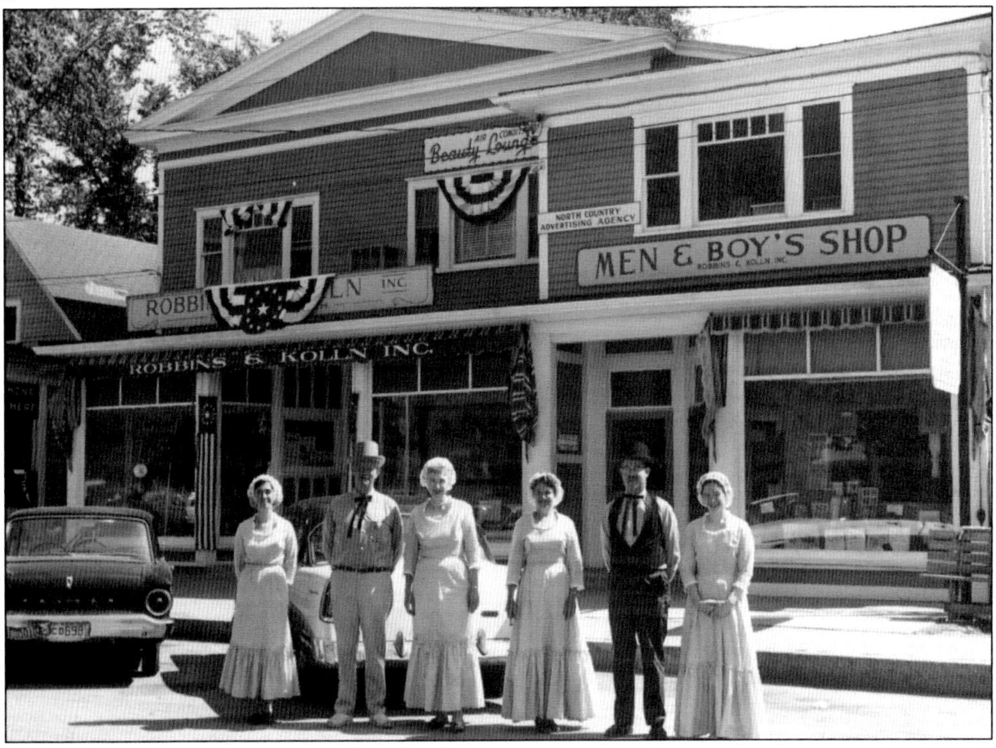

The Gibson Store later became the Robbins & Kolln Country Department Store. Wearing historical attire to celebrate the 1965 bicentennial of the granting of Conway, owners and employees are, from left to right, Mary Lou Ball, John and Florence Kolln, Betty and Maurice West, and Susan Gaudette. Today, the building houses the Penguin Gift Shop. (Conway Historical Society, photograph by Bob Duncan.)

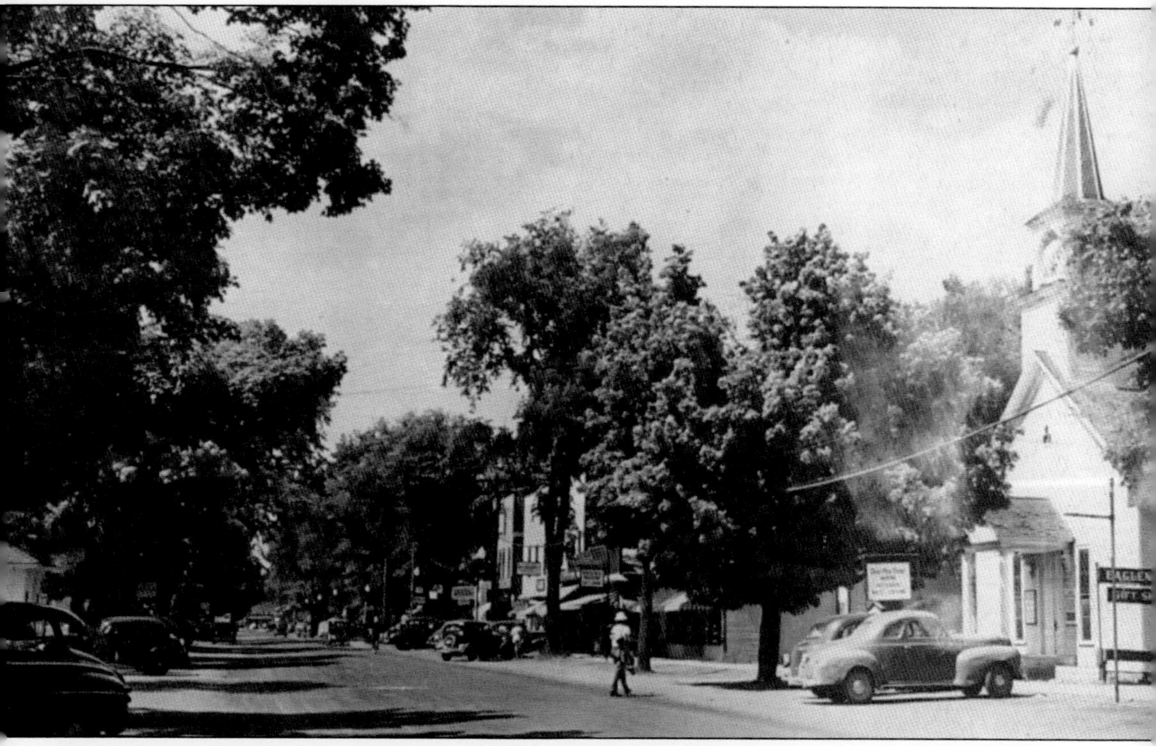

Elm and maple trees line the road around 1950 in front of the First Baptist Church, built in 1838. The 638-pound church steeple bell was purchased from the Revere Copper Company and shipped from Boston for a trucking charge of 50¢. The first known documentation of Baptists in Conway dates from April 1795. Not having their own building, they met for years in homes, barns, and the town meetinghouse. Seen to the right in the image is a sign for the Eagle Nook Gift Shop, and farther north are some of the unique stores and restaurants that make North Conway a tourist destination. At the end of the street is the Whitaker House, and on the far left is a visitor center kiosk. (Henney History Room, Conway Public Library, photograph by Gordon Holland.)

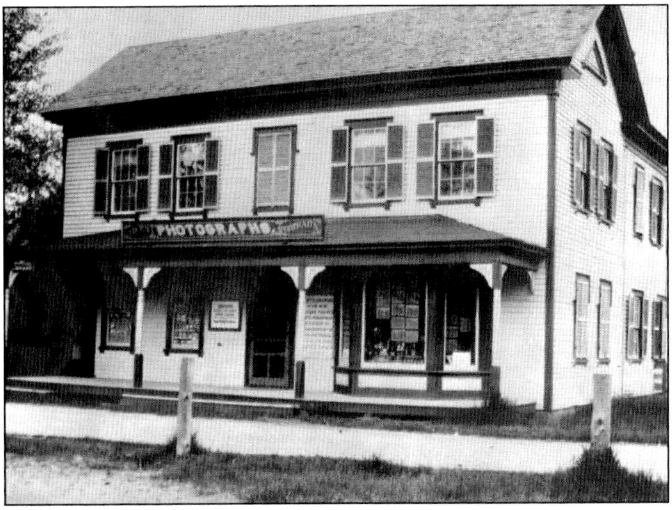

Nathan Pease came to North Conway from Cornish, Maine, in 1858, and five years later, he built the photography shop seen here in 1905. A sign to the left reads, "Public Library," which seems to have moved around a lot in the early days. In 1964, Bob Duncan relocated his camera business to this building, and in 1991, it became Zeb's Old Tyme General Store. (Conway Historical Society, photograph by Nathan W. Pease.)

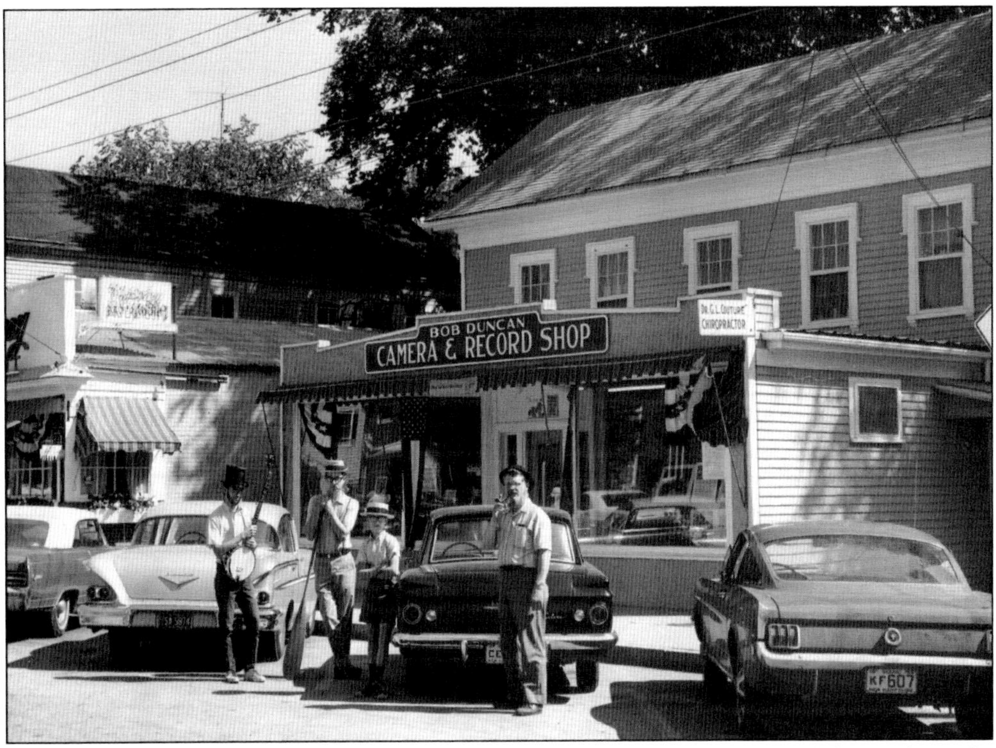

Standing in front of the Bob Duncan Camera & Record Shop in 1965 are, from left to right, Mike Greene, Jeff Carr, Brook Duncan, and Bob Duncan. After six years in this building, Duncan moved the shop next door to the Old Colony Restaurant building. A few years later, he added a second floor. It later became the Mountain Tops Resort Wear store and is currently the Soyfire Candle Shop. (Conway Historical Society, photograph by Bob Duncan.)

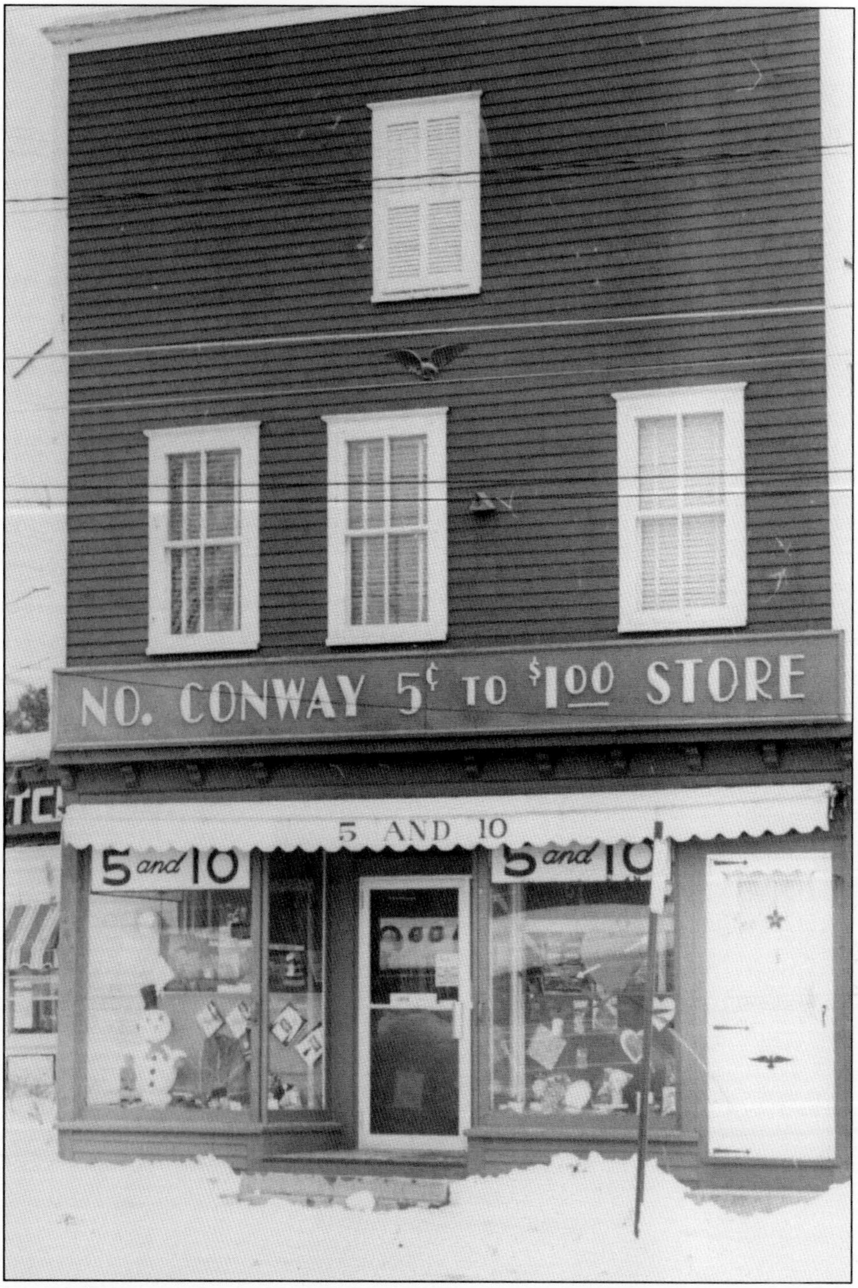

This five-and-dime store, located near the southeast corner of Kearsarge and Main Streets, is the oldest retail business remaining in North Conway and is on the National Register of Historic Places. Established in 1939 by Sidney and Lillian Sweeney, it is one of only two examples of the traditional five-and-dime store known in New Hampshire. The post office was upstairs at one time, as was the office of A.D. Davis Insurance. It is architecturally significant as one of two representations of the boomtown storefront in North Conway and the only unaltered one. This design involves the false-front style often seen in Western movies, with the facade extending upward above the peak of the building's gable roof, which hid the roof and gave the impression of a taller and wider structure. (Henney History Room, Conway Public Library.)

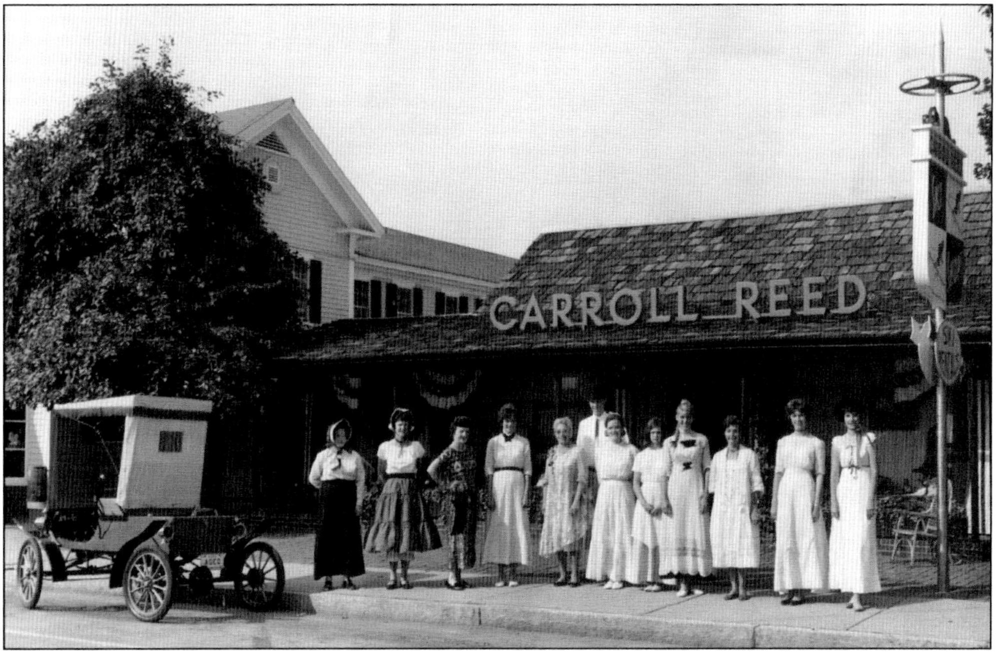

The ski pole–shaped sign on the right for the Carroll Reed Ski Shop still stands today. Reed was an important figure in Mount Washington Valley skiing history. Celebrating Conway's 1965 bicentennial in front of the store are, from left to right, Priscilla Gardner, Edith Macy, Margaret "Peggy" Palmer, Marlee Moulton, Rose Stacy, Patten White, Julie Kennett, Penny Curtis, Bonnie Kitchen, Victoria Brett, Debbie Brett, and Susan Hatch. (Conway Historical Society, photograph by Bob Duncan.)

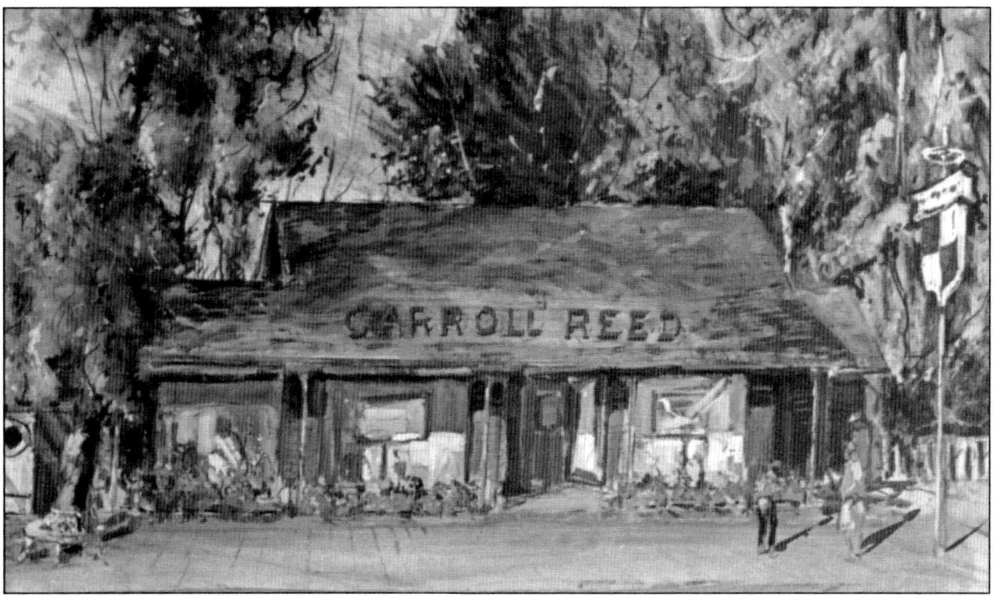

David Baker, the artist behind this rendering of the Carroll Reed Ski Shop, was one of a number of local artists who used art to explore skiing culture, natural wonders, and area history. The Carroll Reed Ski Shop began life as part of the stables of the Mason Hotel, which burned down in 1882, and is now part of the Norcross Circle Shops. (Conway Historical Society.)

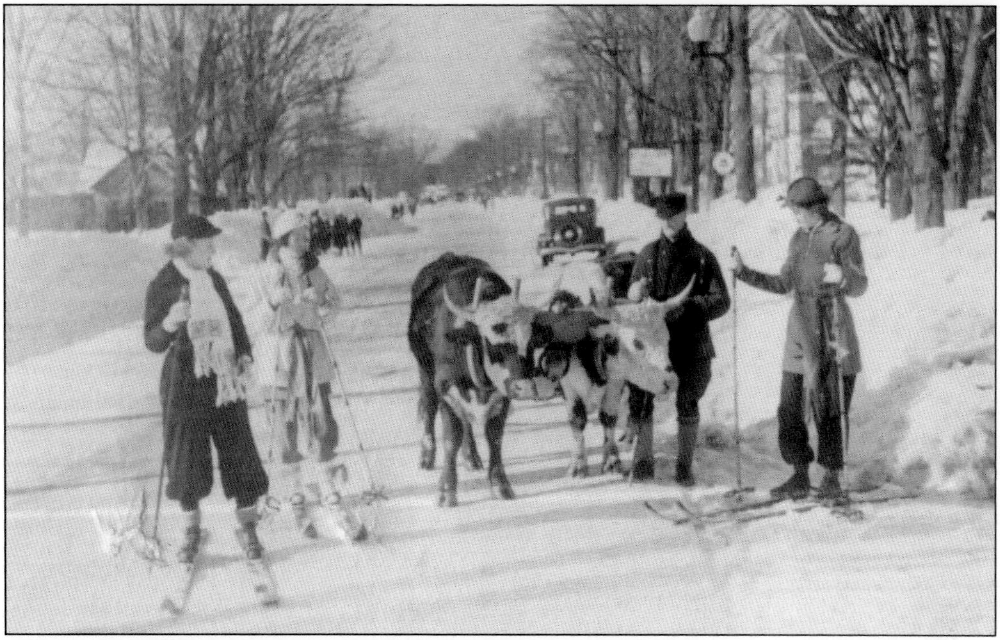

This photograph was used as a "Season's Greetings" card from Kearsarge Hall on Main Street, south of Grove Street. The sign with the Bell telephone symbol reads, "Kearsarge Hall." (Henney History Room, Conway Public Library.)

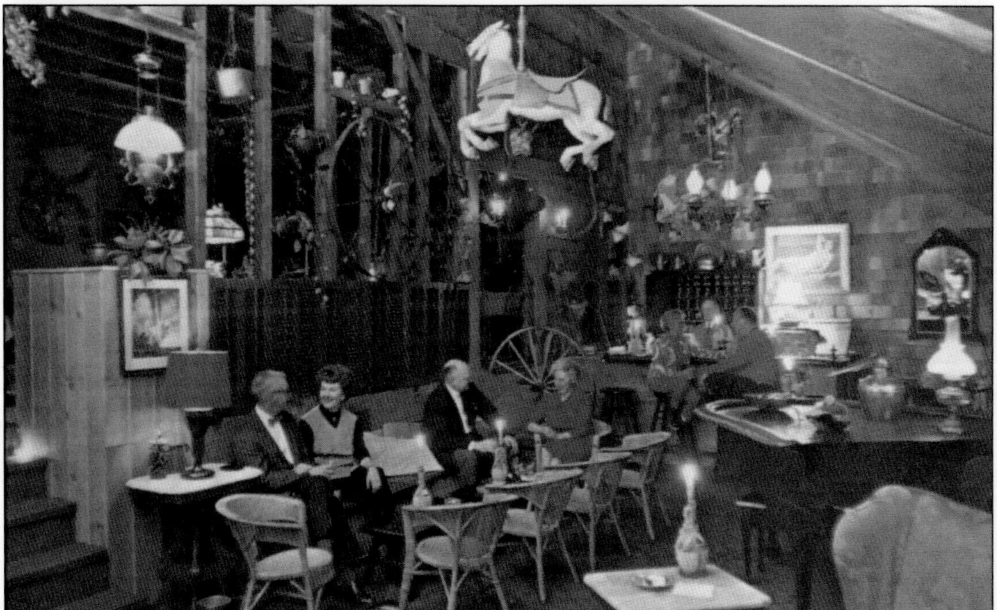

The owners of the Gables Inn, originally built around 1870, transformed a barn into a setting for antiques from all over the world and an old screened-in porch into a cocktail lounge known as the Pony High. In addition to the carousel horse hanging from the ceiling, decorative antiques and collectibles included an antique spittoon, fiasco Chianti bottles wrapped with straw and used as candle holders, and a copper still on the piano. (Conway Historical Society, photograph by Dick Smith.)

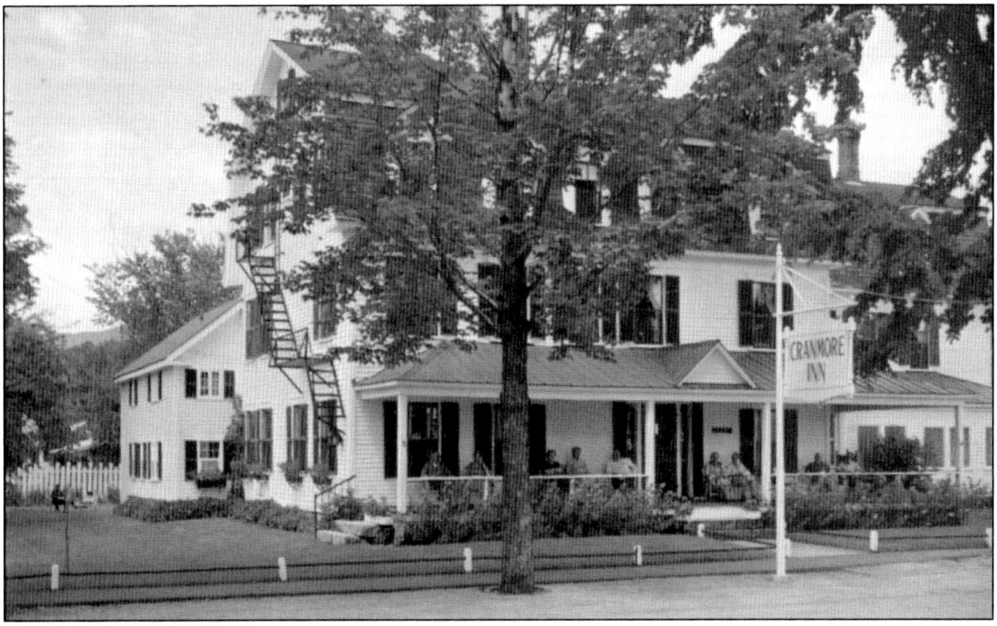

Side streets such as Kearsarge Street are home to more stores, inns, and other businesses, as well as residences. Said to be the oldest continuously operated inn in North Conway, the Cranmore Inn was built in 1863 by either Charles Whitaker or J.A. Whitaker. Over the years, it was operated as the Echo Inn and later as Robertson's Inn. (Conway Historical Society.)

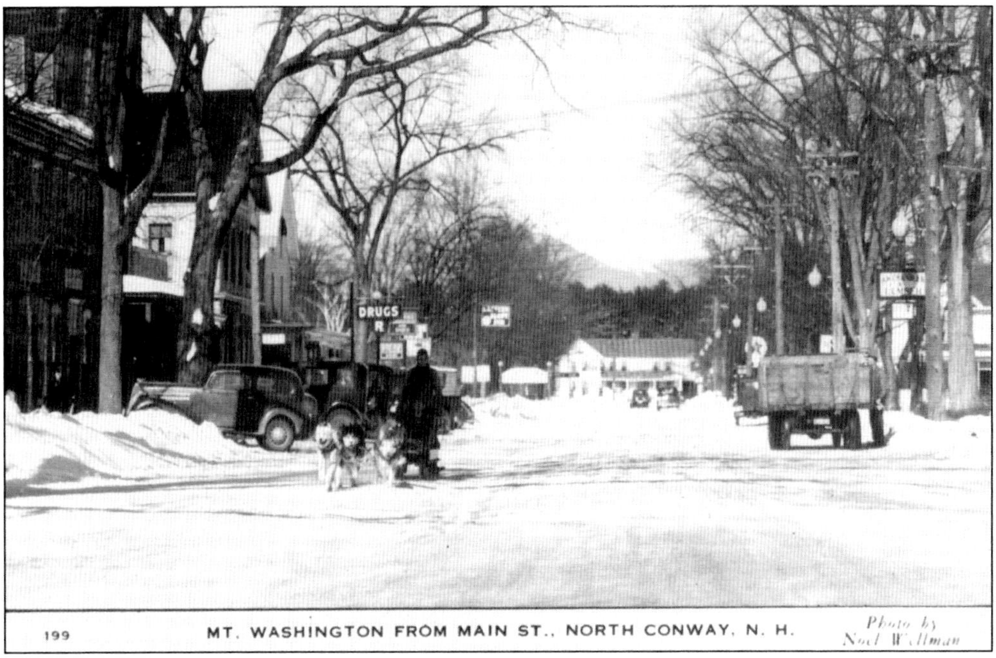

Dogsledding was one of the many activities offered by the Eastern Slope Inn that added to its reputation as a winter wonderland. Looking north, this photograph shows signs for A.W. Chandler Lumber, a Texaco station, a drugstore, and the Eastern Slope Inn. The large white house that appears to be in the middle of the street is the Whitaker family house. (Henney History Room, Conway Public Library, photograph by Noel Wellman.)

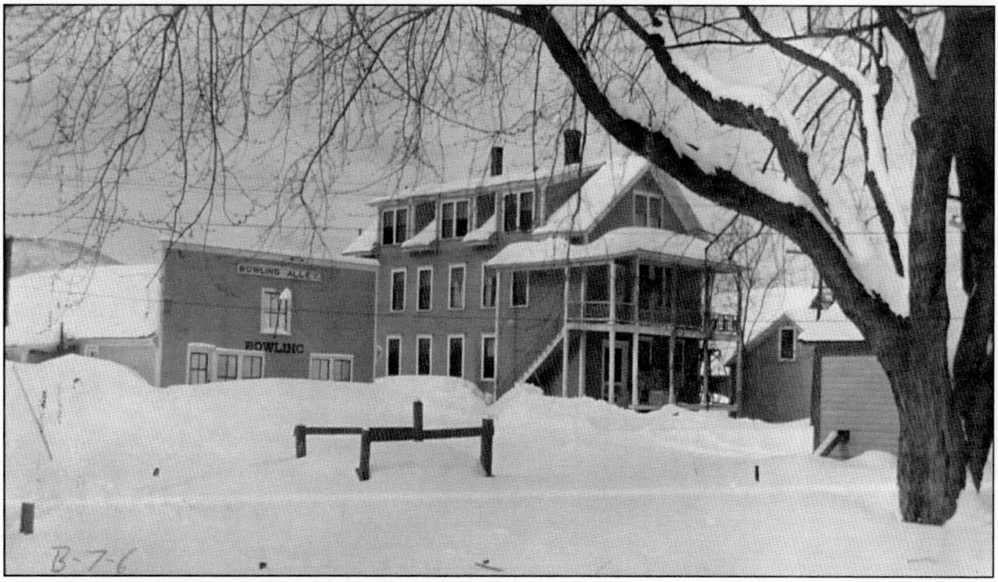

The building to the right was the office and printing press for the *Reporter*, the valley's longest-running newspaper. It began in 1883 as the *Sandwich Reporter* and was published in North Conway from 1893 until 1992. In 2012, it became home to the office of the *Mountainear* newspaper. The bowling alley on the left was 70 feet long, and the small alley next to it is now called Reporter Court. (Henney History Room, Conway Public Library.)

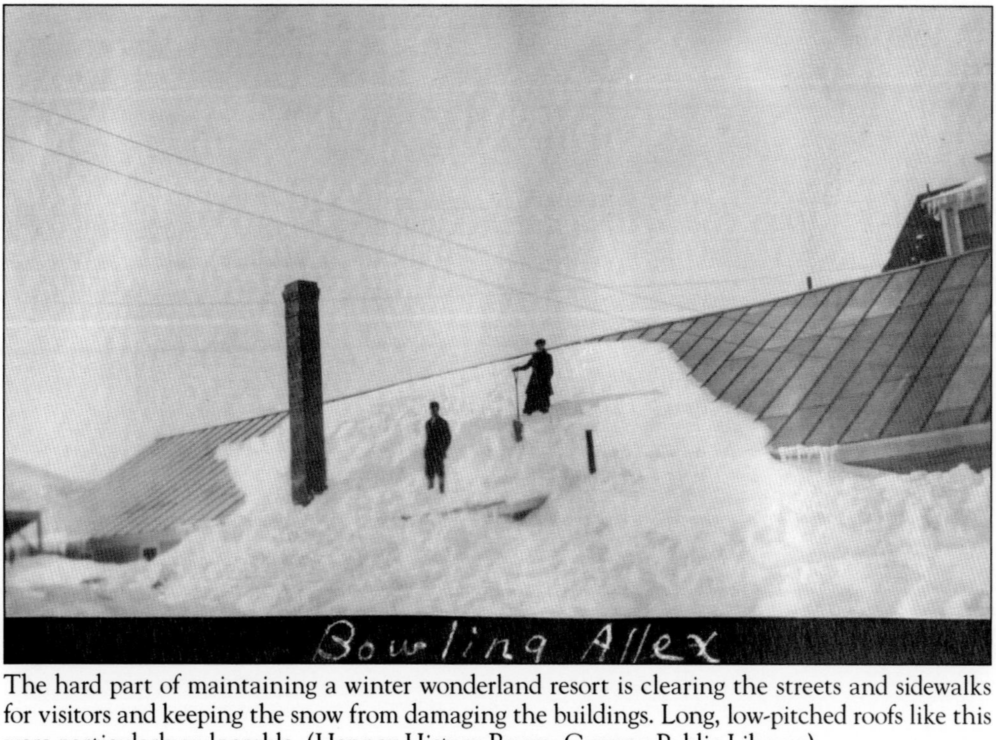

The hard part of maintaining a winter wonderland resort is clearing the streets and sidewalks for visitors and keeping the snow from damaging the buildings. Long, low-pitched roofs like this were particularly vulnerable. (Henney History Room, Conway Public Library.)

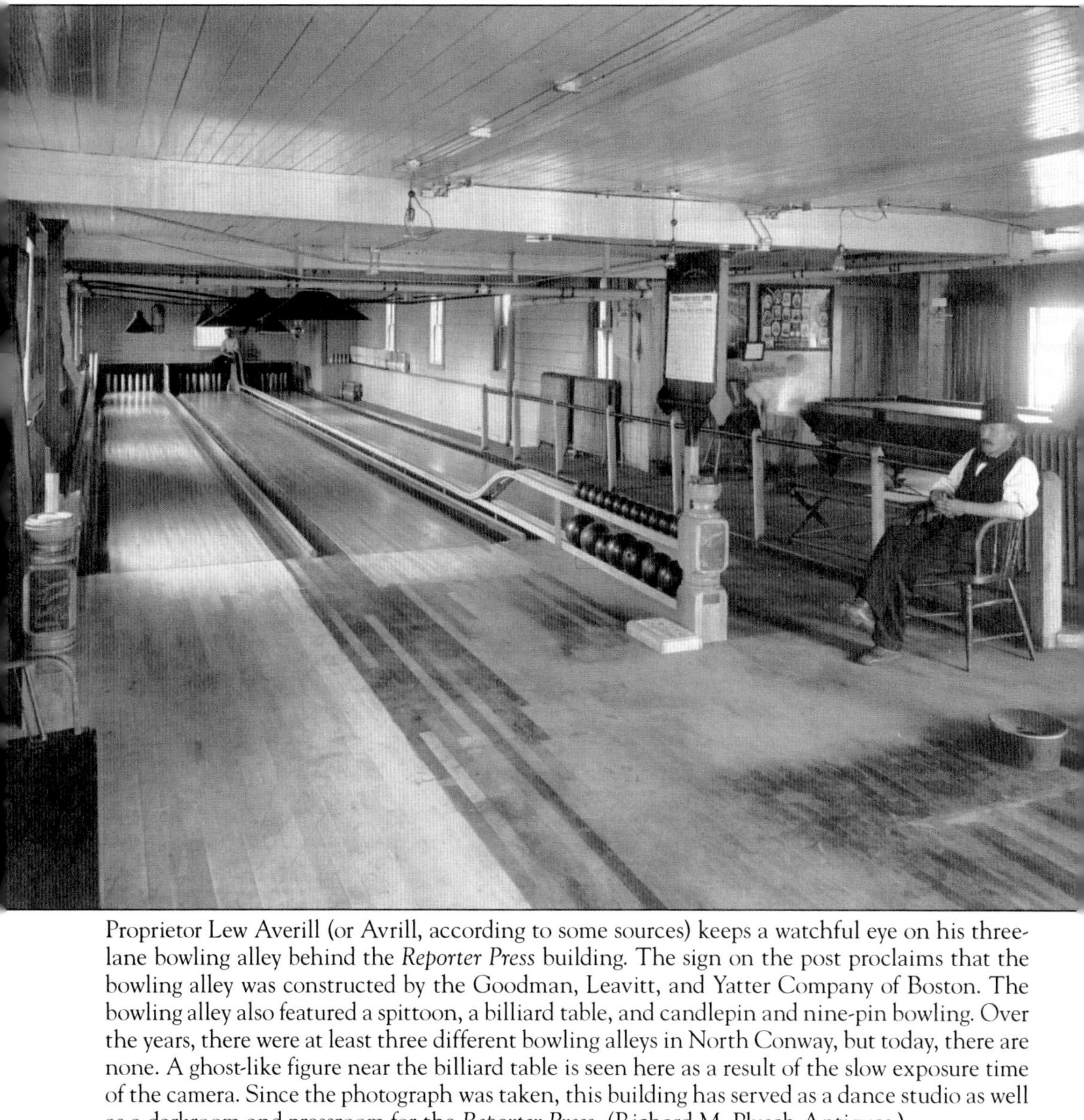

Proprietor Lew Averill (or Avrill, according to some sources) keeps a watchful eye on his three-lane bowling alley behind the *Reporter Press* building. The sign on the post proclaims that the bowling alley was constructed by the Goodman, Leavitt, and Yatter Company of Boston. The bowling alley also featured a spittoon, a billiard table, and candlepin and nine-pin bowling. Over the years, there were at least three different bowling alleys in North Conway, but today, there are none. A ghost-like figure near the billiard table is seen here as a result of the slow exposure time of the camera. Since the photograph was taken, this building has served as a dance studio as well as a darkroom and pressroom for the *Reporter Press*. (Richard M. Plusch Antiques.)

Dr. James Schouler had this library built in memory of his wife, Emily, on the northeast corner of Main and Mechanic Streets. Designed by Philadelphia architect Clarence Clark Zantzinger (1872–1954) using granite donated by James A. Whitaker from a quarry on nearby Oak Street, it was constructed in 1911 on the site of the North Conway House. Additions were made in 1917 and 1988. (Henney History Room, Conway Public Library.)

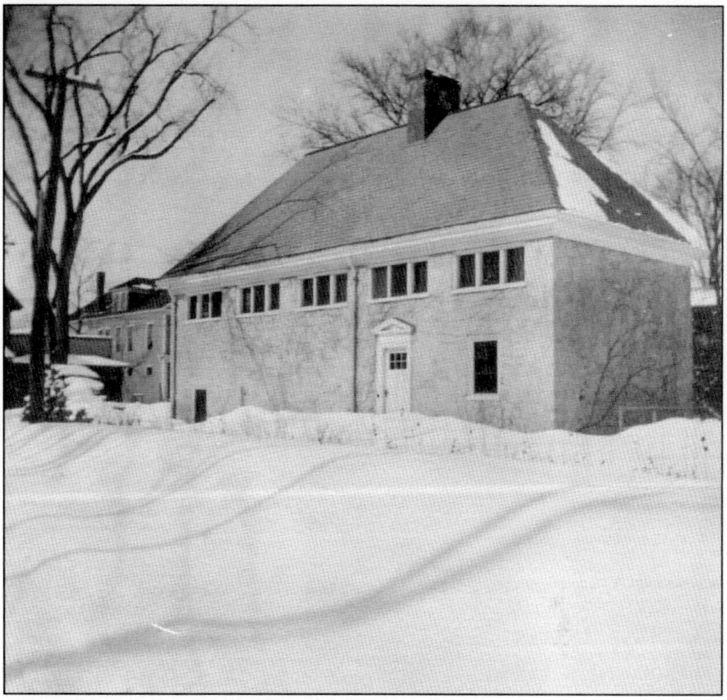

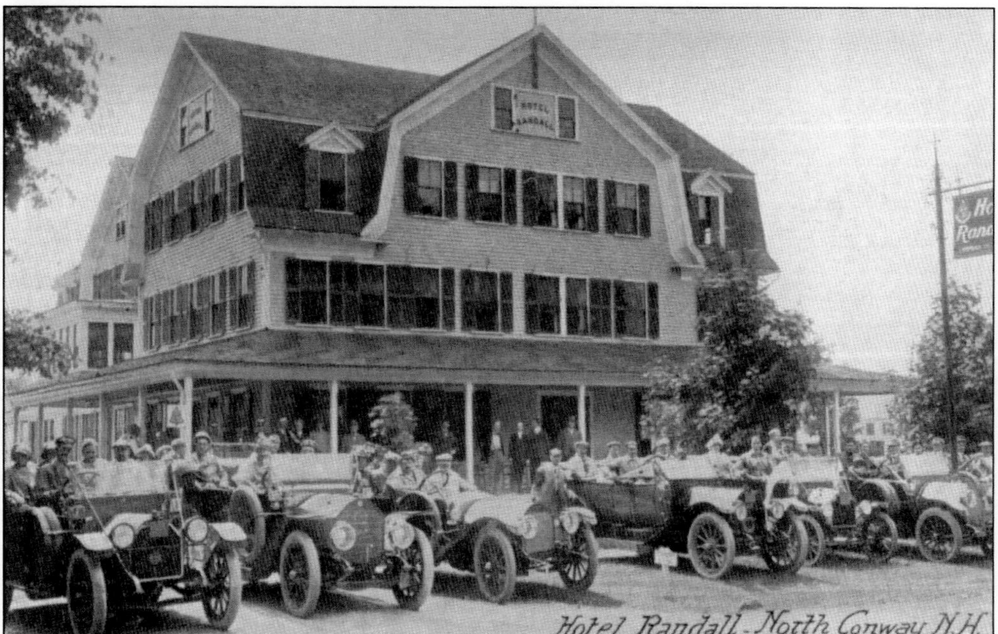

In 1864, Moses Randall bought a boardinghouse and christened it the Randall House. It burned down in 1902, and Randall built a new, state-of-the-art hotel in 1903. The 50-room inn had 10 plate-glass scenery windows and cypress-paneled sleeping rooms with electric bells, electric lights, and modern steam heat. It also featured a telephone, as the Bell sign indicates. (Henney History Room, Conway Public Library.)

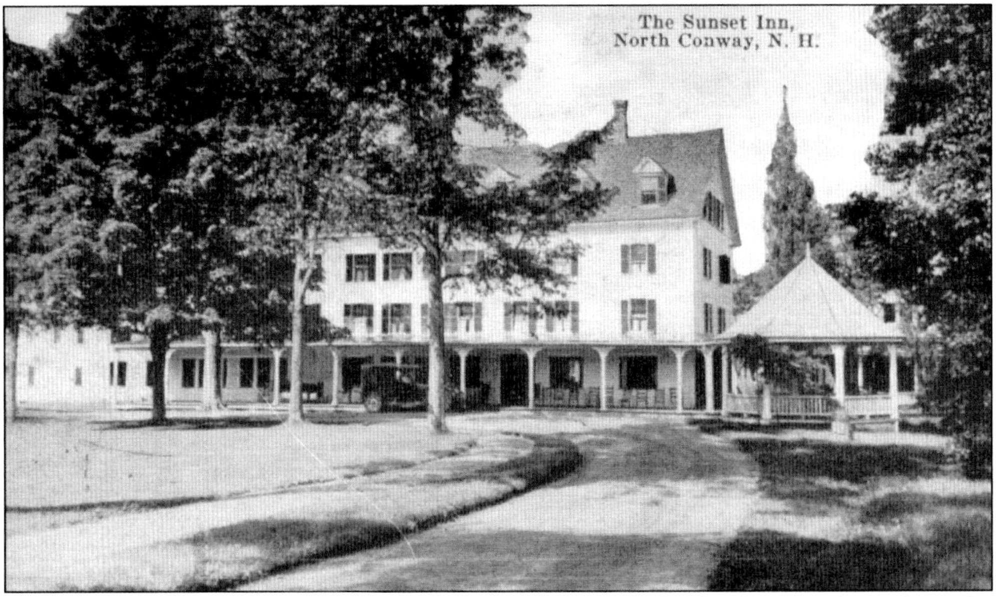

The Sunset Inn and Music Hall, originally the site of a medical school operated by Alexander Ramsey, is now the Eastern Slope Playhouse. Actors associated with the theater include David Strathairn from such films as *Good Night and Good Luck* and *The Bourne Ultimatum*; Brian Clark, best known for a guest role on *Cheers*; Gordon Clapp of *NYPD Blue*, and filmmaker John Sayles. The building was spared when a 1940 fire destroyed the hotel. (Henney History Room, Conway Public Library.)

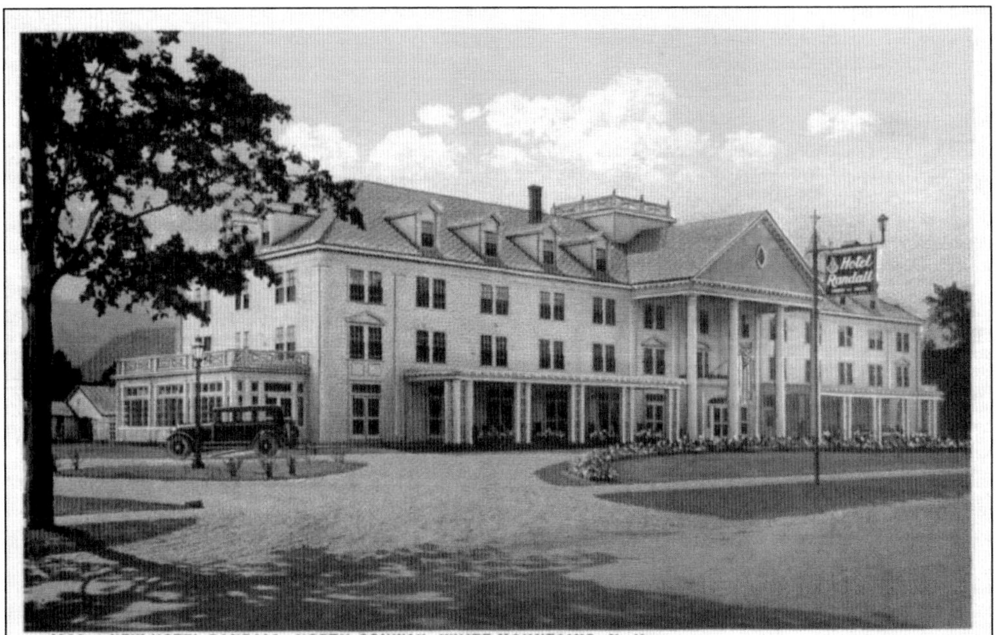

The third Hotel Randall was built in 1925, but Harvey Dow Gibson purchased it in 1926 and renamed it the Eastern Slope Inn. It is now on the National Register of Historic Places. On top of the main roof was an observation platform that offered sweeping views of the Presidential Range and the Mount Washington Valley. (Henney History Room, Conway Public Library.)

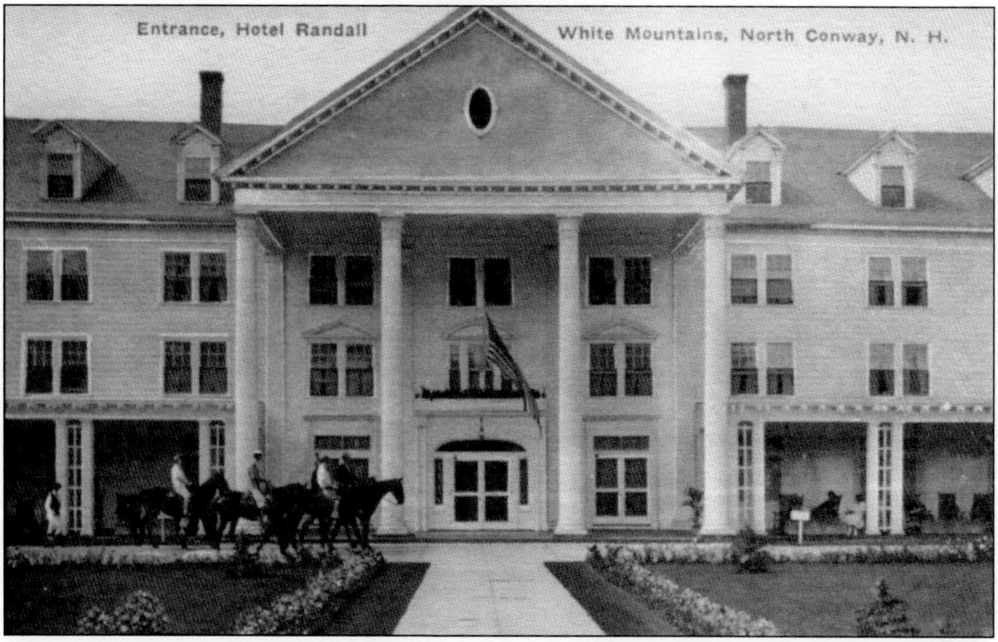

Horses were used to pull wagons, carriages, coaches, and farm equipment as well as for pleasure and sport. (Henney History Room, Conway Public Library.)

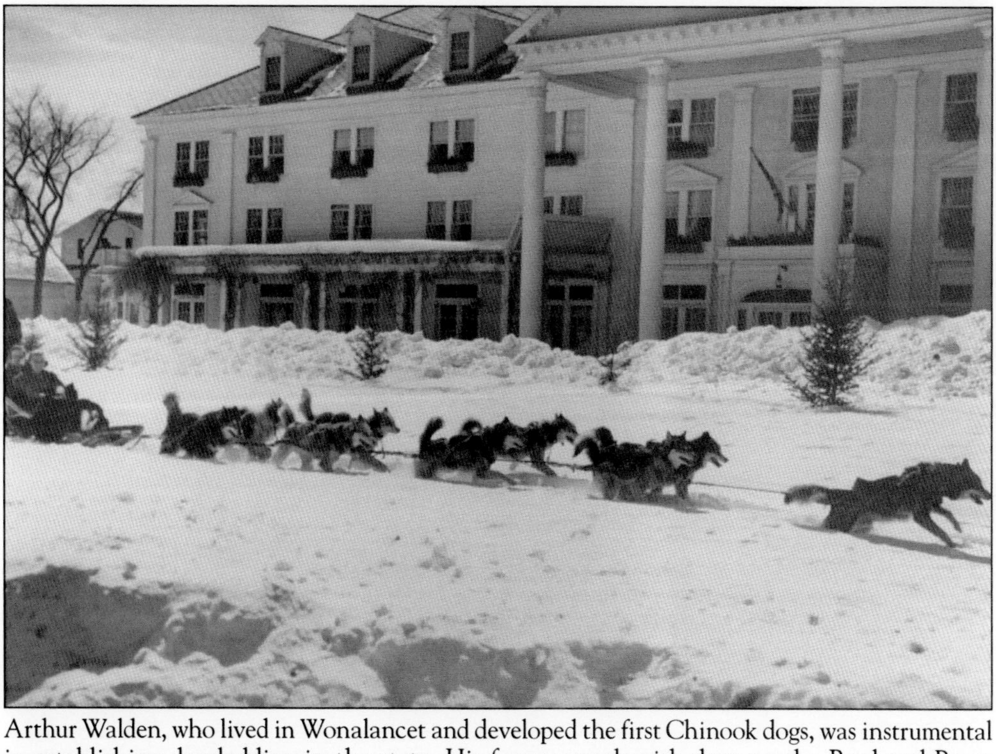

Arthur Walden, who lived in Wonalancet and developed the first Chinook dogs, was instrumental in establishing dogsledding in the state. His famous work with dogs on the Byrd and Peary expeditions to the North and South Poles popularized dogsledding and racing in the region. (North Conway Public Library.)

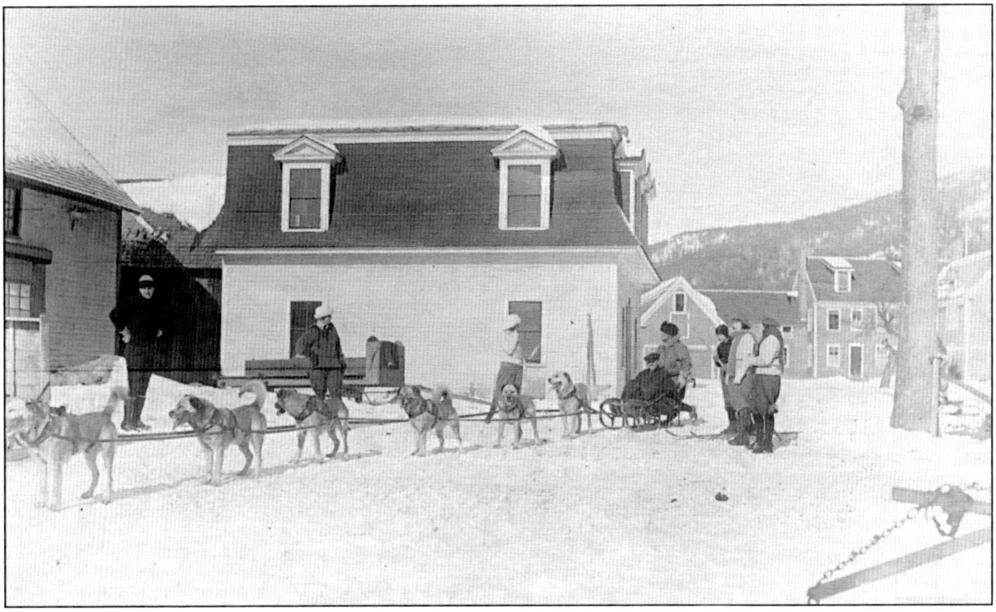

The White Mountains of central New Hampshire have been the center of American dogsledding since the early part of the 20th century. Chinook dogs, now the state dog of New Hampshire, are an important, rare breed and were frequently seen in North Conway with their original breeder, Arthur Walden, pictured here wearing his distinctive fur hat as he drives the sled. (Henney History Room, Conway Public Library.)

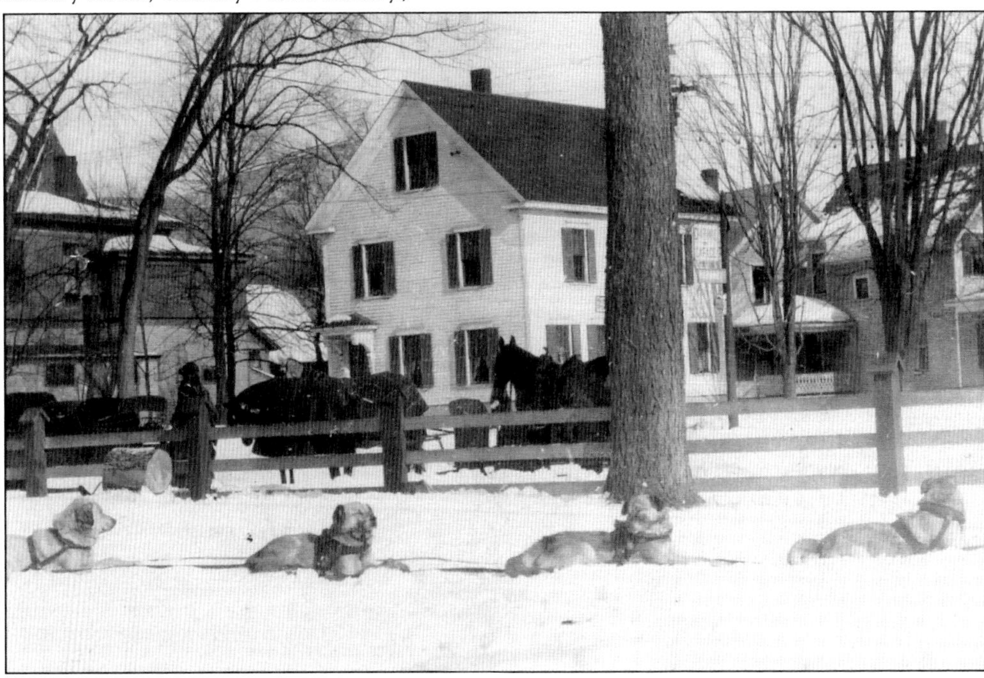

A team of Chinooks, driven by Arthur Walden, made the first ascent of Mount Washington by dog team in 1926. Signs in the background suggest this photograph was taken near the White Mountain Steam Laundry and Chapman's Garage on Seavey Street. (Henney History Room, Conway Public Library.)

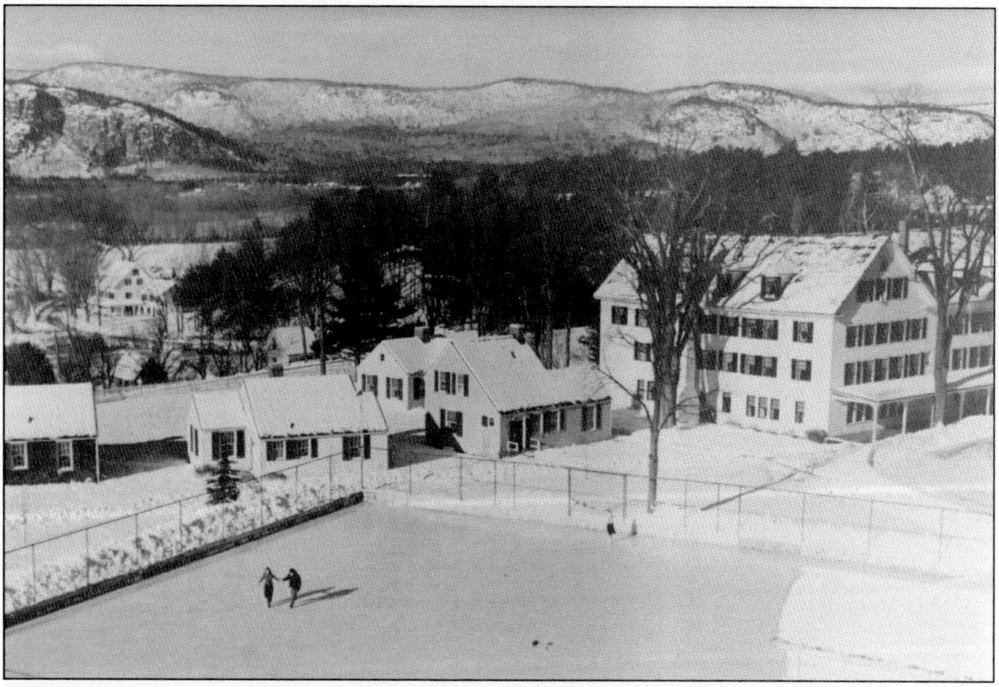

The Sunset Inn and Cottages in the background burned down in the summer of 1940. During the winter, the tennis courts were flooded to create an outdoor ice-skating rink. In the summer, tennis tournaments were held at Eastern Slope, and later the Volvo Classic was held at Cranmore. (North Conway Public Library, photograph by James M. Bray.)

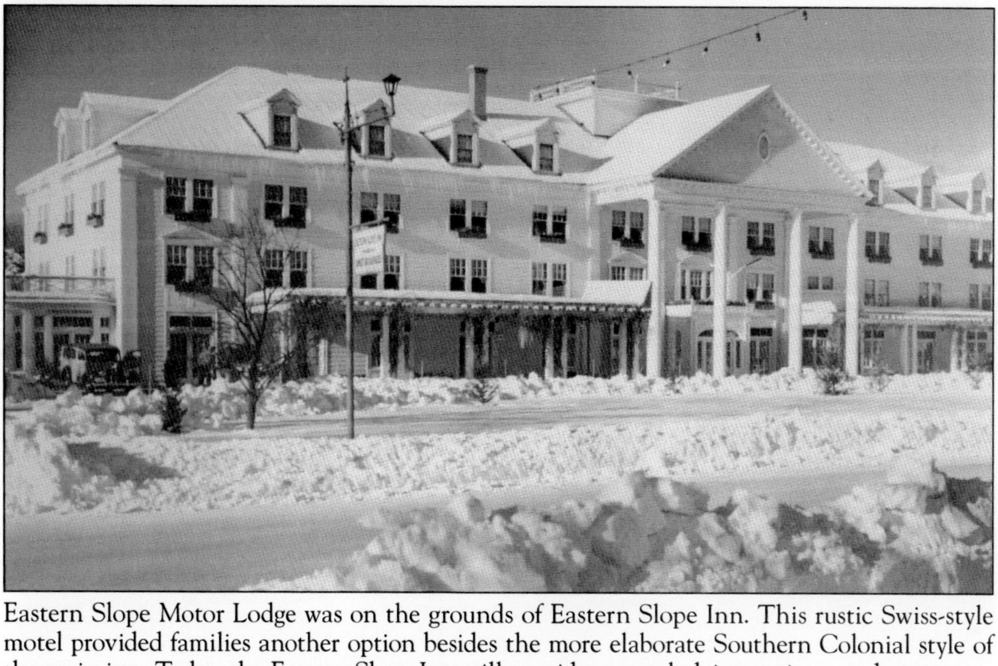

Eastern Slope Motor Lodge was on the grounds of Eastern Slope Inn. This rustic Swiss-style motel provided families another option besides the more elaborate Southern Colonial style of the main inn. Today, the Eastern Slope Inn still provides many lodging options, and guests can enjoy a variety of cottages, townhouses, suites, and the nearby Oxen Yoke Inn. (Conway Historical Society, photograph by Dick Smith.)

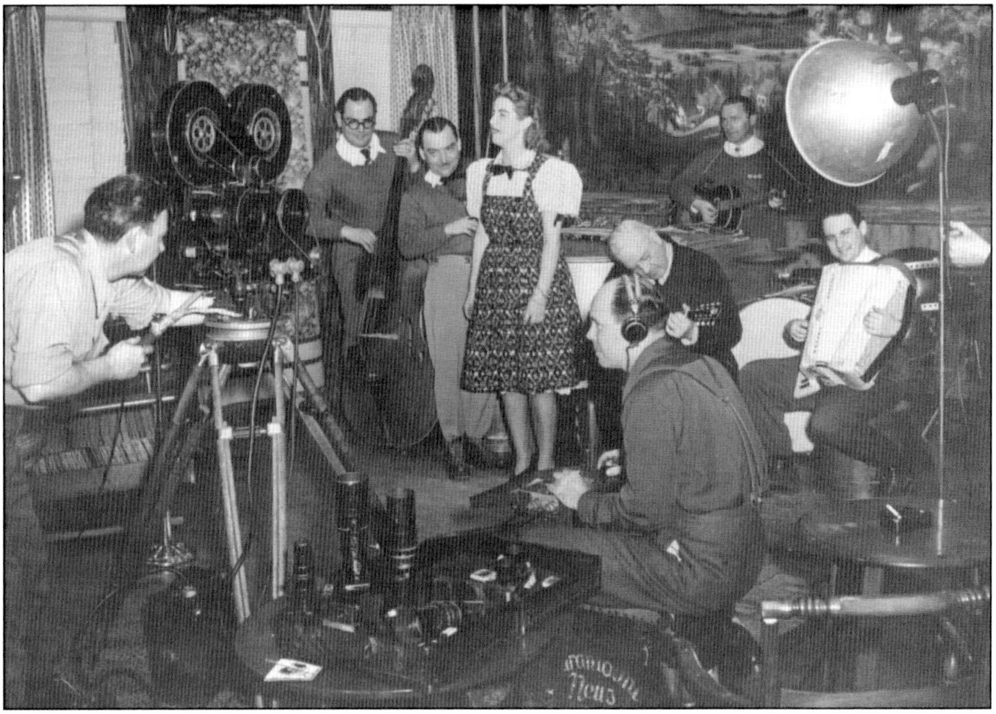

Charles Zumstein and his Swiss Orchestra, formerly of the New York and Paris World's Fairs, was the house band at the Eastern Slope Inn. Here, Harvey Dow Gibson sits in the center as he plays his mandolin. The orchestra is seen playing in the Currier and Ives Room, which features wall murals based on well-known prints, such as this famous 1860 Fanny Palmer print of North Conway. (North Conway Public Library, photograph by James M. Bray.)

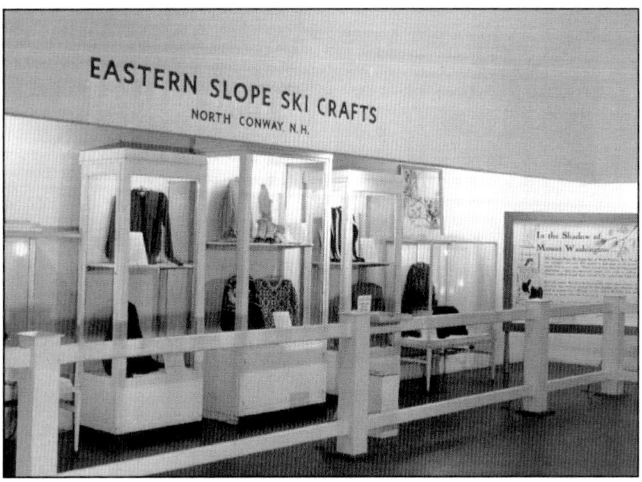

Eastern Slope Ski Crafts was established in 1939 to employ women around North Conway and promote historical craft traditions. The sign explains that its sweaters will keep out the cold at 20 degrees below zero and yet not be too heavy when the snow thaws in the spring. Today, the Conway Home Industries and the League of New Hampshire Craftsmen continue this heritage of handcrafted items. (North Conway Public Library, photograph by James M. Bray.)

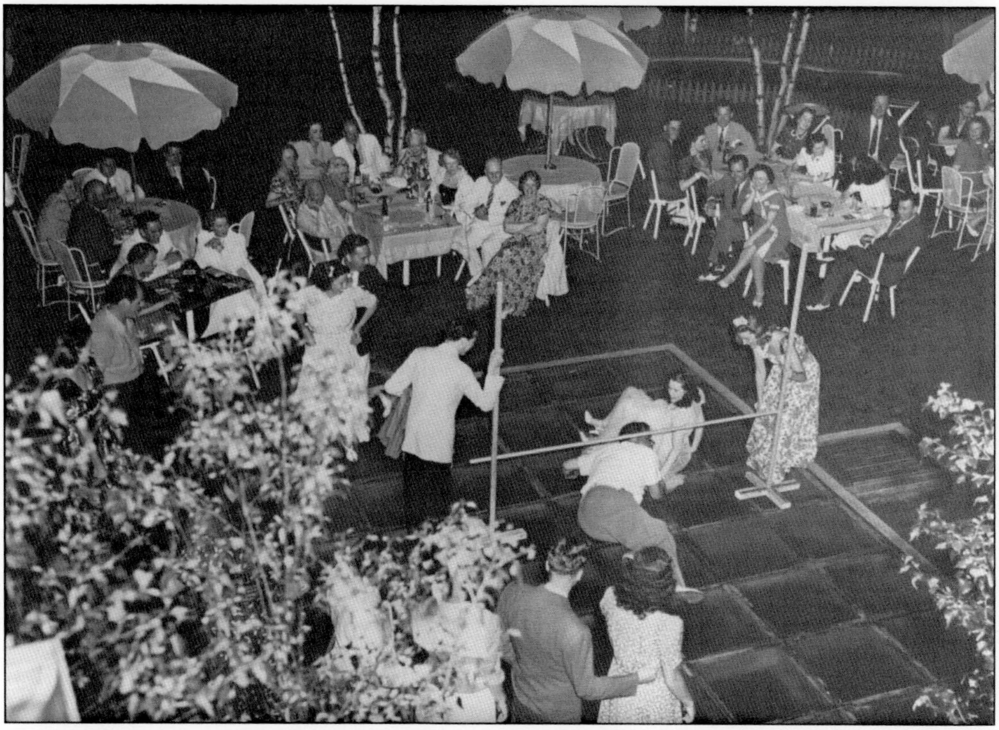

The southwest courtyard of the Eastern Slope Inn had a unique dining and dancing patio called the Terrace Garden, famous for its "sub illuminated glass dance floor"; it was touted as the only outdoor one of its kind in America. (North Conway Public Library, photograph by James M. Bray.)

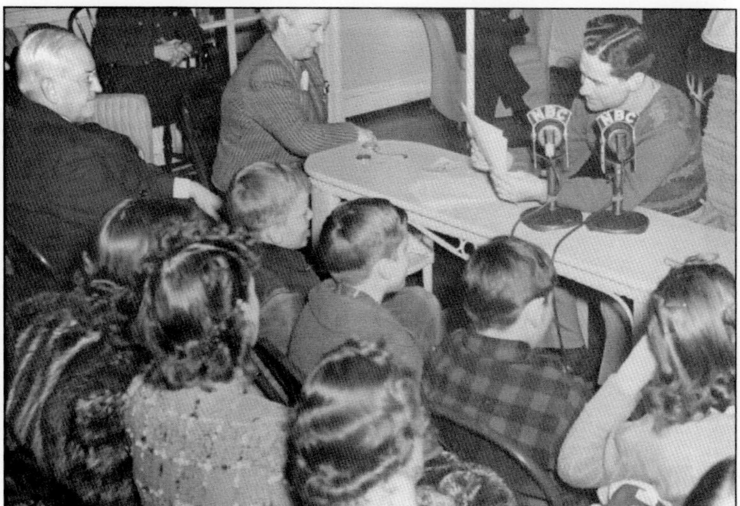

Lowell Thomas reports from the Eastern Slope Inn in 1939. This national radio broadcast featured an interview with skier Hannes Schneider. Anxious to learn to ski, children were invited to sit in the front row. Promoter Harvey Dow Gibson is on the left. (North Conway Public Library, photograph by James M. Bray.)

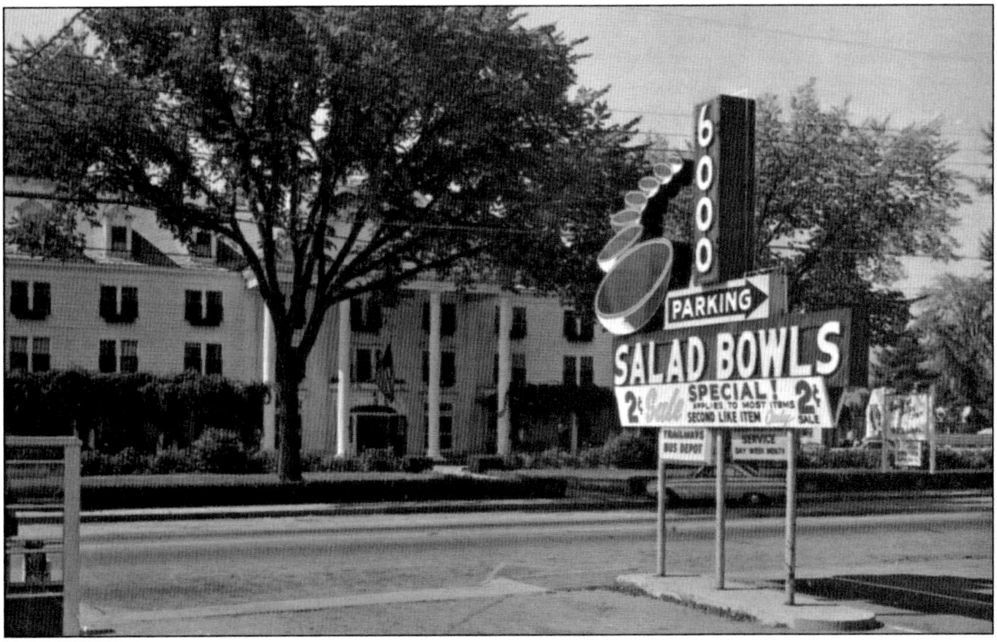

Across the street from the Eastern Slope Inn was one of the most unique landmarks in the area, which was owned by Betty Louise (McAllister) Hoyt, whose famous native bowls were shipped all over the world. The site was also the home of the Trailways Bus Depot. In 1973, the 6000 Salad Bowls shop was memorialized by a group of rock-climbing enthusiasts in the name of a climbing trail on Crawford Notch's Mount Willard. (Conway Historical Society.)

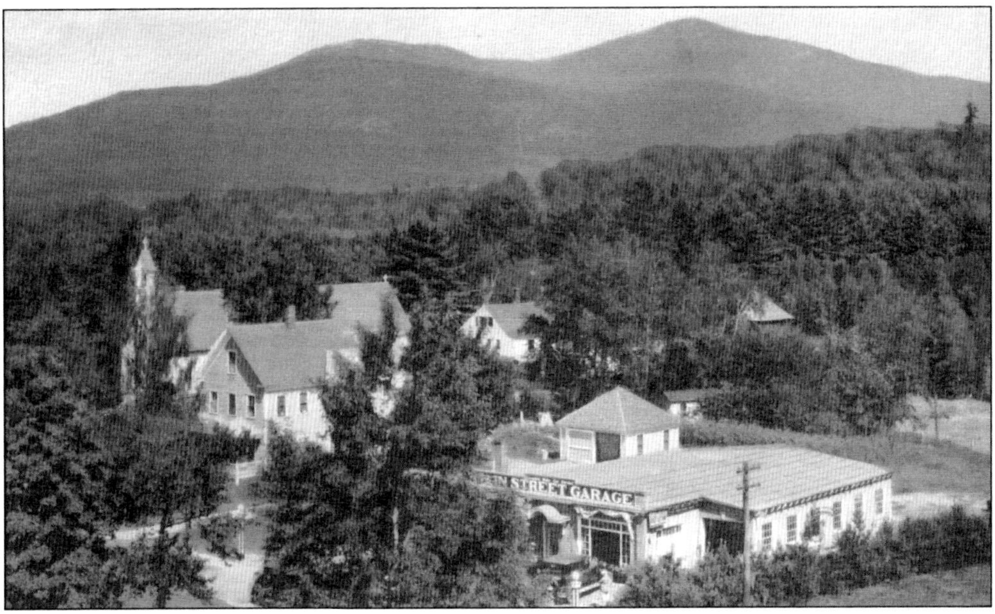

Probably taken from the parapet of the Eastern Slope Inn, these buildings were replaced by several brick buildings now housing the Mount Washington Observatory Museum and Citizen's Bank. To the far left is Christ Church Episcopal. A fire tower on Mount Kearsarge that protected the area's forests can still be visited today. (Henney History Room, Conway Public Library.)

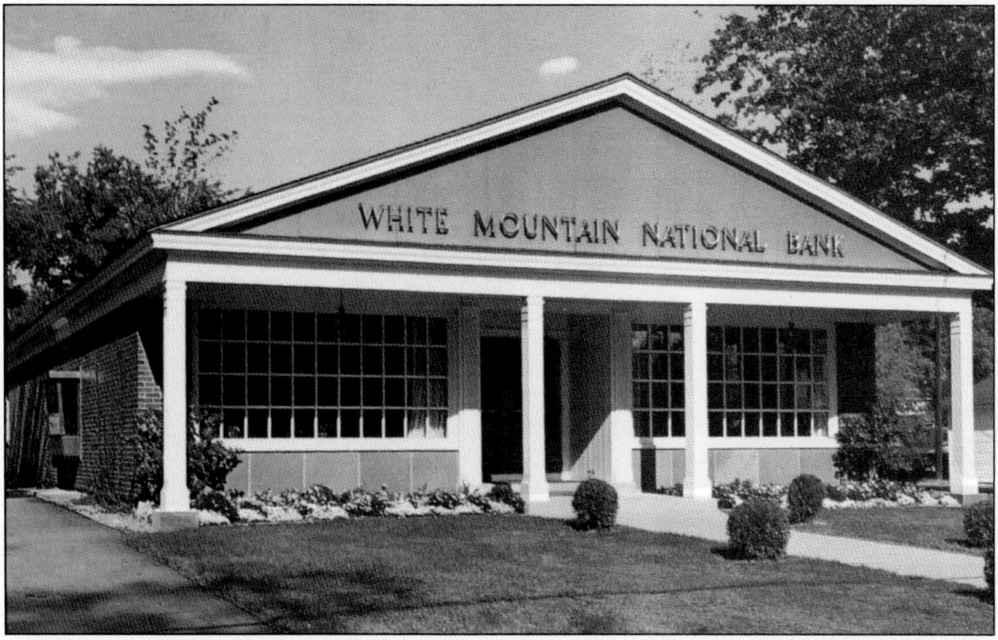

This branch of White Mountain National Bank (now Citizen's Bank) and several other branches display a fine collection of White Mountain art. A connected annex houses the Mount Washington Observatory Weather Discovery Center, which is home to important archives of White Mountain historical materials, including early newspapers printed at the summit of Mount Washington. (Conway Historical Society.)

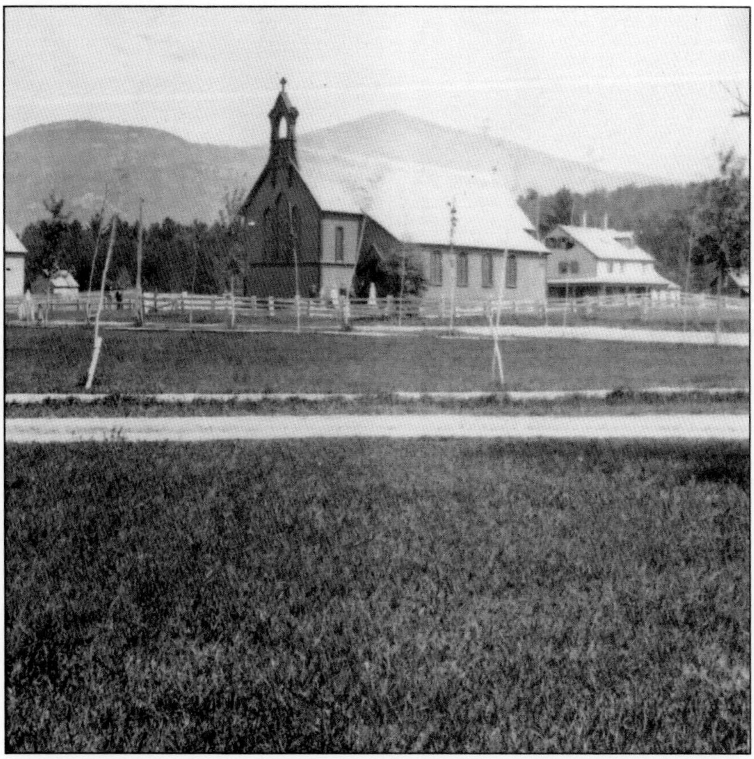

Christ Church Episcopal, built in 1876, was located on the southeast corner of Main and Pine Streets, about 3.5 miles north of the Saco River Overlook. Thomas Murphy, whose wife, Lady Blanche Murphy, was of British royal descent, lived near Humphrey's Ledge and was the organist and choir director. Some of his original musical scores still exist. (Henney History Room, Conway Public Library.)

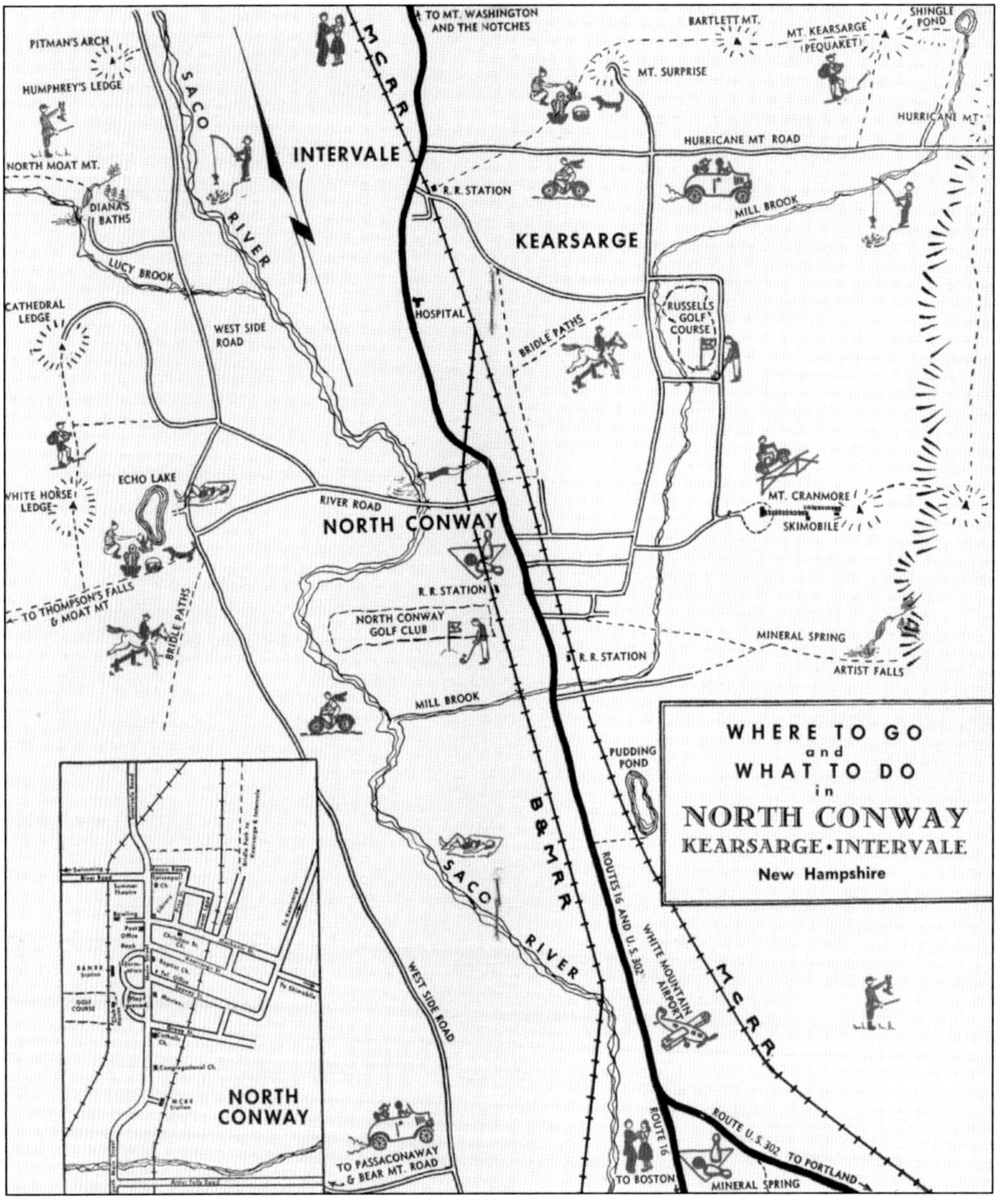

This chamber of commerce map from the 1940s or 1950s shows "Where to Go and What to Do in North Conway." There are symbols for the bowling alleys, bridle trails, waterfalls, golf courses, and other activities. When asked, many natives would say that North Conway begins at Bowling Alley Hill, seen on the bottom of this map with a bowling alley symbol, and runs up to the Bartlett town line at Hurricane Mountain Road. The map shows another bowling alley to the north near the North Conway Golf Club and the railroad station. (Henney History Room, Conway Public Library.)

Two

THE SOUTHERN GATEWAY

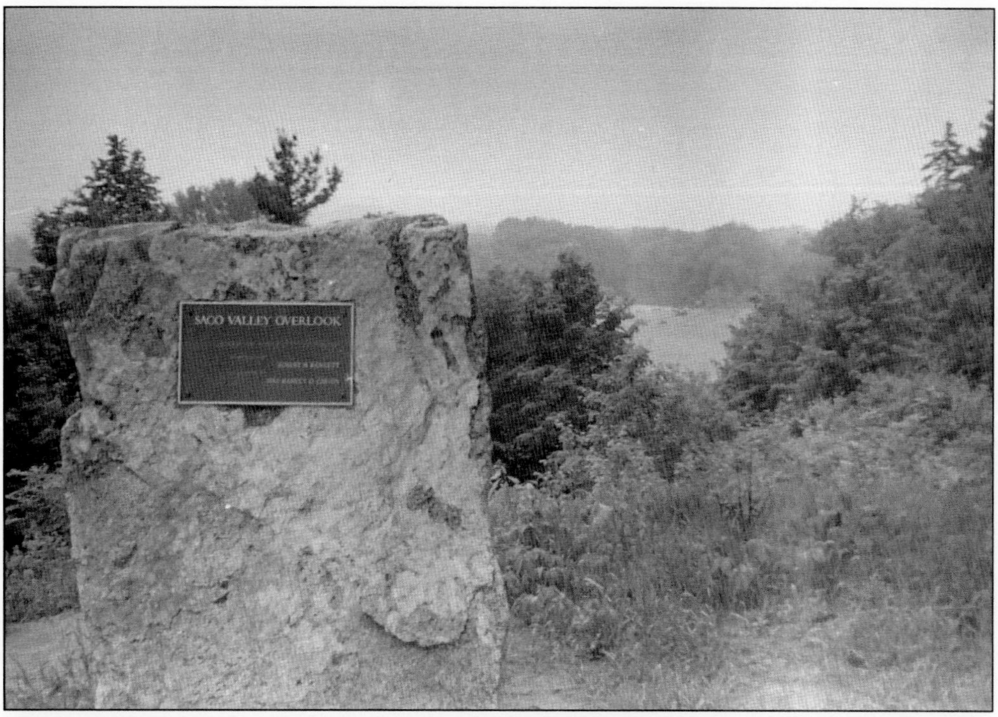

While some natives place the southern boundary of North Conway at Bowling Alley Hill, others place it a half mile south at the Saco River Overlook, which is about five miles from the Bartlett town line. The bronze plaque on the granite monument reads, "Saco Valley Overlook. Given in 1973 by the Pequawket Foundation. In memory of Robert H. Kennett. In honor of Mrs. Harvey Dow Gibson." (Henney History Room, Conway Public Library.)

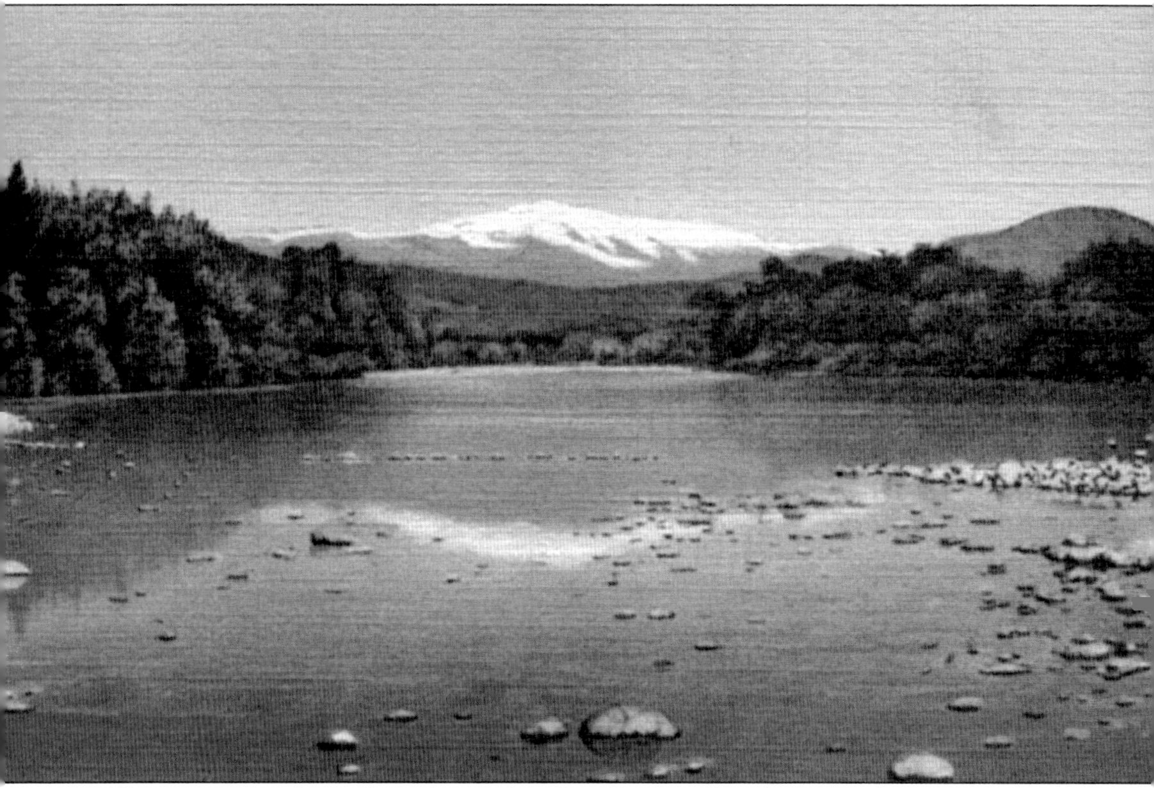

There are many places along the winding Saco River within this view of Mount Washington, including one spot just below the Saco River Overlook near a rope swing and swimming hole. Canoeing and kayaking have long been popular pursuits, and a number of outfitters provide rentals. Between here and the beginning of North Conway's downtown area is the Dahl Audubon Sanctuary. (Conway Historical Society.)

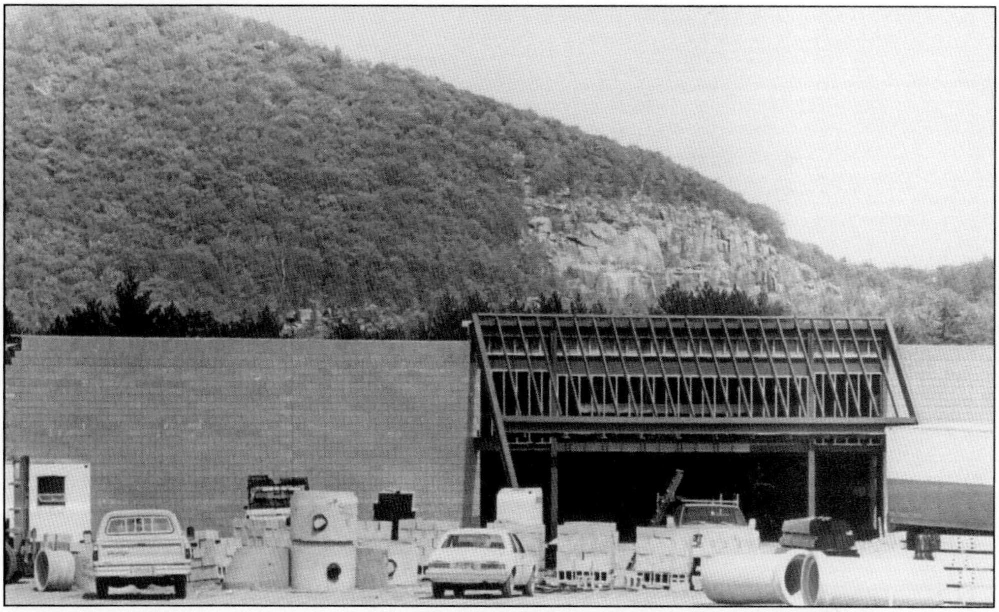

Beyond the old Howard Johnson's site is the road leading to the Mountain Valley Mall, pictured here under construction in 1980. Recently, the mall was renovated, and only a few of the key stores remain, as some have been replaced by bigger chain stores. (Henney History Room, Conway Public Library.)

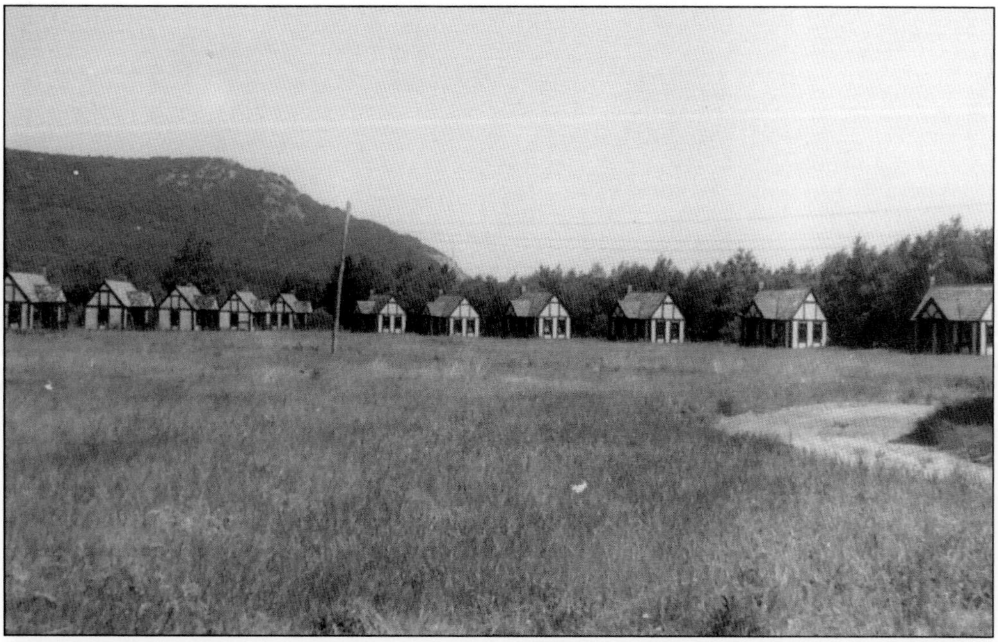

Green Granite Cottages was established in the early 1930s, and these small cabins were expanded and developed into the 90-room Green Granite Inn and Conference Center. The cottages and center were named after the green granite from the quarry seen in the background, with its tall derricks for hoisting and moving stone. A number of granite relics from the quarry are displayed at the inn. (Henney History Room, Conway Public Library.)

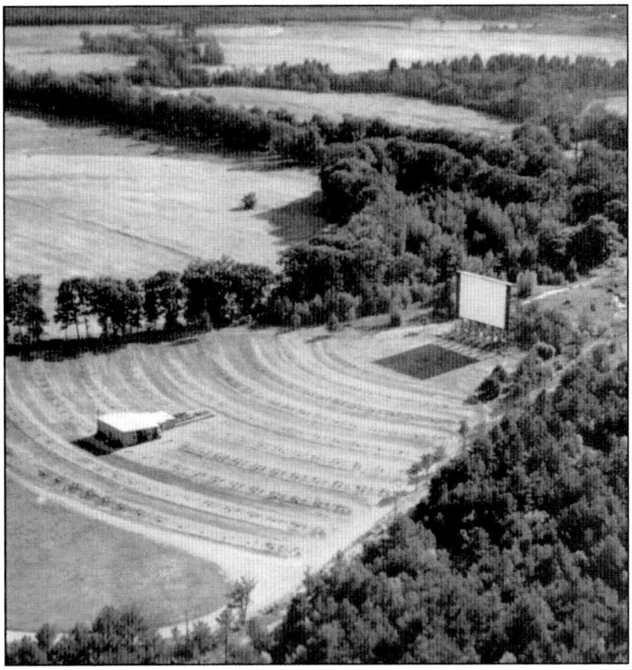

The marquee sign for what was billed as "New England's most beautiful outdoor movie theatre" still remains. With a 300-car capacity, it had a "colorful free playground for kiddies" with Miracle Whirls, hobbyhorses, swings, and slides. A free baby bottle–warming service was provided, and children under 12 were admitted free. It is now the site of the defunct Yankee Settlements housing development for seniors. (Henney History Room, Conway Public Library.)

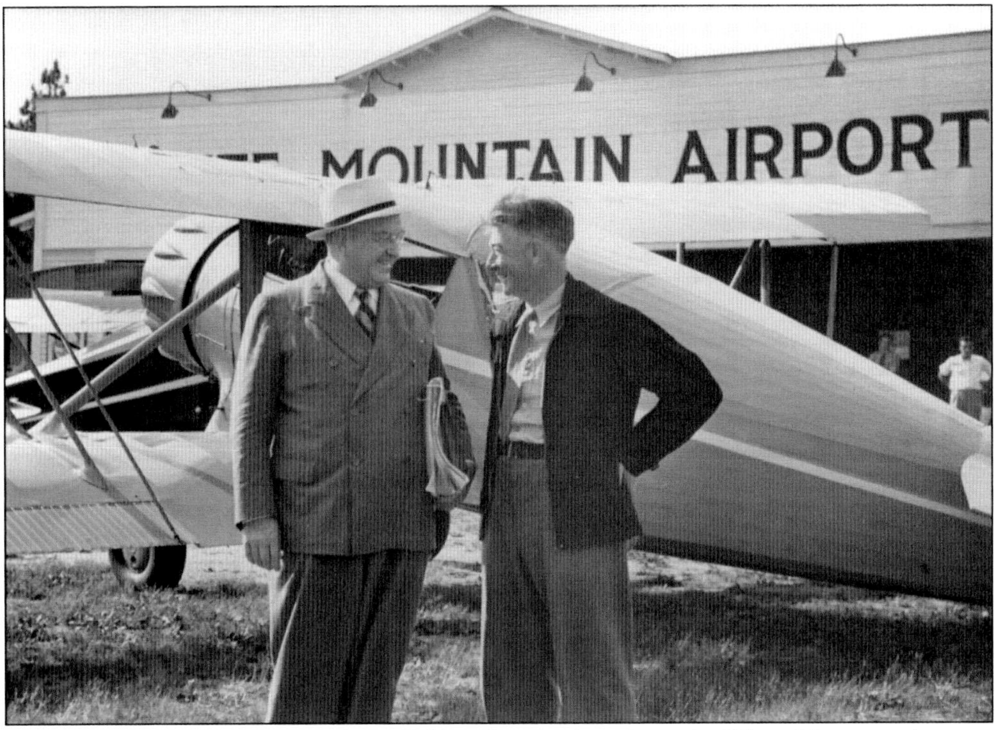

Pictured here are Harvey Dow Gibson (left) and Wylie Apte Sr. at the White Mountain Airport. Built in the 1920s on a horse track, the airport closed in 1980s, and the site now holds Settler's Green Outlet Village Shops, with the former hangar renovated as a storefront. A biplane weather vane is on the roof, and in front of the building is a granite marker commemorating Apte as a pioneer aviator. (North Conway Public Library, photograph by James M. Bray.)

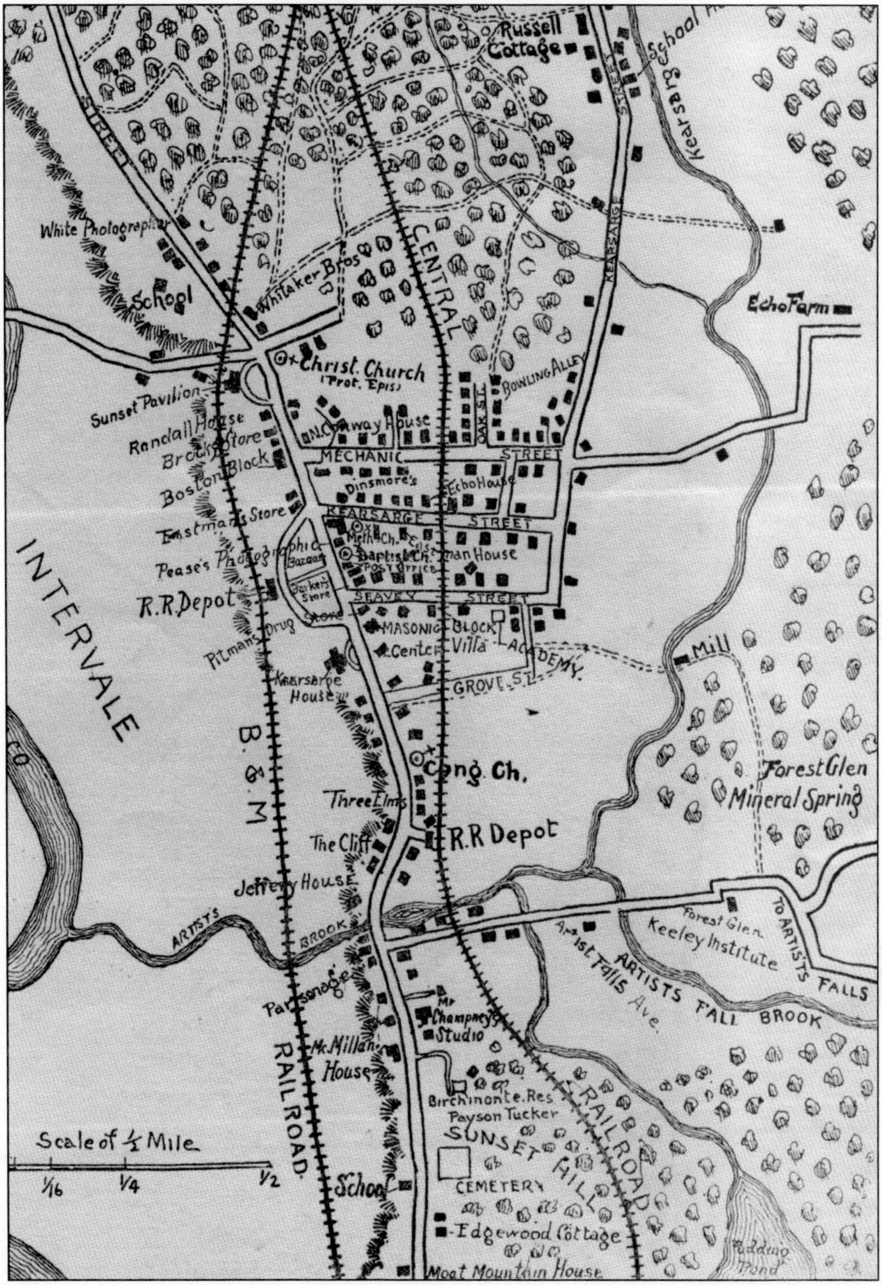

Showing the north half of Pudding Pond on the right, this map illustrates Russell Cottage in the north. A network of trails indicated by dashed lines lead to attractions throughout North Conway. Guests from the Russell Cottage could take a trail to the bowling alley at the end of Oak Street or to the studio of "White Photographer," as it is referred to here. Trails from Seavey and Grove Streets lead to a mill on Kearsarge Brook and continue on past the Forest Glen mineral spring to Artists' Falls Road and the Keeley Institute. The map shows all of the railroad depots, inns, stores, and attractions the rambling tourist would need to find. The hatched lines behind the buildings along the main street represent the high ledge upon which North Conway was built, protecting it from the periodic floods of the Saco. (Conway Historical Society.)

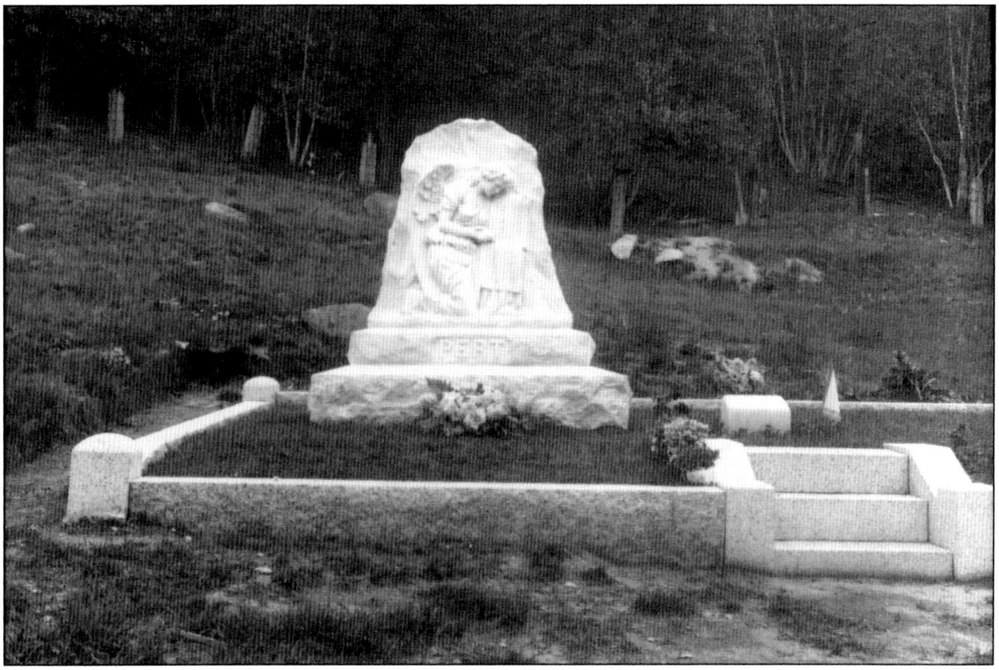

This cemetery, which is noted on the rambler map, is about two miles north of the Saco River Overlook. The photograph offers an example of the fine workmanship of marble and granite found in the area cemeteries. Many of these tombstones were produced by local stonecutters working at town quarries. (Henney History Room, Conway Public Library.)

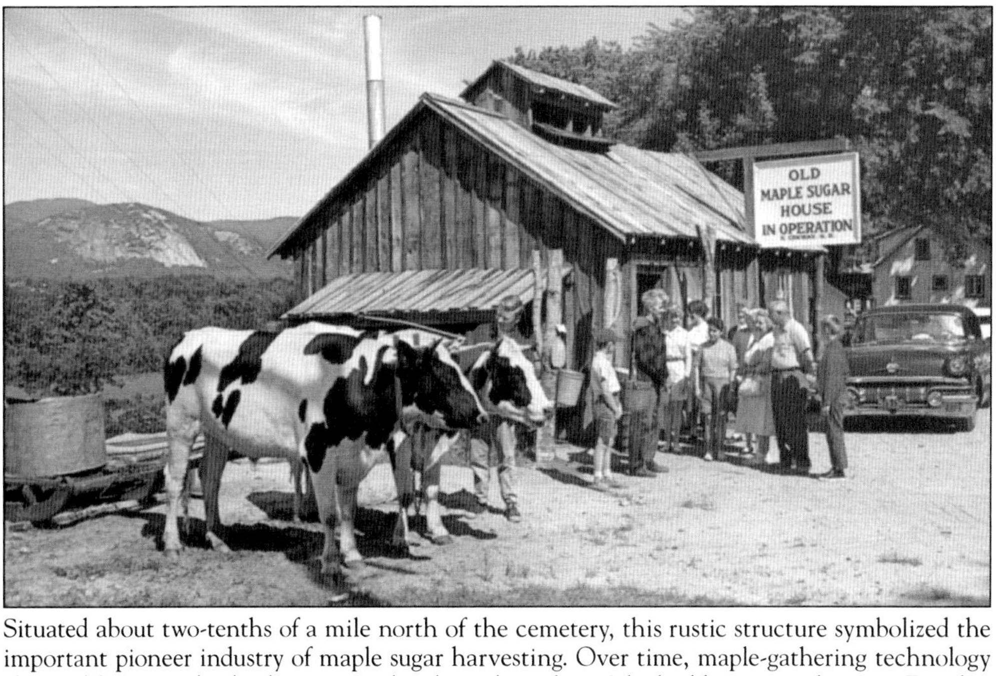

Situated about two-tenths of a mile north of the cemetery, this rustic structure symbolized the important pioneer industry of maple sugar harvesting. Over time, maple-gathering technology changed from wooden buckets to metal pails to plastic bags. The building is now home to Emerlyn Technology, developers of high-tech medical software. (Conway Historical Society, photograph by Dick Smith.)

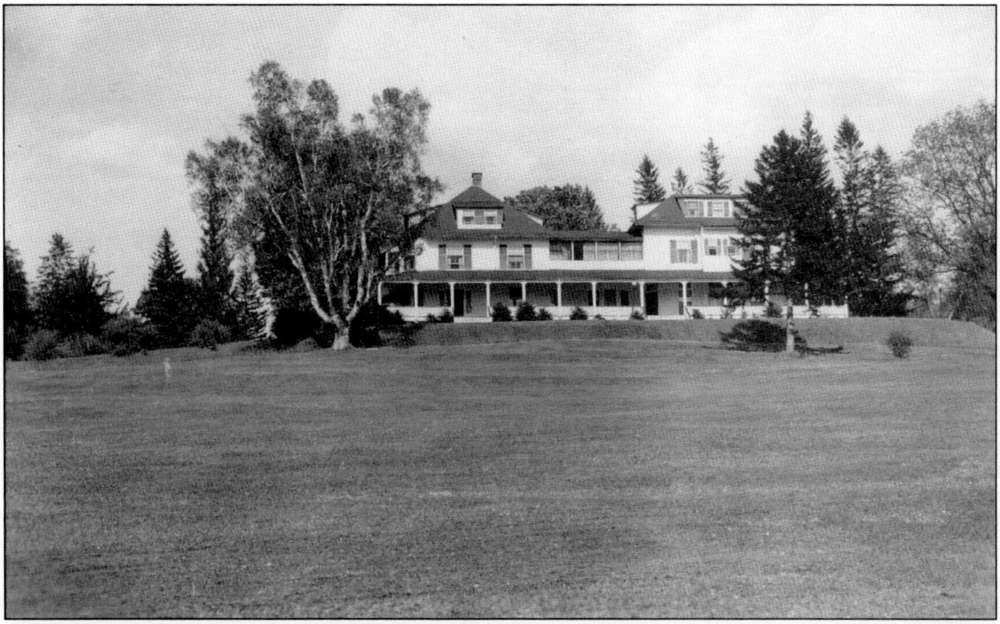

Birchmont was built on the crest of Sunset Hill as a country seat for Payson Tucker, the president of the Maine Central Railroad, in 1890. Tucker constructed a rail spur to it so his guests could arrive by private railway car. Later, Harvey Dow Gibson ran it for 20 years as an executive retreat for the Manufacturers' Trust, of which he was president. It later operated as an inn until it burned down in 1970. (Conway Historical Society, photograph by Bob Knapp.)

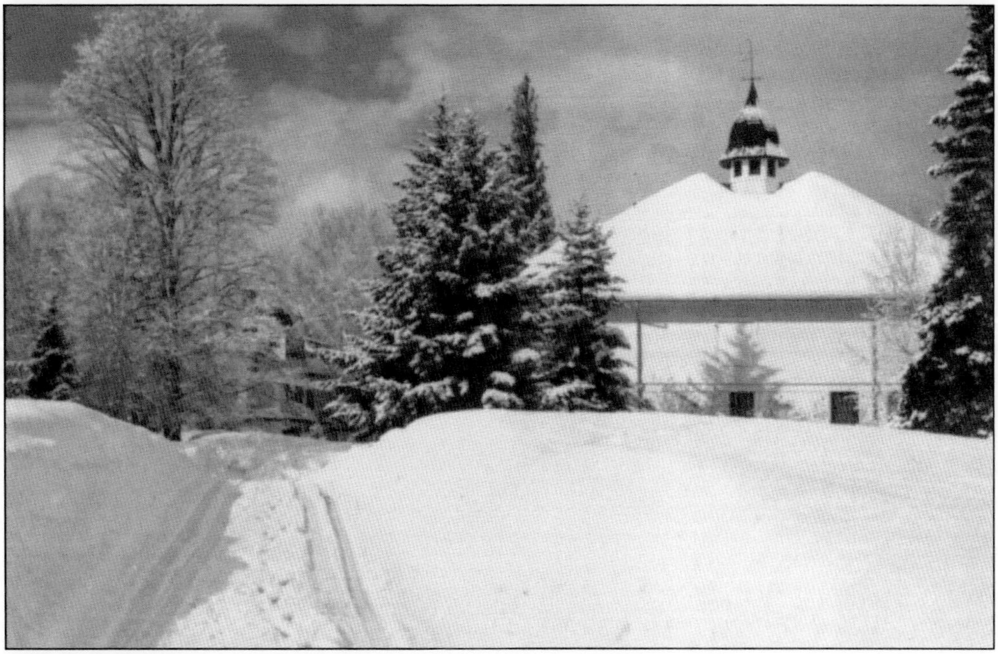

The carriage house and nearby icehouse survived the 1970 fire. They were built with similar architectural details, including a distinctive arched cupola and flared walls with fish-shaped shingles. Over the years, the carriage house was used as a tavern and a fitness center, while the icehouse is still used for storage. (Conway Historical Society, photograph by Bob Knapp.)

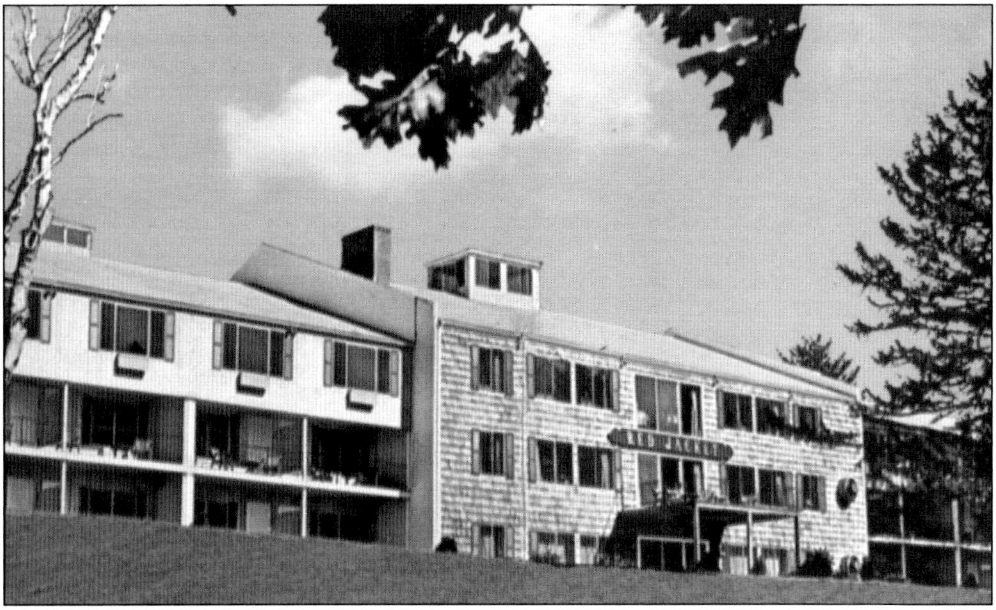

The site of Birchmont now holds Kahuna Laguna, the largest indoor water park in New England, with four waterslides, a wave pool, a water basketball court, a waterfall, and a 25-person hot tub. Along this ridge, some of the most famous views of the White Mountains were sketched and painted. Unfortunately, much of the vista is now blocked by trees and development. (Conway Historical Society, photograph by J. Lazarus.)

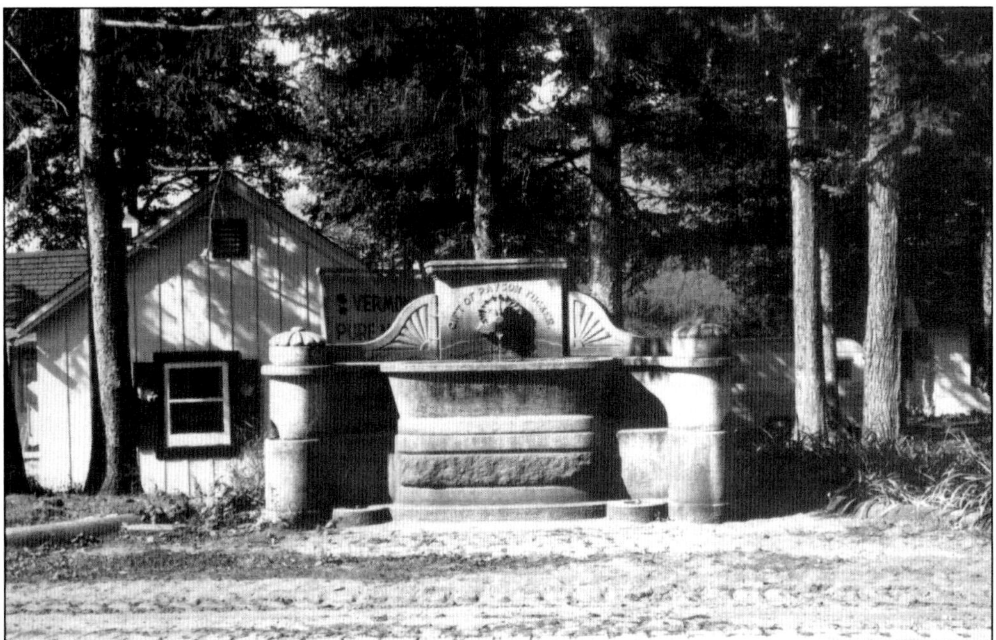

This granite public fountain with carved artistic flourishes was a gift to the town from Payson Tucker in 1894. It has several levels of watering sources for horses, people, and dogs. The fountain was later moved a half mile north to Rotary Park at the northeast corner of Main Street and Depot Road. (Henney History Room, Conway Public Library.)

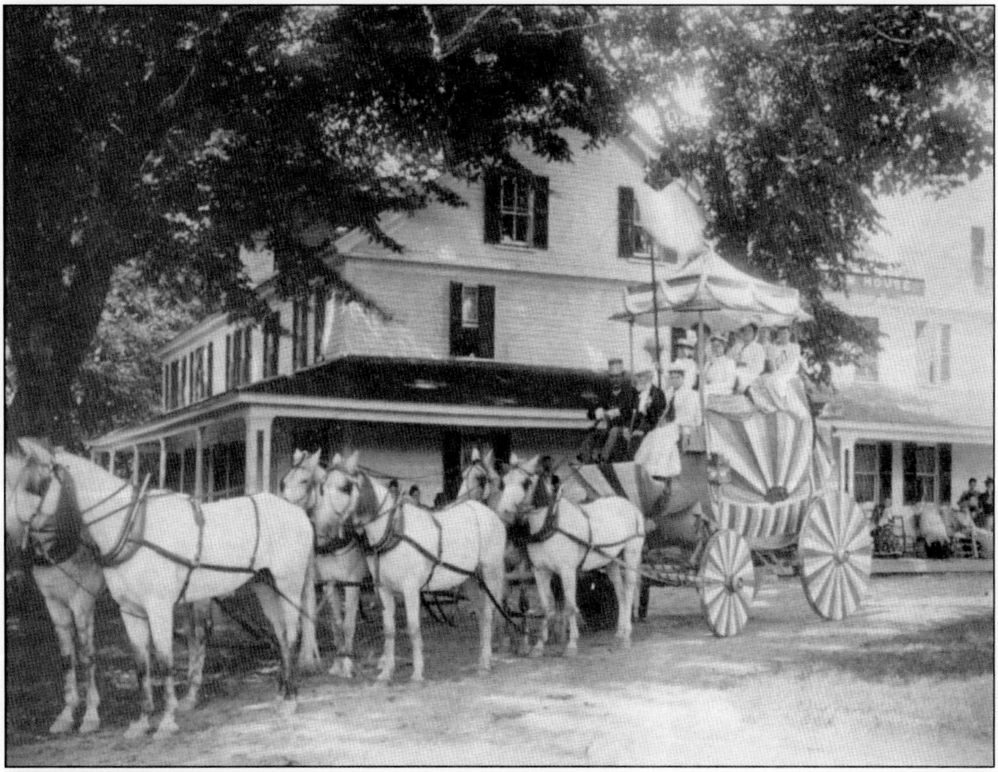

The McMillan House is between the driveway to Birchmont and Champney Studio. Historian David Emerson pointed out that although Eleazar Rosebrook is sometimes credited with opening the region's first inn around 1803, Andrew McMillan was operating his hostel in North Conway as early as 1784. The McMillan House was destroyed by fire in September 1899. (Henney History Room, Conway Public Library.)

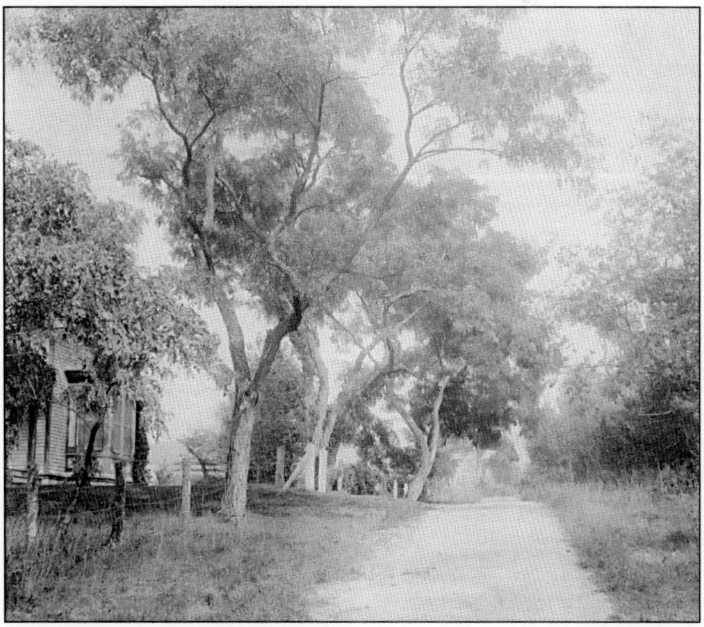

Once known as Hansen's Lane, Locust Lane is now the exit from the Red Jacket Resort. The bay window of the Alpheus Furber house, seen on the left, is now the Red Elephant Inn. Due to their rot-resistant nature, the twisting locust trees seen lining this road were prized for their wood, which were made into fence posts, connected here by barbed wire. Locust trees also provide beautiful and sweet smelling flowers in spring. (Henney History Room, Conway Public Library.)

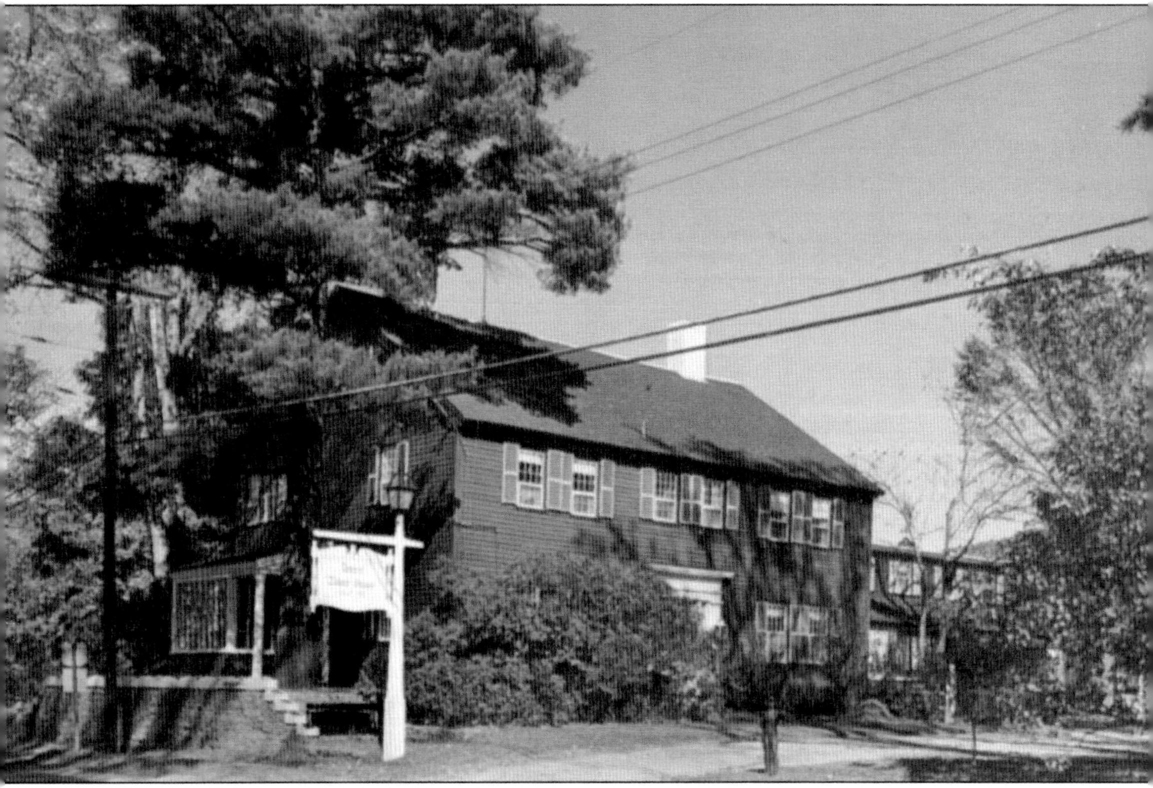

About 2.5 miles north of the Saco River Overlook sits the 1768 Country Inn, built for the Eastman family just three years after the town's charter was obtained from His Majesty George III in 1765. It was originally erected near Kearsarge Brook but was moved here to higher ground after the devastating freshet of 1785 in which the Saco flooded the intervale along its banks. It was common for houses to be moved in days before plumbing and electrical connections. A number of jacks, some skids, a little snow, and 20 or so yoke of oxen could do the job. (Conway Historical Society, photograph by Don Sieburg.)

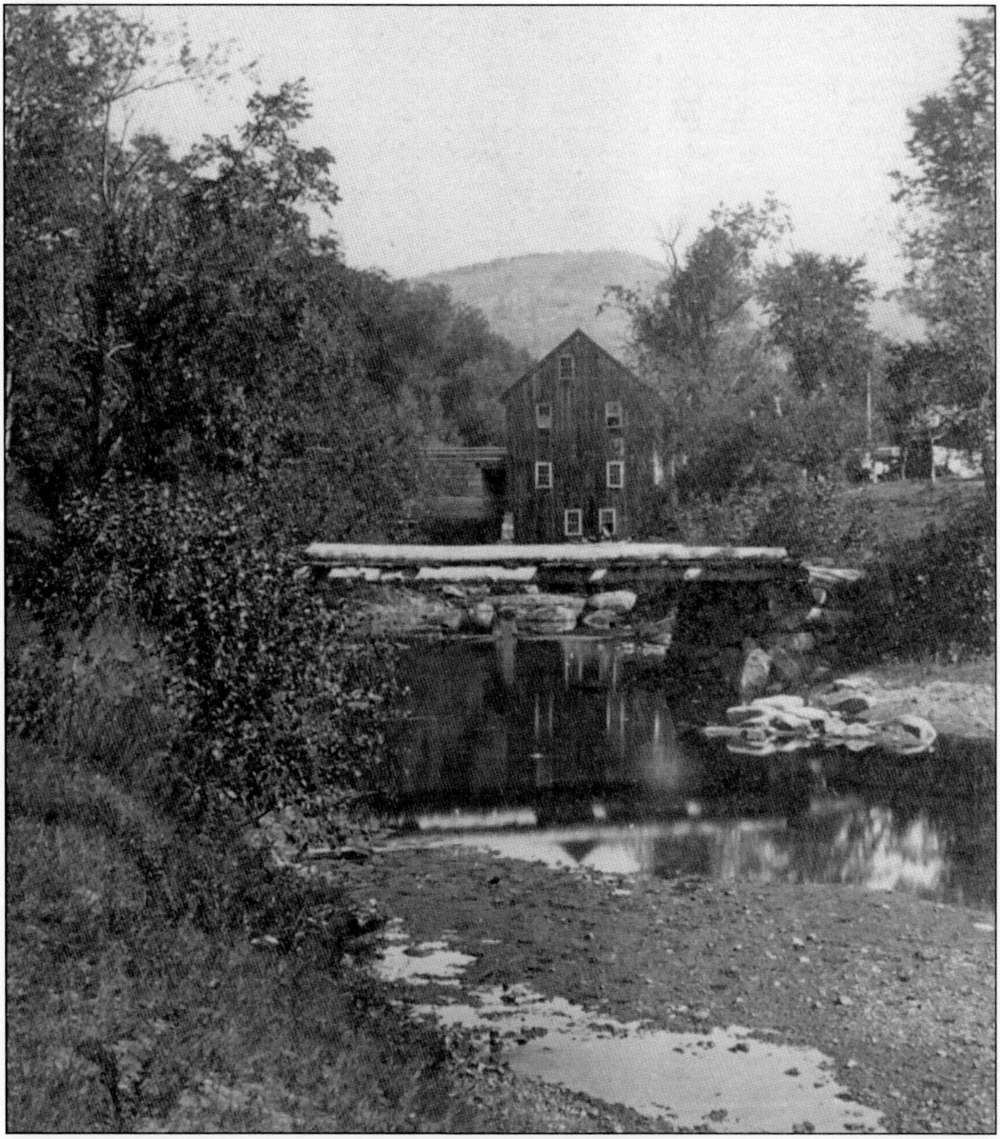

This intersection of Main Street and Artists' Brook was at the center of North Conway's art scene. Just a short distance from Benjamin Champney's house and studio, it was a rendezvous point and avenue for artistic exploration. Champney was a leading force in the White Mountain art tradition for over 60 years, a motivator to artists of his own generation, and a mentor to numerous younger artists. Many of the views they made famous are within just a mile or two of this point. Now the site of the Muddy Moose Restaurant, this mill was one of the few industrial buildings seen in White Mountain art, and this view was produced as a Currier and Ives print. It was listed as a sawmill on an 1860 map with a millpond behind the milldam, and on the 1892 map, it was listed with a blacksmith shop. (Conway Historical Society, photograph by Nathan W. Pease.)

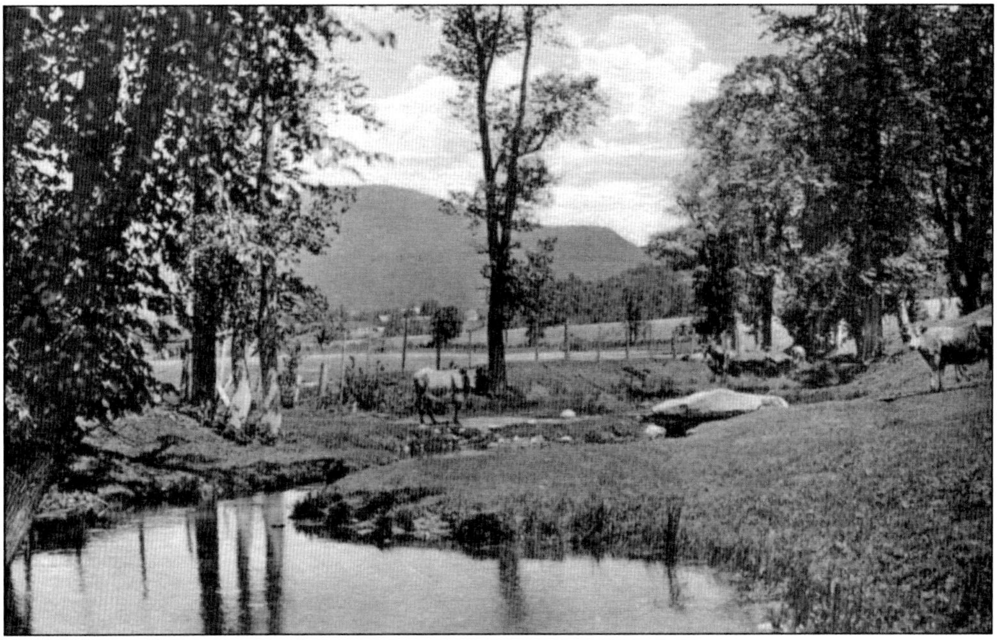

The meadows along Artists' Brook offered popular aesthetic viewpoints. The cool, refreshing air under the shaded maples and elms and the sound of the water made it a strong draw for city dwellers. The trails and fields were kept open by grazing livestock and farming crops, especially hay. Cattle and hay wagons are often seen in White Mountain art. (Conway Historical Society, photograph by Nathan W. Pease.)

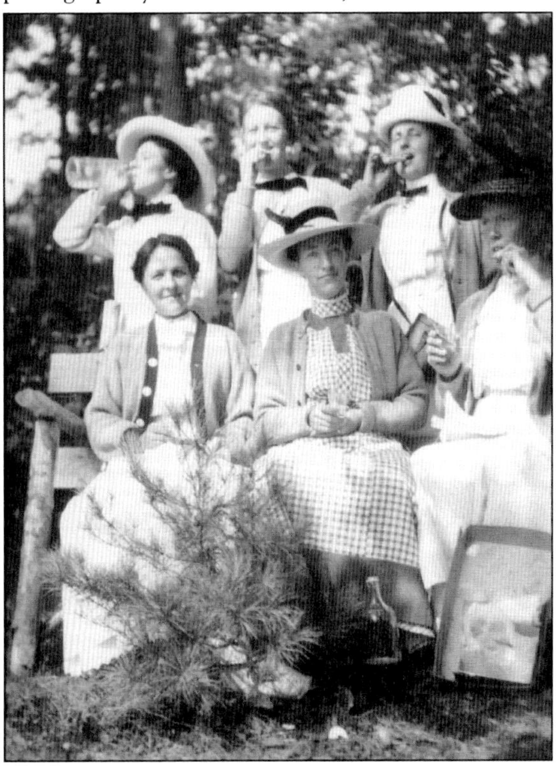

Clean water was an obsession for Victorians like these, who are most likely drinking water from one of two local mineral springs or another refreshing watering spot like the falls. Allowing livestock access to open water, along with other period activities, made many water sources suspect, and beer and cider were popular because alcohol kills germs. (Henney History Room, Conway Public Library.)

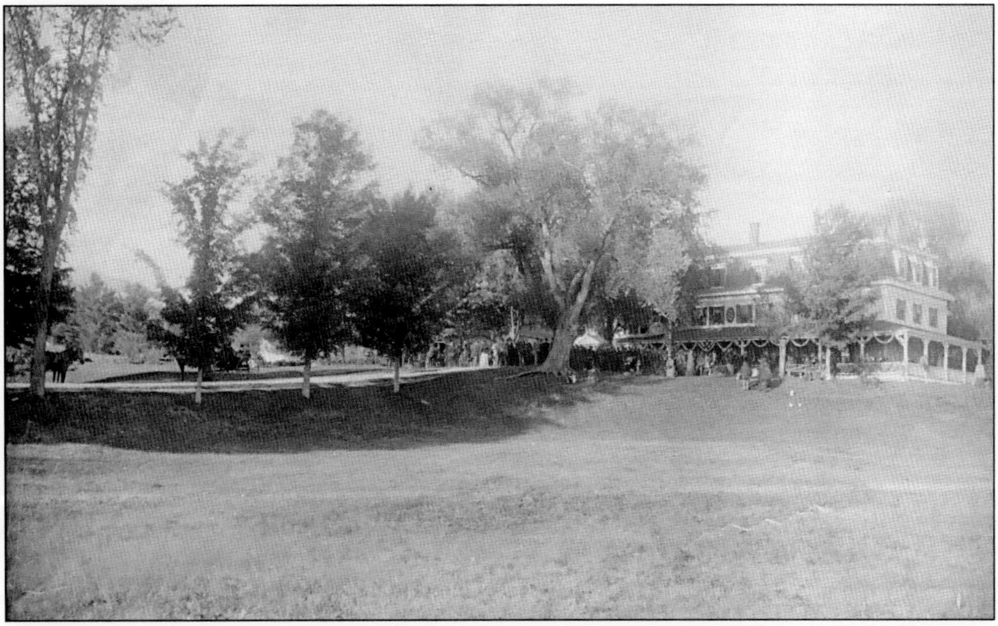

After being a patient at Dr. Leslie E. Keeley's sanatorium to cure alcohol, tobacco, and opium addiction in Dwight, Illinois, recovering alcoholic Payson Tucker decided to open a Keeley Institute in North Conway. He converted the former Artists' Falls House into the first sanatorium in the eastern United States. The Keeley Institute advertised accommodations as fine as any local hotel and that patients were allowed to bring their families to stay with them. Waters from the nearby mineral spring, as well as a mixture of noxious chemicals, figured in the health-restoring treatments. The above photograph features the distinctively shaped Keeley sign and a large number of guests on the lawn. Later, the building was enlarged and modernized as the Forest Glen Inn, as pictured below. It burned down in 1969. Today, the site is part of a 27-unit timeshare resort, complete with a sauna, hot tubs, and shuffleboard. (Both, Henney History Room, Conway Public Library.)

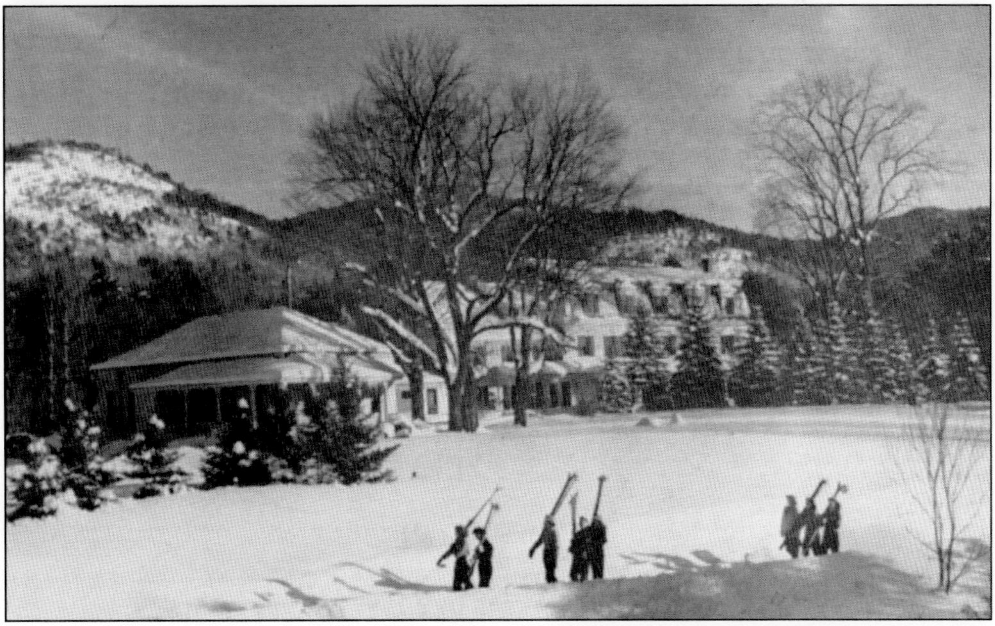

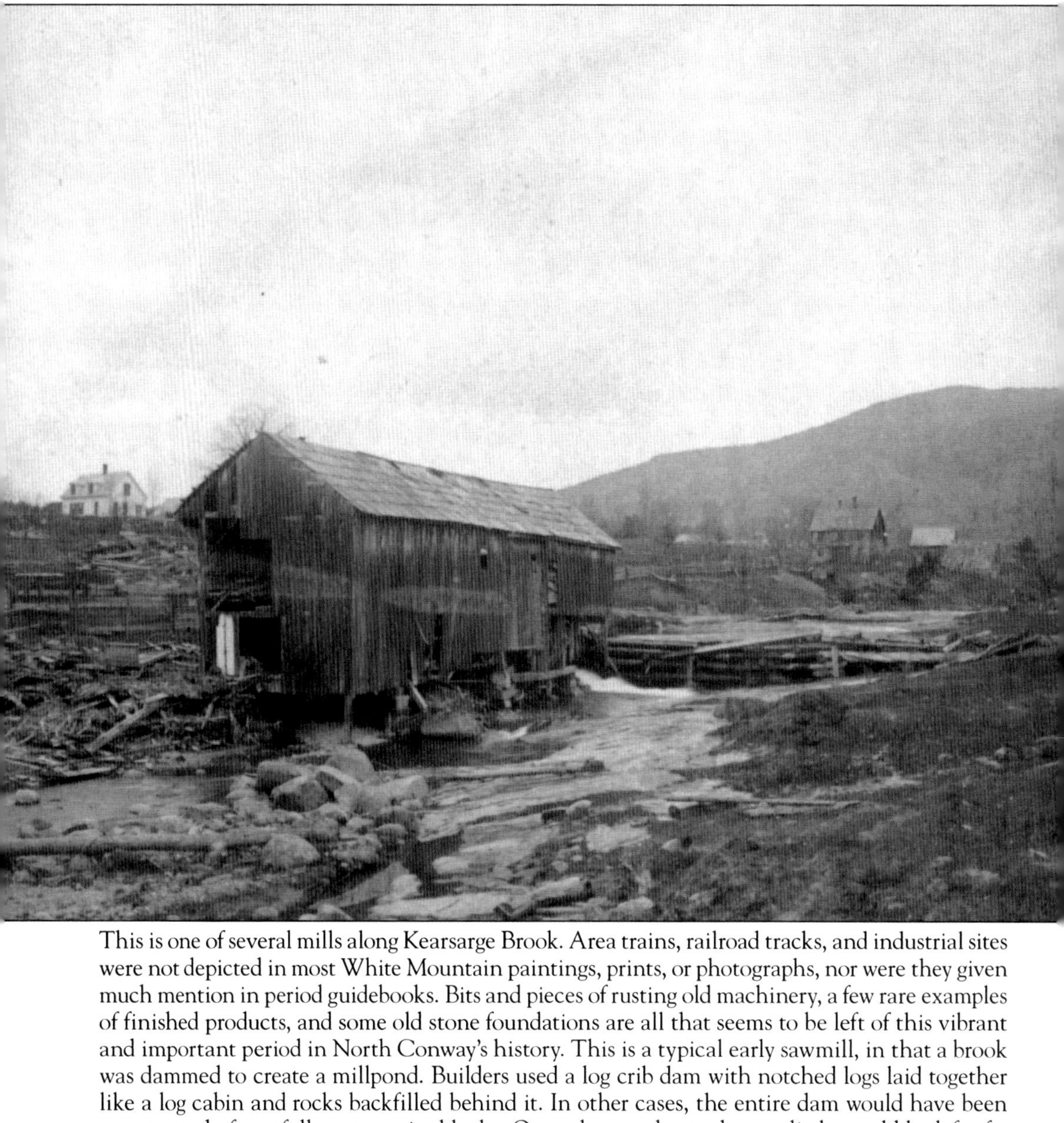

This is one of several mills along Kearsarge Brook. Area trains, railroad tracks, and industrial sites were not depicted in most White Mountain paintings, prints, or photographs, nor were they given much mention in period guidebooks. Bits and pieces of rusting old machinery, a few rare examples of finished products, and some old stone foundations are all that seems to be left of this vibrant and important period in North Conway's history. This is a typical early sawmill, in that a brook was dammed to create a millpond. Builders used a log crib dam with notched logs laid together like a log cabin and rocks backfilled behind it. In other cases, the entire dam would have been constructed of carefully cut granite blocks. Once the wood rotted away, little would be left of a crib dam to indicate the presence of a mill, but cut granite dams remain hidden throughout the woods as monuments to the active period. (Conway Historical Society.)

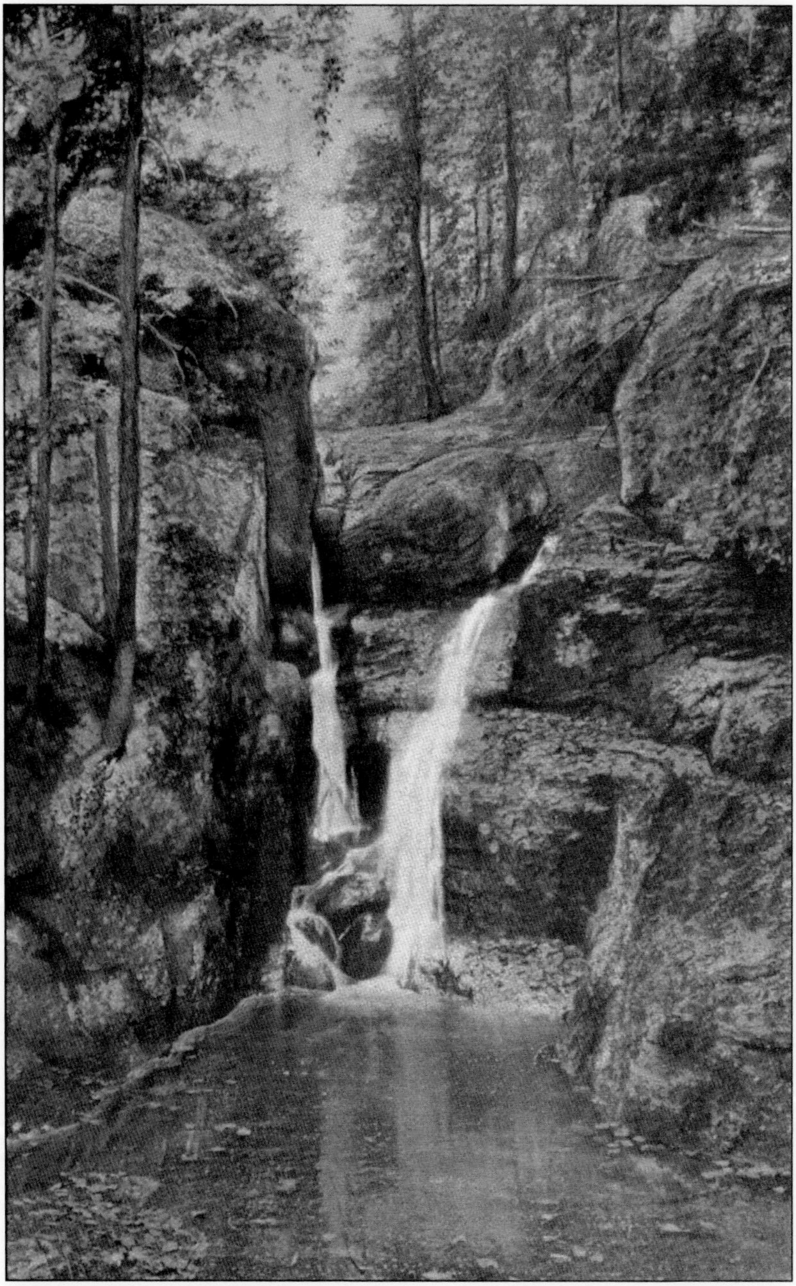

This waterfall was a key tourist attraction and source of drinking water. Tucked away off the main street in what is now a residential neighborhood, these falls were an inspiration to many local photographers and artists, most notably Benjamin Champney. The White Mountain art master had a home and studio on Main Street next to what is now the Red Jacket Resort, just a short walk to the Artists' Falls. The river split into two cascades over the falls, and the double falls splashed upon a large rock below. The rock itself looks like a carved sculpture with its soft curving lines and shape. The stone walls alongside the falls flare out away from it, and the combination of all these elements creates a beautifully serene landscape favored by artists. (Conway Historical Society.)

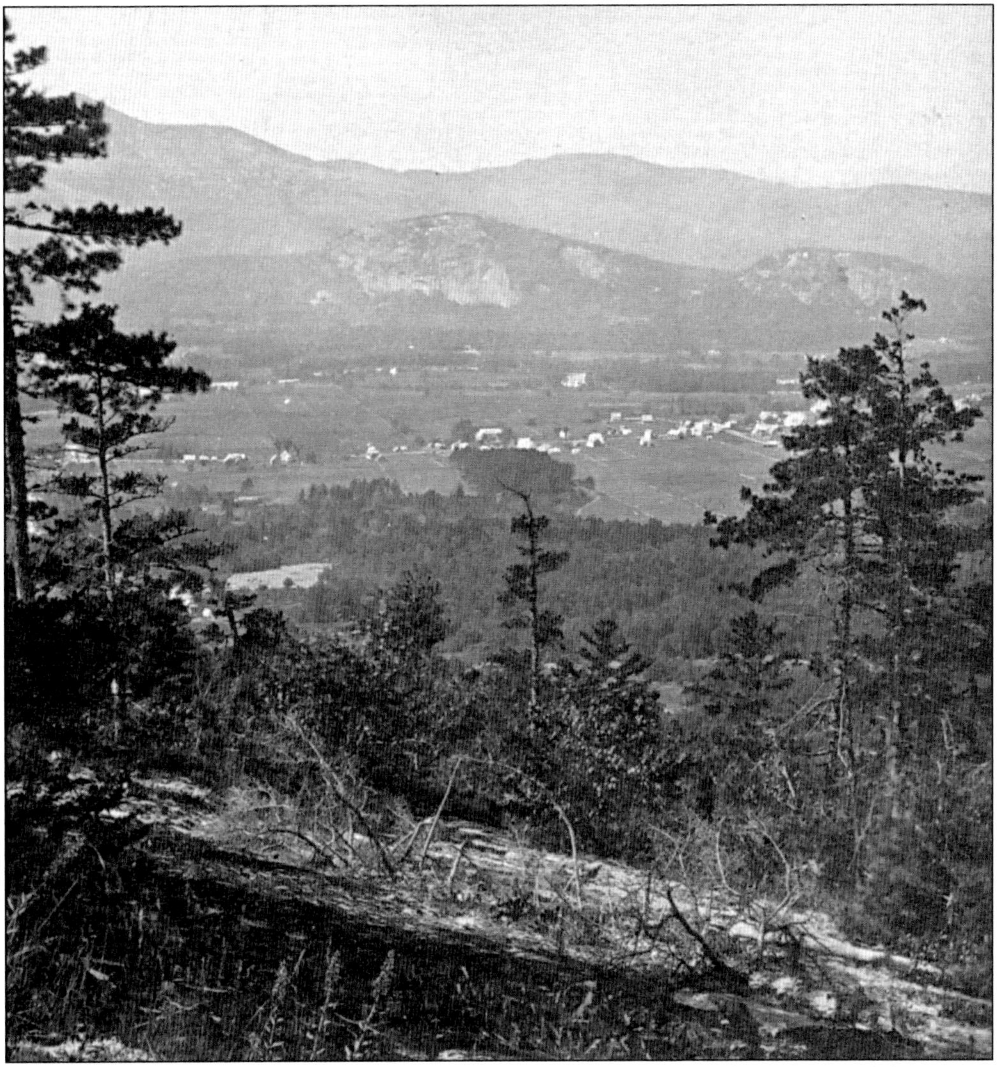

The trail from which this photograph was taken heads up toward the summit of the Green Mountains east of town and moves along Artist's Brook to Artist's Ledge. This was a popular spot to take in the view and gather blueberries in the late summer. In the middle ground are the typical New England farming patterns on which North Conway was originally built. A single main street is centered in the broad, flat, fertile valley between two mountain ranges. In the background are the peaks of White Horse and Cathedral Ledge followed by the Moat Mountain Range. The outlines of the fields are defined by small lanes and farm access roads radiating east and west from the main street. The main street leads north to the clustered center of North Conway village, where the larger hotels and church spires are. (Henney History Room, Conway Public Library, photograph by Nathan W. Pease.)

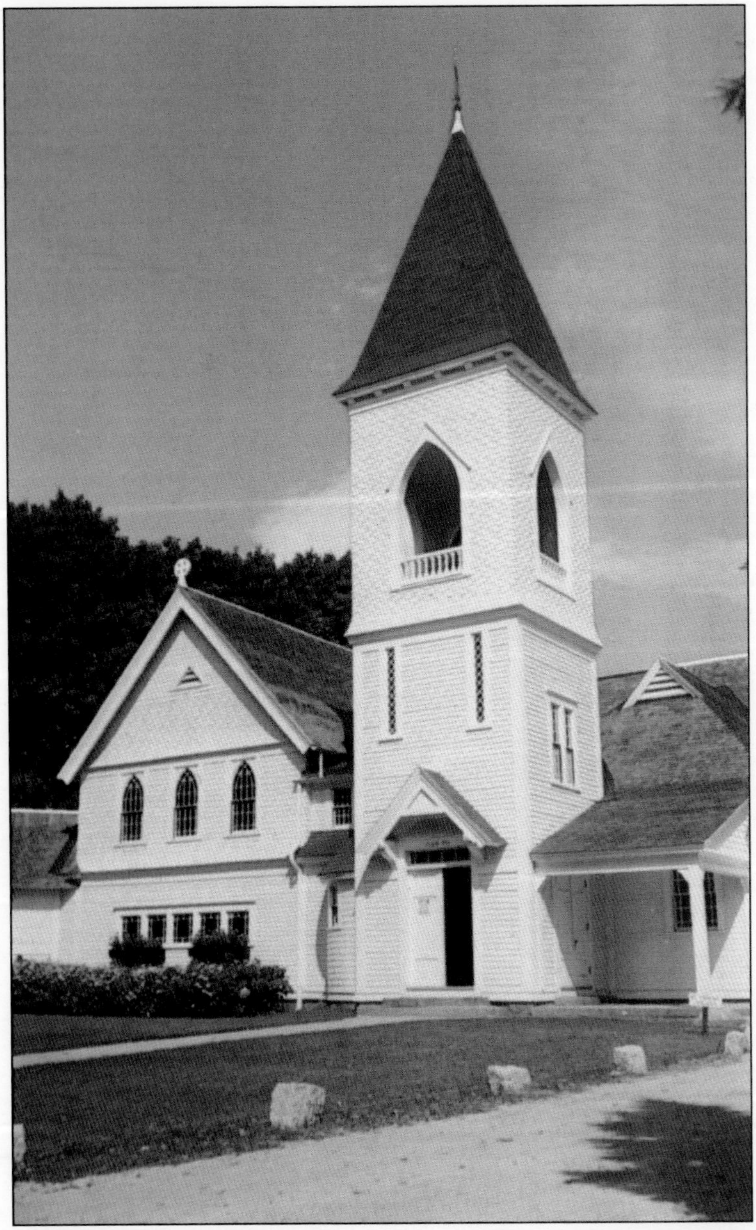

The First Church of Christ Congregational, built in 1884 just south of Grove Street on Main Street, has been added on to several times but maintains much of its original Gothic-style detailing. Helen Bigelow Merriman completed the financing for the church in honor of her father, Erastus B. Bigelow of Bigelow carpet fame. She was aided by her husband, Dr. Daniel Merriman, pastor of the Congregational Church of Worcester, Massachusetts. For 20 years, the only kindergarten in the village was held here under the direction of Carrie Gleason. It also offered a clinic for children and adults aided first by Mrs. Scott Simpson and later by Dr. Clarence Vaughan. In 1965, Dr. Vaughan established a trust that eventually resulted in Vaughan Community Service, Inc., to promote health and well-being for the individual, the family, and the community. The Vaughan programs are housed in the Reverence for Life Building, which was constructed in 1972 with funds provided by Helen Whitney Gibson. (Conway Historical Society, photograph by Dick Smith.)

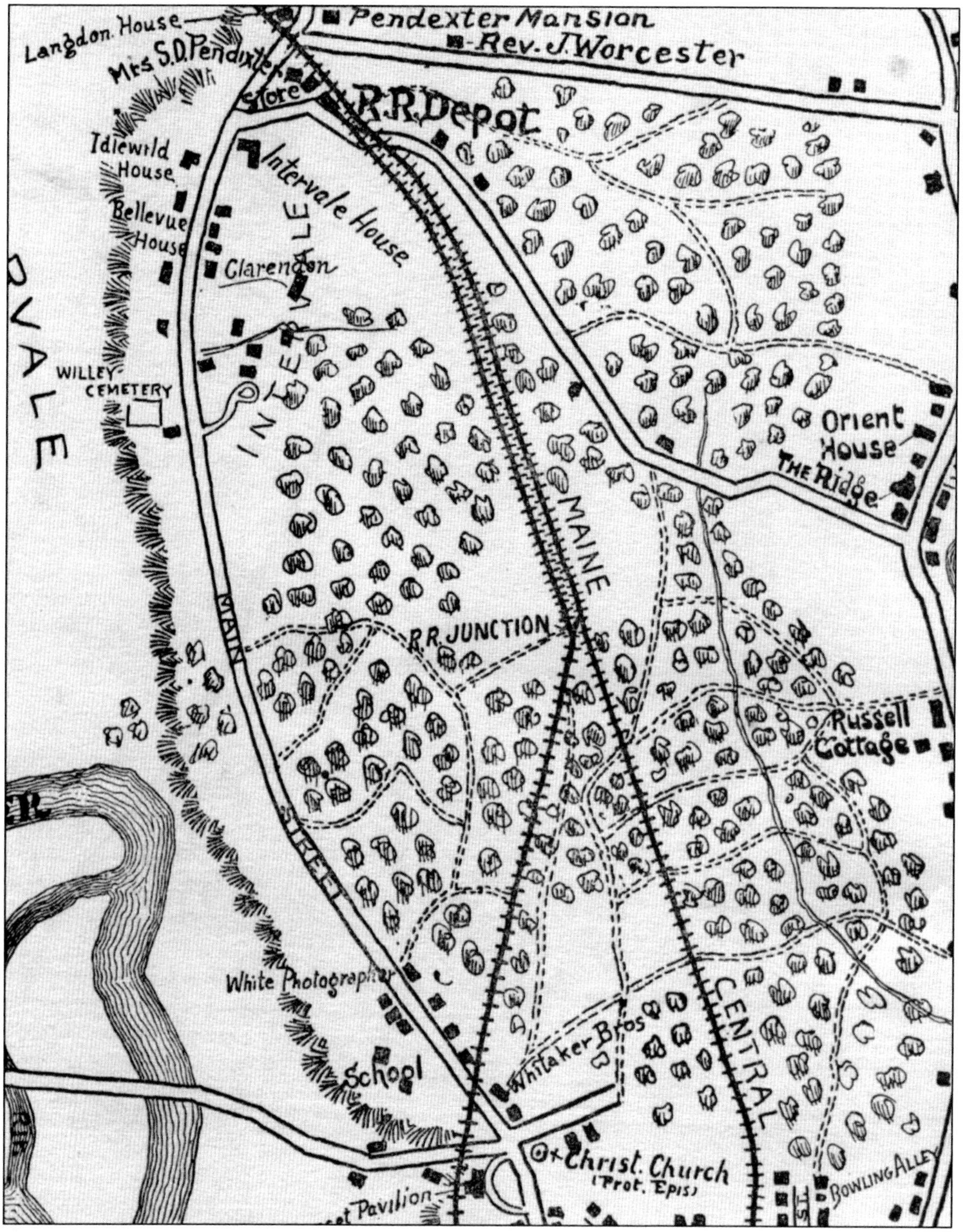

The character of North Conway changes as one goes north on Main Street and crosses the train tracks. The buildings are fewer and more dispersed, and the area is wooded until one reaches another cluster of buildings around the Intervale railroad depot. The extensive walking paths for which this area was famous meander from one attraction to another. These trails are now part of the town's Whitaker Woods recreation system, named in honor of the Whitaker family, whose home is near the bottom of this map. The tourist accommodations Russell Cottage, the Ridge, and the Orient House on the east and the Intervale House, Idlewild, Bellevue, and Clarendon to the west cluster around natural areas that offer broad views over open meadows toward the surrounding mountains. These sites all proclaimed the benefits of fresh air, clean water, recreation, and exercise, which were so attractive to city dwellers of the era. (Conway Historical Society.)

Three

North of the Center

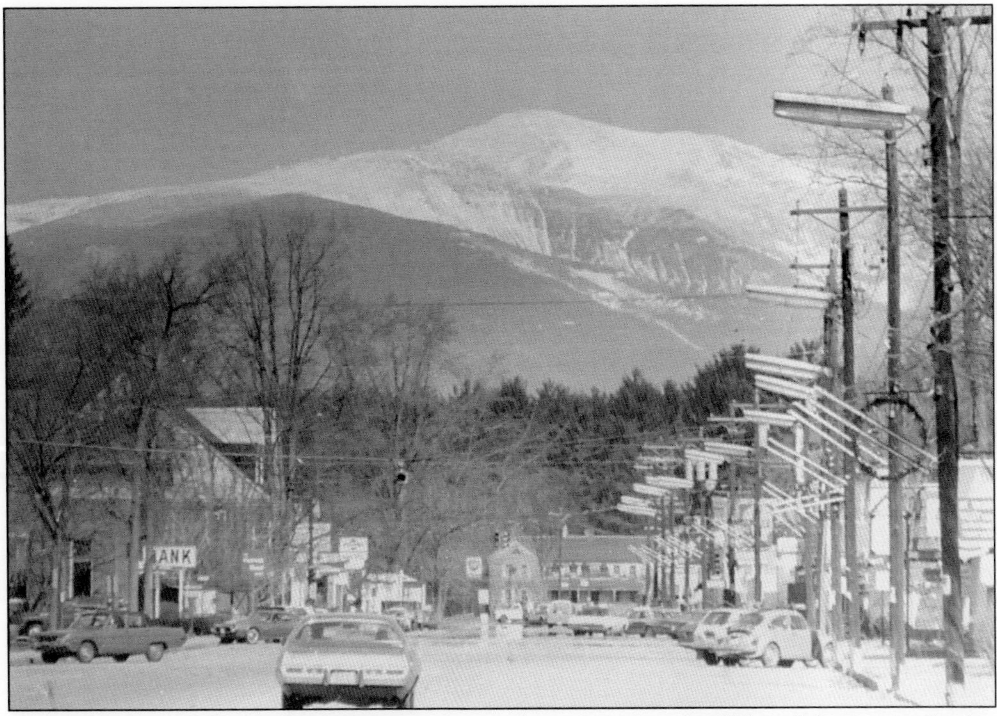

The north end of North Conway is known as the gateway to the White Mountains. In this photograph, Mount Washington in its crowning glory is covered with snow, as it is for most of the year. In this image, captured from just south of the railroad crossing, the Whitaker house seems to be in the middle of the road, but the road makes a sharp turn to the left directly before it. (Conway Historical Society.)

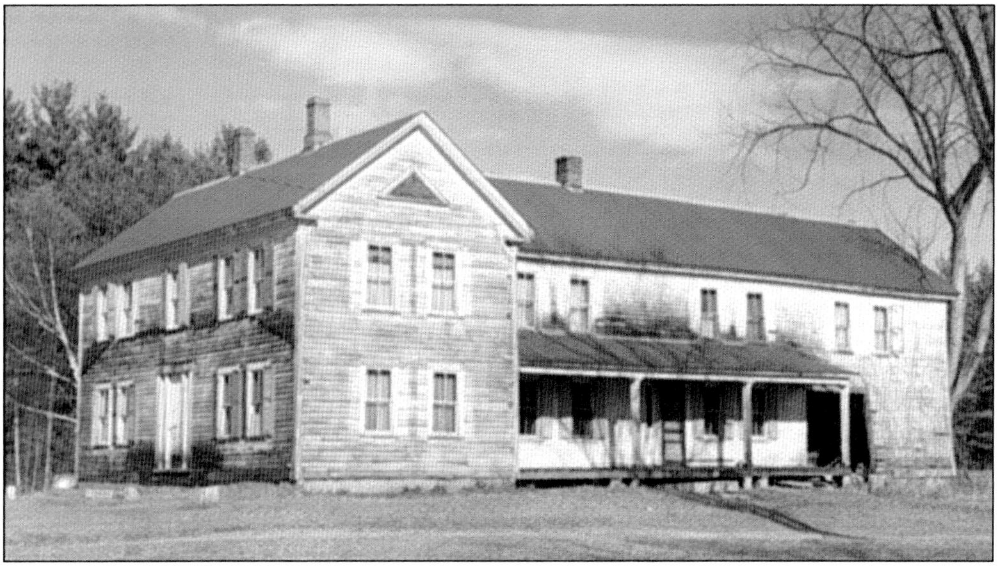

Built around 1830, this house was home to generations of Whitakers and their extended families. The town acquired the adjacent Whitaker Woods in 1971, but Whitaker heirs are still allowed to cut wood for domestic use. Charles "Chubby" W. Whitaker later remarked he would have preferred the town give it an "Indian"-type name. The historic home burned down in 1996, but the barn and nearby Horatio Carter blacksmith shop have been preserved, and a recreation center was built on the site. The fields behind it are now used for baseball, soccer, and lacrosse. A warming hut with toilet facilities, picnic benches, and a small office is also available. (Both, Conway Historical Society.)

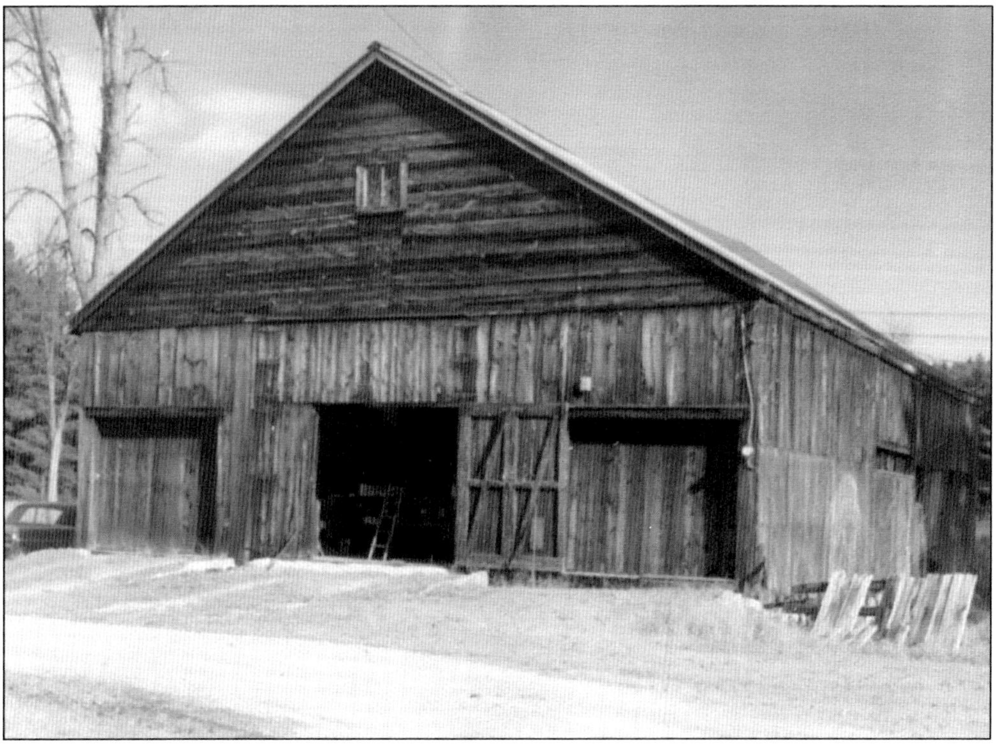

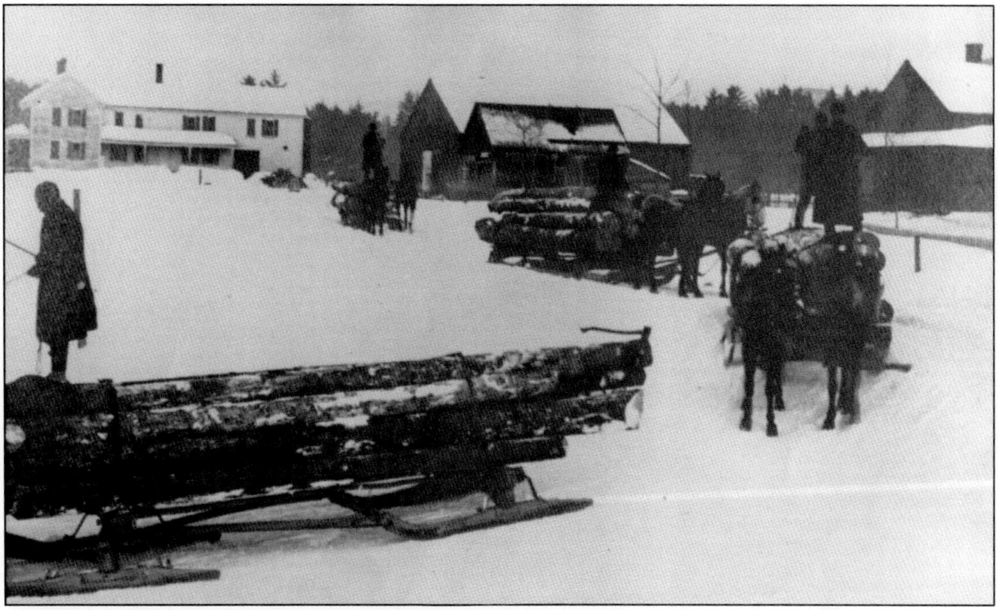

North Conway's wooded natural resources provided both pleasure and profit over the years. The photograph above shows a horse-drawn sled loaded with logs heading for the mill in front of the Whitaker homestead. Driving the horse teams while standing on loaded sleds was daring and dangerous work. The snow was an essential part of the process, allowing the sled to move; work was stopped if there was not enough snow for the men to work on. Below is an example of the woods being used for recreation. While the gentleman with skis on the left is unidentified, Abbie Downs, Vesta Tibbetts, and Evelyn Hill are smartly dressed for winter fun. Whitaker Woods is now part of the Mount Washington Valley Ski Touring Center and used for cross-country skiing and snowshoeing. (Both, Henney History Room, Conway Public Library.)

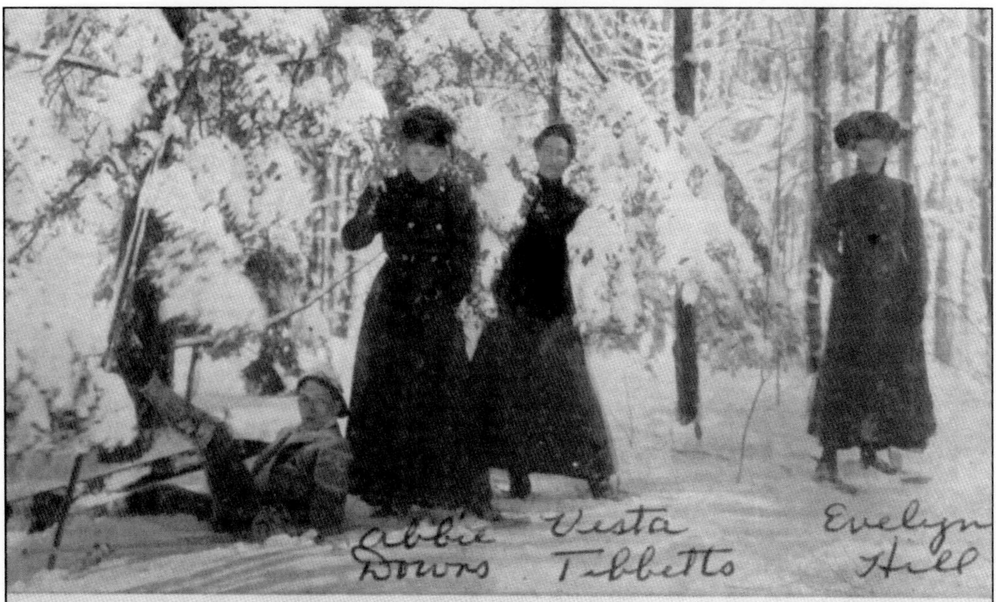

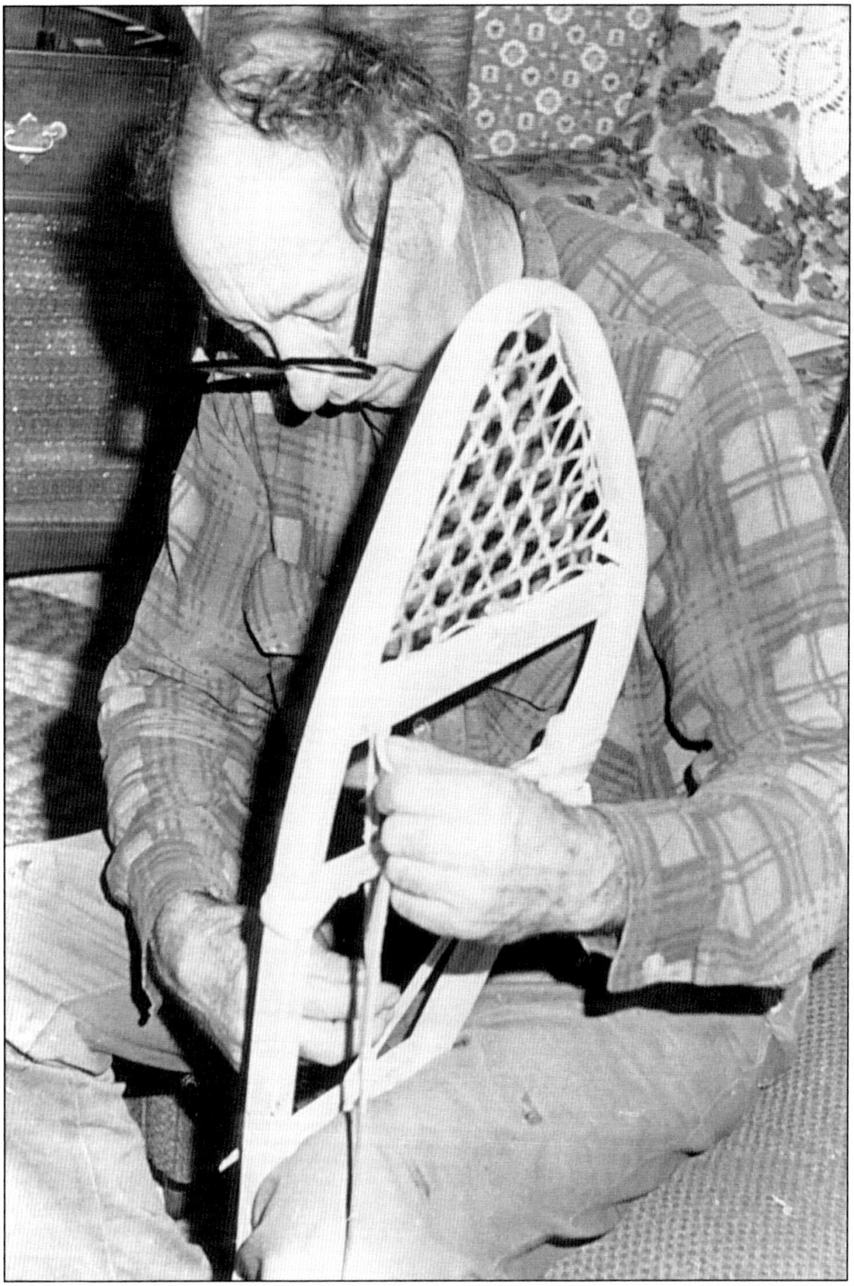

Snowshoeing, a tradition learned from Native Americans, became a popular pastime around 1900. Historically, most New England villages were relatively self-sufficient, with many products made locally. Treffle Bolduc operated Baldy's Store and the Kancamagus Snowshoe Company for over 40 years on nearby Kancamagus Highway, which led into the White Mountain National Forest. He also did carpentry, made birch bark canoes, and was one of a number of Native Americans who expressed their heritage through the traditional products they made and sold. He also had a fine collection of artifacts on display in his store. A master of many trades, he was an accomplished musician and a concertmaster with the New Hampshire State Symphony for five years. (Henney History Room, Conway Public Library.)

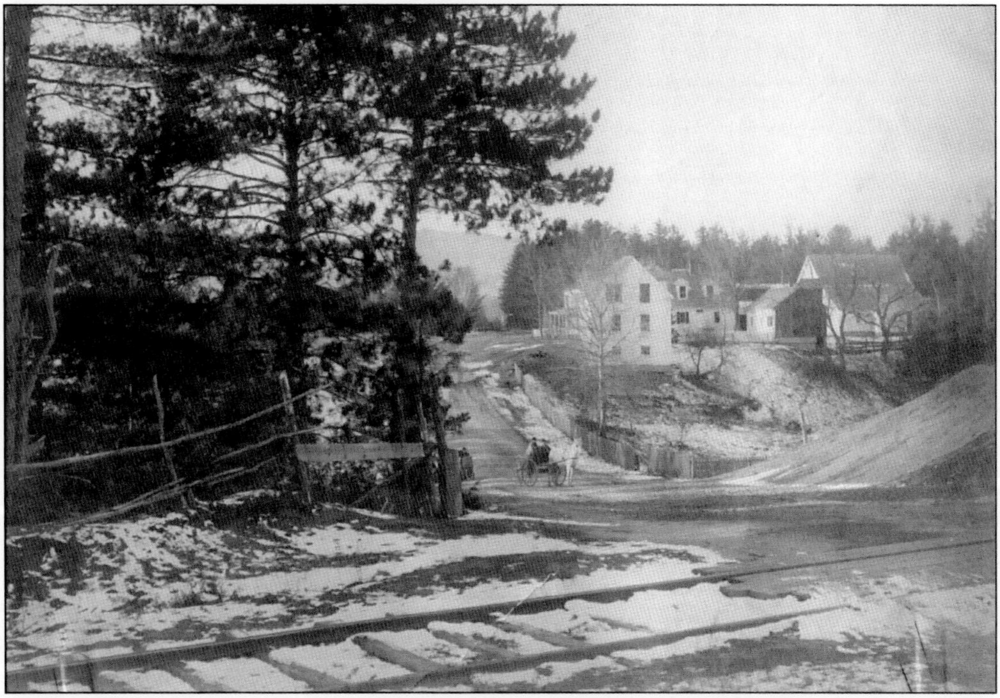

Shortly after the Whitaker homesite, the street crossed the railroad tracks and made a large dip into what was known as Crawford Hollow. The snow-covered railroad line can be seen in the foreground, and a wagon drawn by a single white horse rests at the bottom of the hollow. Today, the road has been built up, and the hollow is hardly noticeable. The Whitaker home and the Episcopal church are in the background of this photograph, which was taken facing south from Crawford Hollow. (Both, Henney History Room, Conway Public Library, photographs by T.E.M. White.)

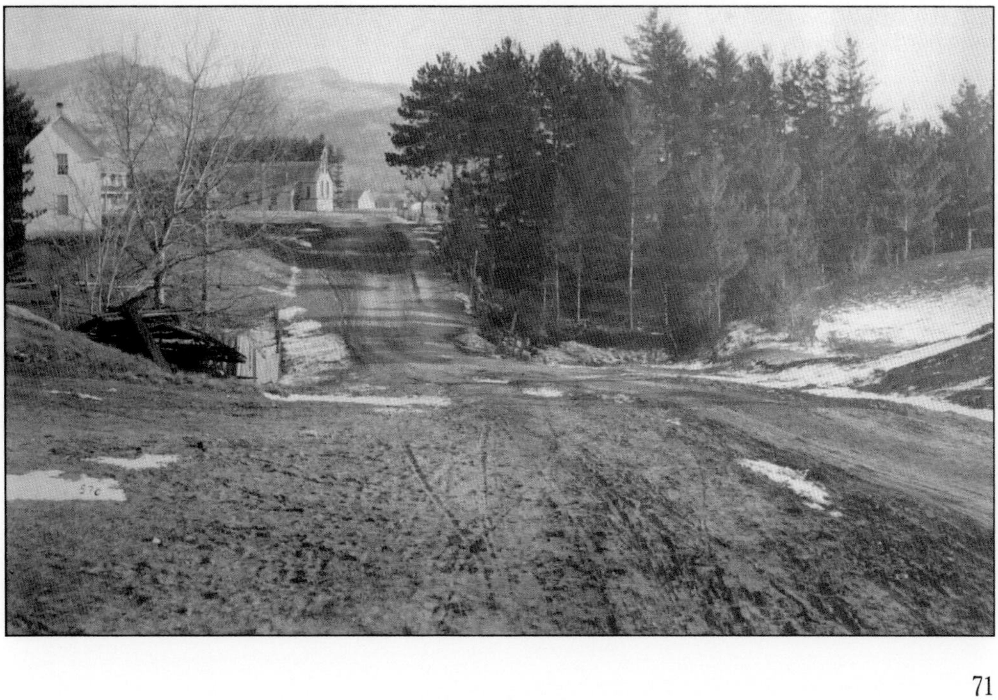

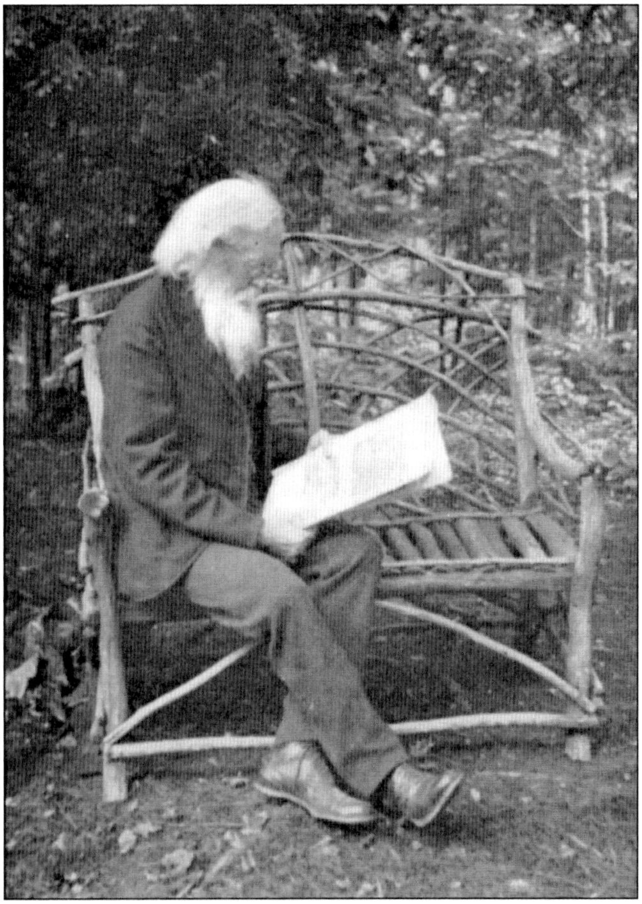

One of the trails through the woods led to Tanglewild, the home and studio of Thomas Edward Mulliken "T.E.M." White and his wife, Gabriella F. White, both photographers. In the image to the left, Gabriella, who was also an accomplished painter, captured her silver-haired husband sitting on a rustic bench near their home. An appreciation booklet published shortly after his death on December 16, 1909, reports that T.E.M. was an acknowledged "nature worshipper" and would whistle entire opera scores while he worked. He was an enthusiastic swimmer, mountain climber, rower, and ice-skater. He and his wife gave poetic stereopticon exhibitions and frequent magic lantern slide shows on the lawn to entertain their guests. (Both, Henney History Room, Conway Public Library, photographs by Gabriella F. White.)

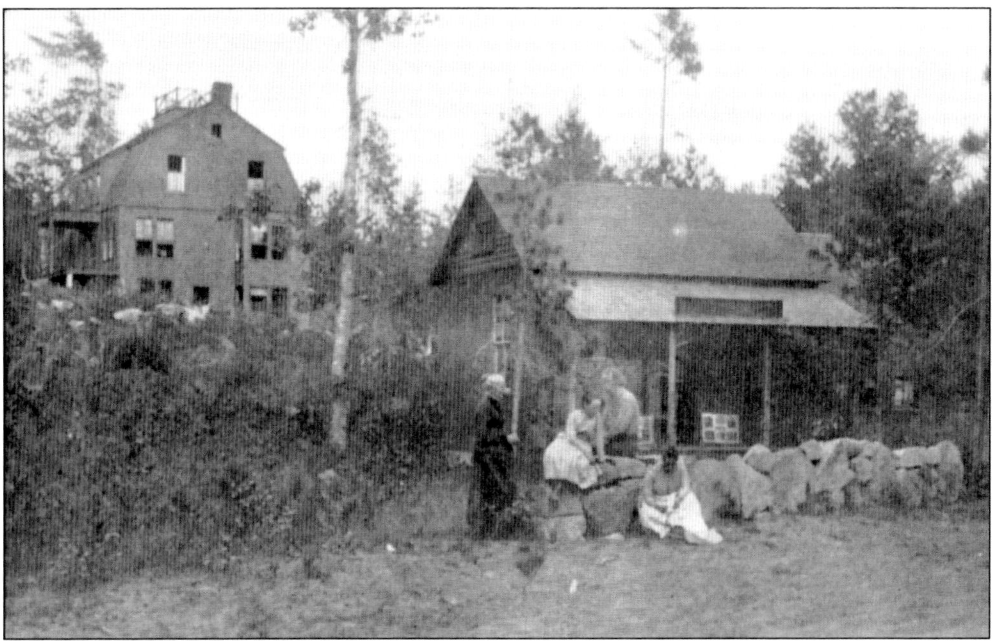

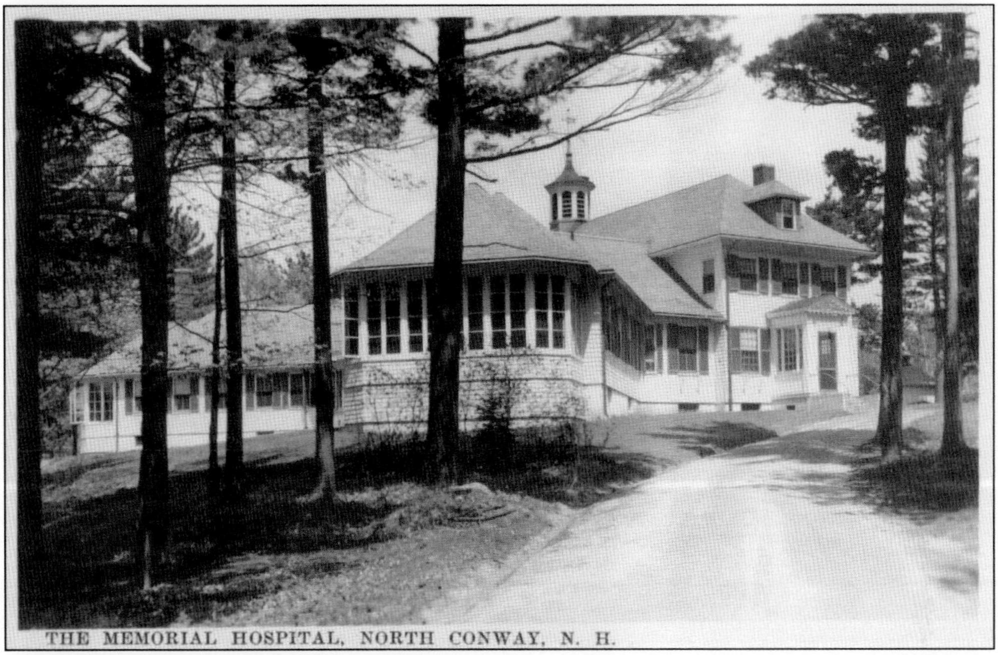

The slate-roofed, wood-frame Memorial Hospital opened in 1911 with 25 beds; its construction was funded by Helen Bigelow Merriman. Dr. George Harold Shedd was named physician-in-charge, and his staff included his brother Dr. John Z. Shedd and Drs. B.F. Horne and S.S. Mullen. Contributions of fruits, vegetables, used clothing, and furnishings helped support the hospital. (Henney History Room, Conway Public Library.)

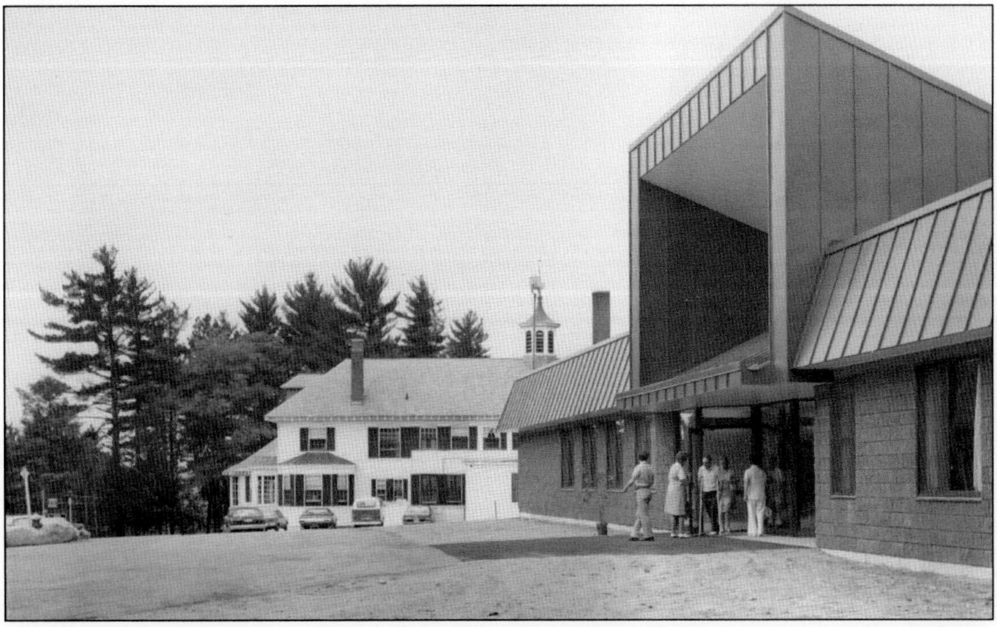

The hospital celebrated its centennial in 2011. The original building remains, along with the original icehouse, but as the population of the area increased and modern medical services became more complex, several additions over the years have expanded its size and operation, including the 1976 wing at right. (Henney History Room, Conway Public Library.)

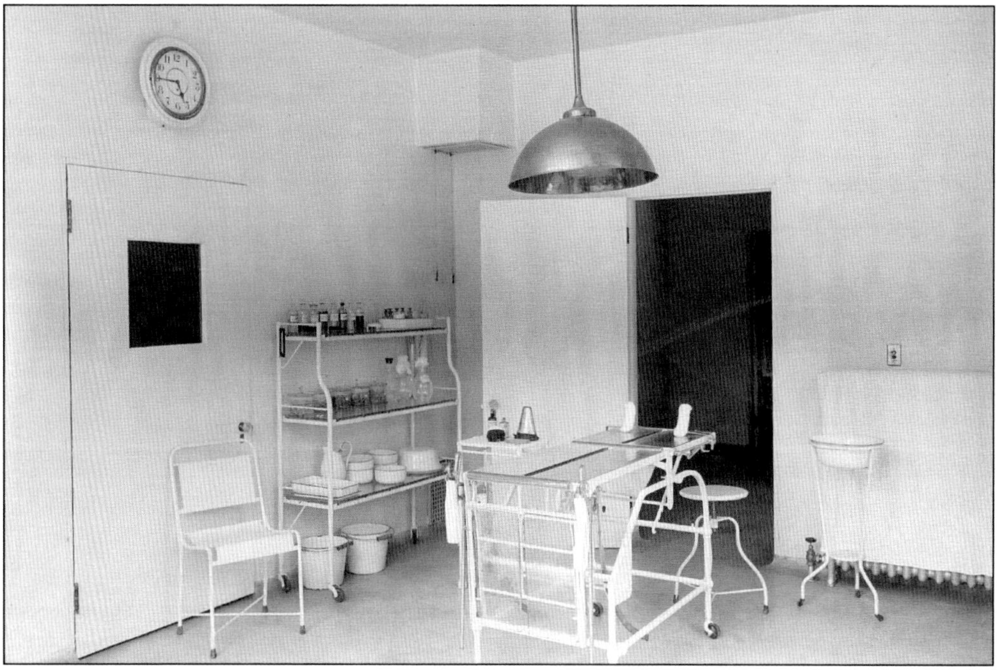

White enameled dishes and glass-stoppered bottles were standard in this early operating or exam room around 1915; white was considered clean and sterile at the time. Enameled metal was also deemed to be more hygienic than porous wood; therefore, it replaced all the older furnishings. The radiator was covered to facilitate cleaning. (Henney History Room, Conway Public Library.)

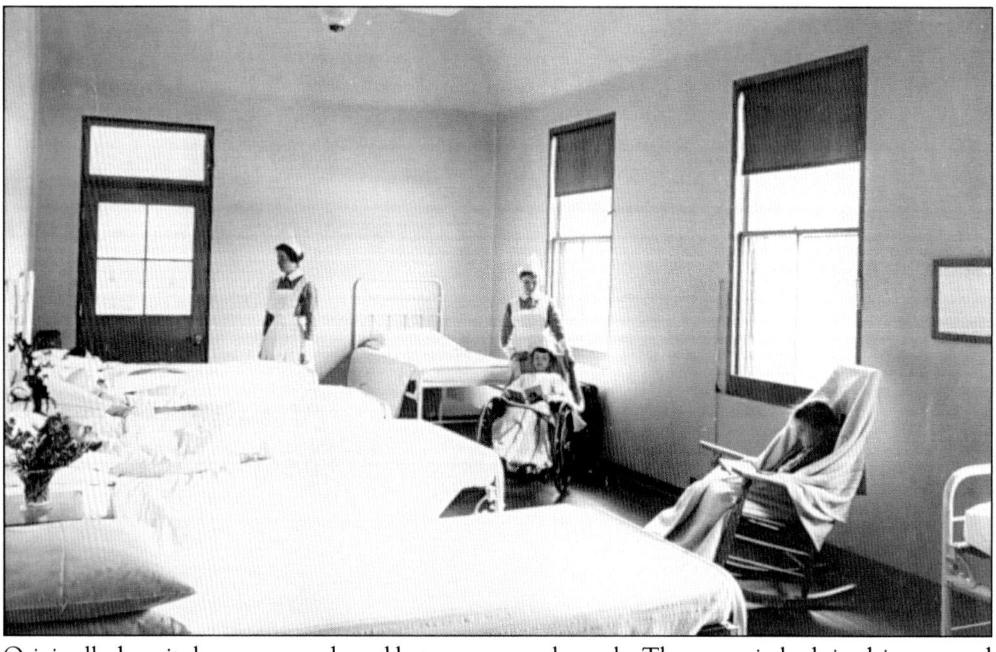

Originally, hospital rooms were shared between several people. There are six beds in this cramped room. The rooms were also very austere, with the only furnishings being enameled metal beds, a rocking chair, and a mirror, with the only light being an overhead fixture. (Henney History Room, Conway Public Library.)

Three generations of Shedd doctors played a major role in the town's medicinal development. Dr. Harold Shedd, seen here, was the chief-of-staff at Memorial Hospital as well as a pioneering ski doctor, making innovations in the treatment of limbs commonly broken by skiers. He devised a new way to cast broken limbs, leaving openings to accommodate swelling and allowing patients to spend less time in the hospital. (Henney History Room, Conway Public Library.)

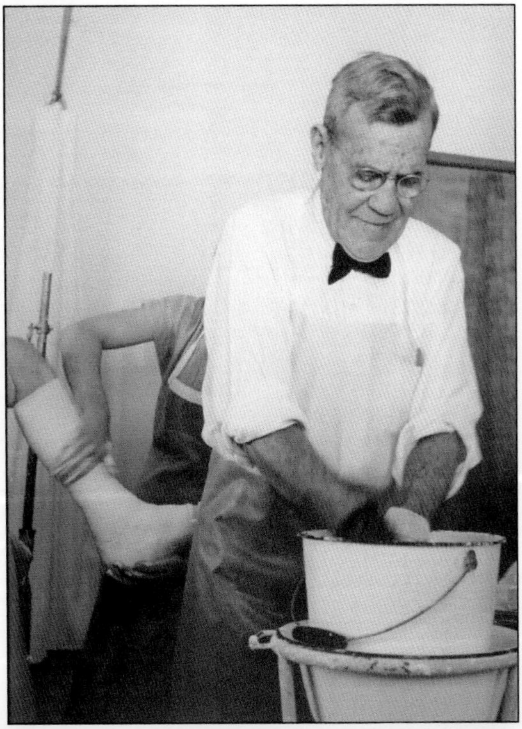

A young student works on a cast as part of the teenage medic program established at the hospital. Teaching new generations is as critical in the medical profession as finding new medical innovations. New technologies like hyperbaric oxygen therapy for wound care are now available at Memorial. (Henney History Room, Conway Public Library.)

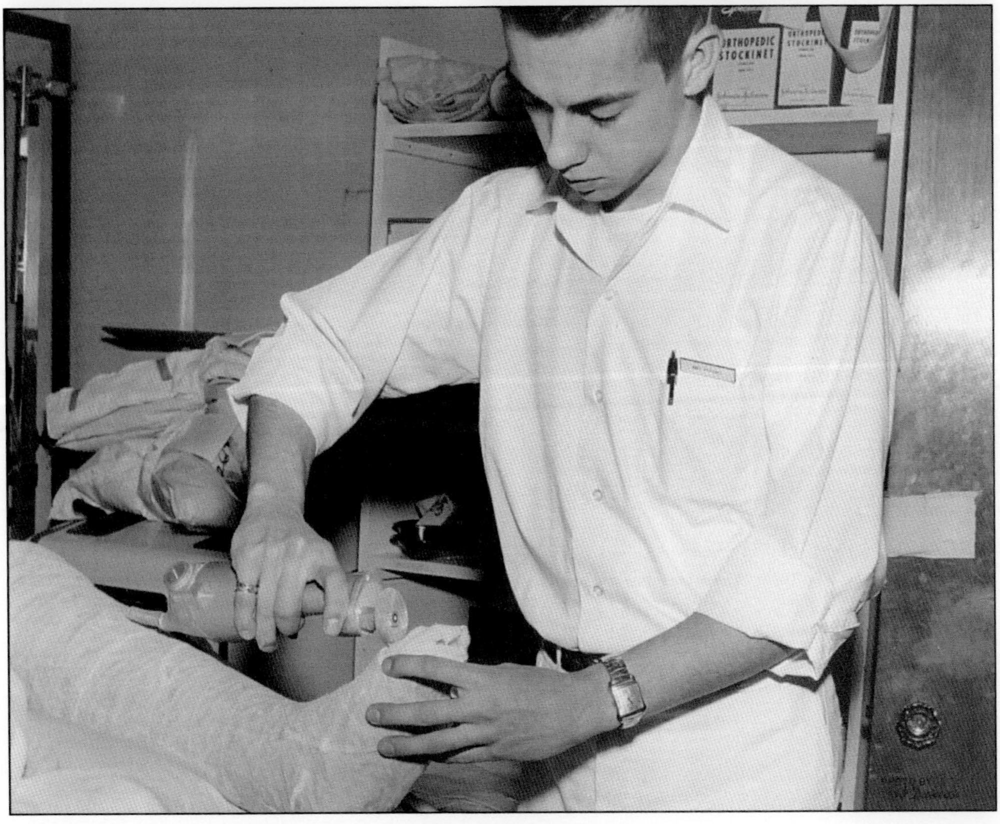

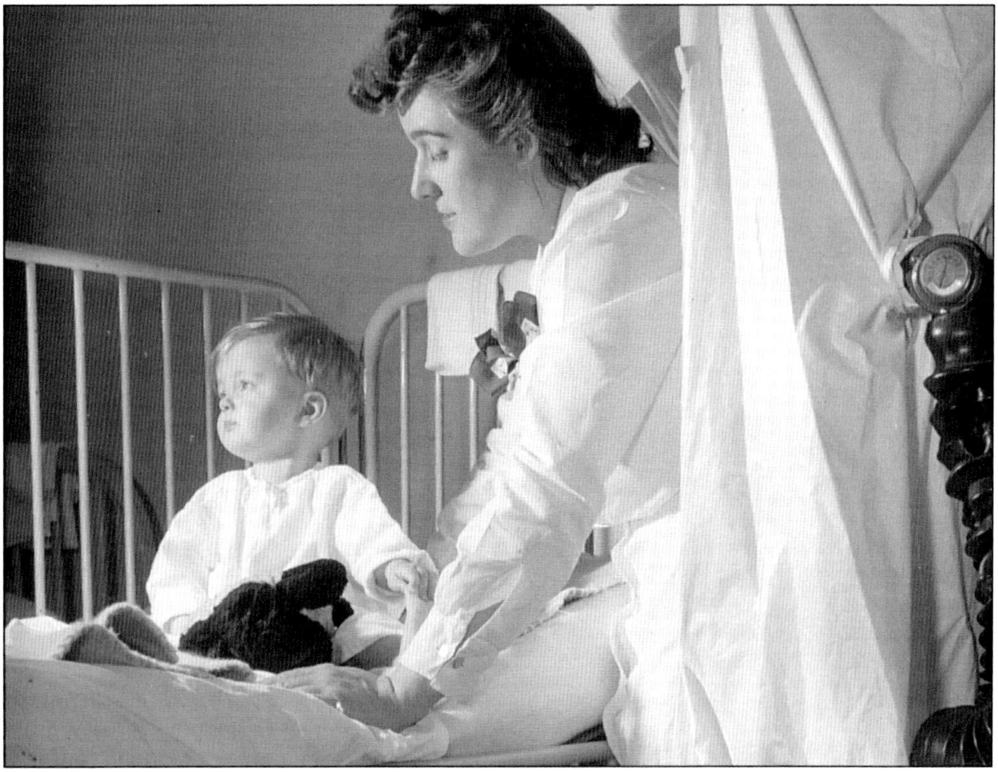

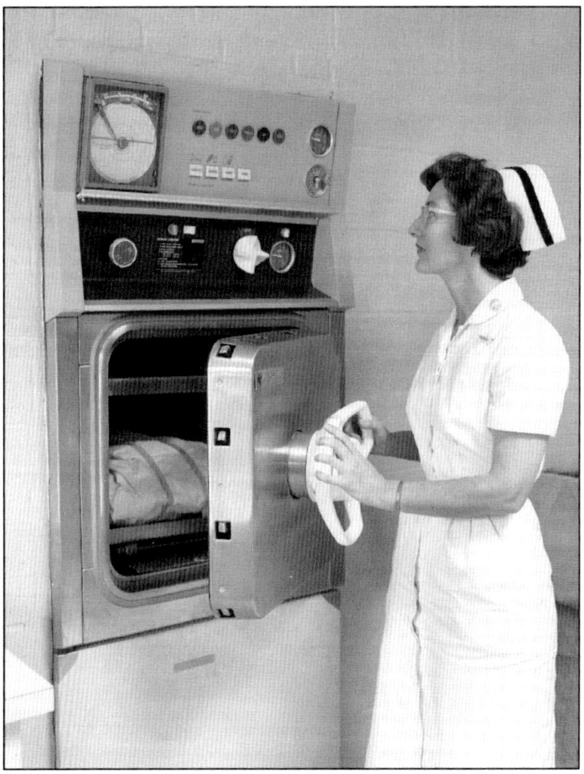

Nurse Alice Grant, who would later become a hospital administrator, tends to a small child in 1960. The children's beds were also made of white enameled metal for its perceived hygienic qualities. Rooms for young children had multiple beds. (Henney History Room, Conway Public Library.)

Nurse Alice Proctor operates a hospital autoclave, an instrument used to sterilize medical equipment and supplies by subjecting them to high-pressure saturated steam at 121 degrees Celsius for 15 to 20 minutes. White uniforms were also standard at the hospital, furthering the notion that white represented a clean, sterile environment. (Henney History Room, Conway Public Library.)

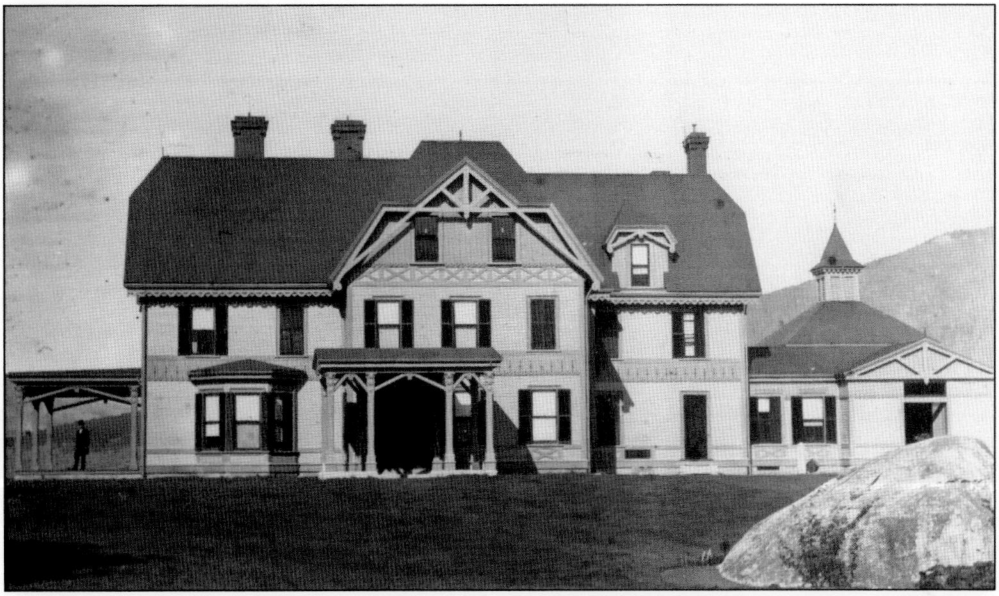

The Manor was originally built in 1874 as the summer estate of the Bigelow family of Bigelow Carpets—at one time, the largest carpet manufacturing company in the world. Above is the original house, built in stick-style architecture, which burned down and was then rebuilt. Notice the location of the rock in both images; it still exists today near a giant outdoor chess set. The second and current Stonehurst Manor is below. In 1895, Helen Merriman wanted to create a more impressive, elegant home and began a complete refurbishment and enlargement of the main house, which took 10 months to complete. The finished home was the English Manor–style shingled mansion below. Merriman eventually turned the estate into the center for the North Conway society. She was an artist and patron of the arts, writing several books and traveling extensively. Together with her husband, Dr. Daniel Merriman, she founded numerous institutions, including Memorial Hospital and the Worcester Art Museum. In 1946, Stonehurst became a hotel and resort. (Both, Henney History Room, Conway Public Library.)

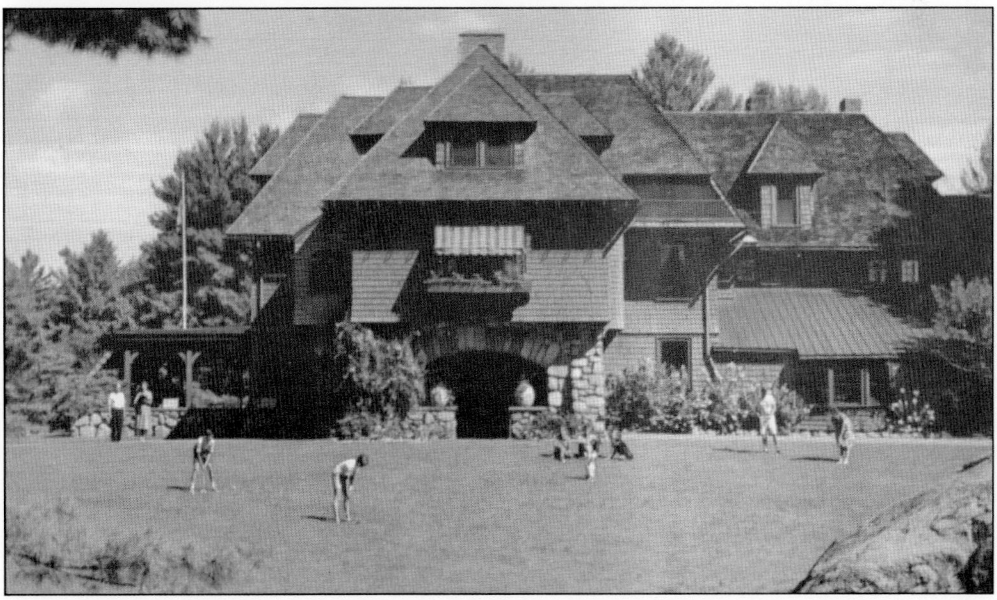

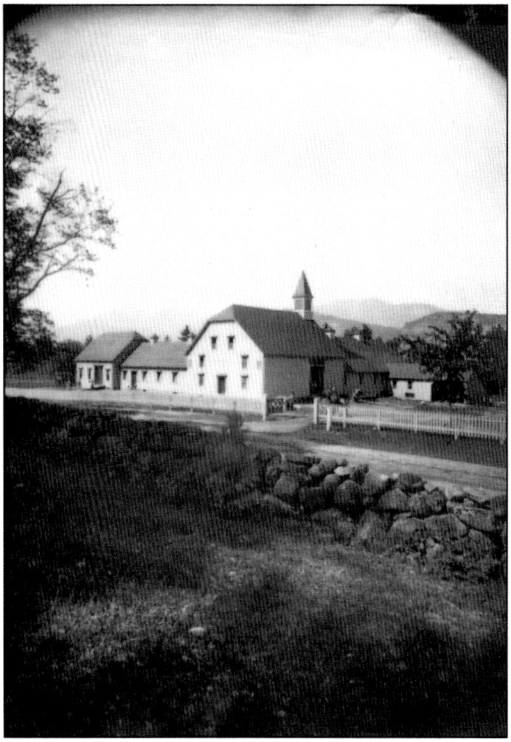

Surrounding the main house was an extensive gentlemen's farm with numerous state-of-the-art outbuildings. They can be identified today with the distinctive jerkin-style roof, in which the gable is cut back. Over the years, these buildings have been sold off and have operated as individual businesses. This large barn became the Carriage Inn, then a craft store, and eventually a sausage factory. Today, it houses an organic grocery and restaurant. (Henney History Room, Conway Public Library.)

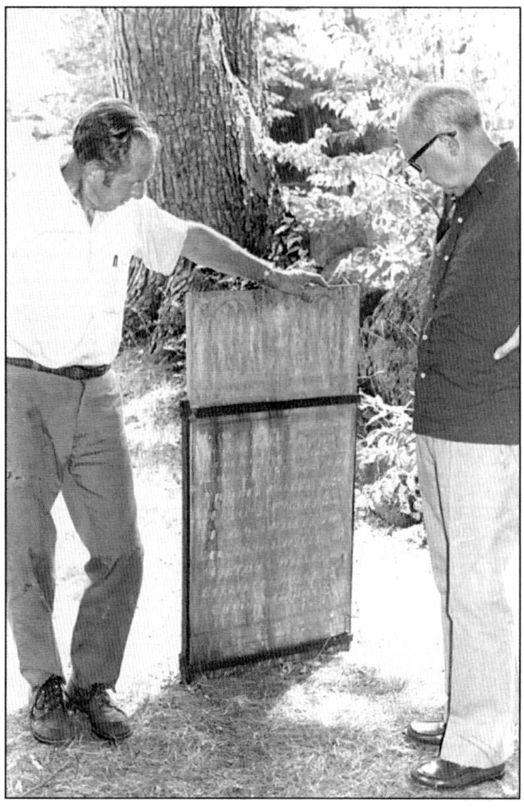

Some of the land upon which Stonehurst Manor was built originally belonged to the Willey family. In this photograph, Herb Willey (left) and Maurice Lovejoy stand by the commemorative marker for the Willey family, who perished in the infamous August 1826 landslide that created a national sensation and drew tourists to Crawford Notch for many years. The marker lists the names of the parents, their five children, and two hired men. (Henney History Room, Conway Public Library.)

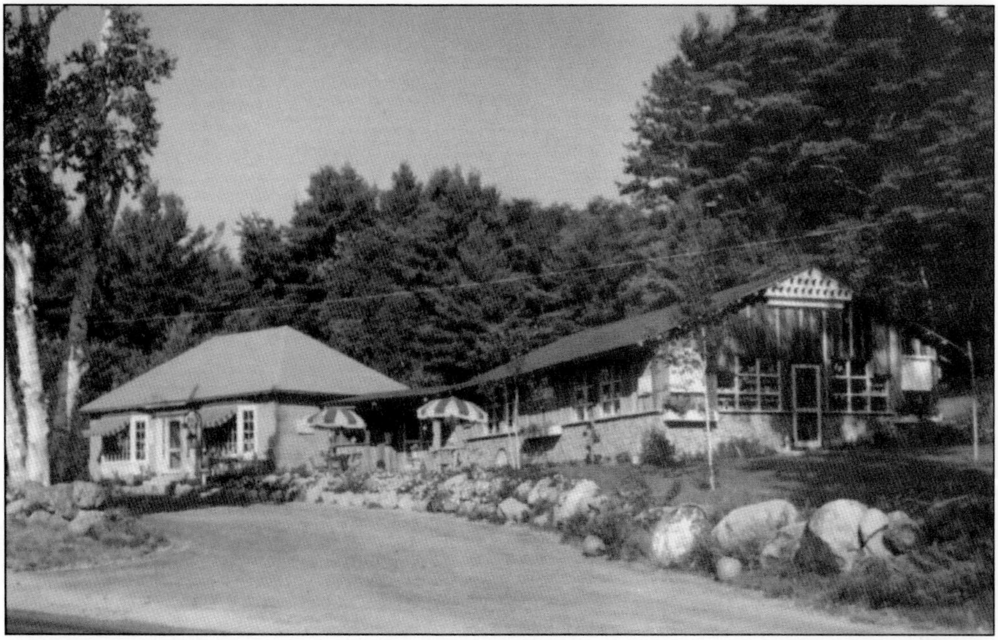

The Shop in the Woods was a very distinctive gift shop established in 1916. Originally located on West Side Road near Echo Lake, it was owned and operated by Marion Howard, a graduate of the School of the Museum of Fine Arts, Boston. The store not only sold interesting gifts but displayed items from around the world. The store and its contents were later purchased by Judy and Paul Burtis, moved to this location on Route 16, and operated until 1985. Later, it was a cigar shop, a barbershop, and a tattoo parlor. (Both, Henney History Room, Conway Public Library.)

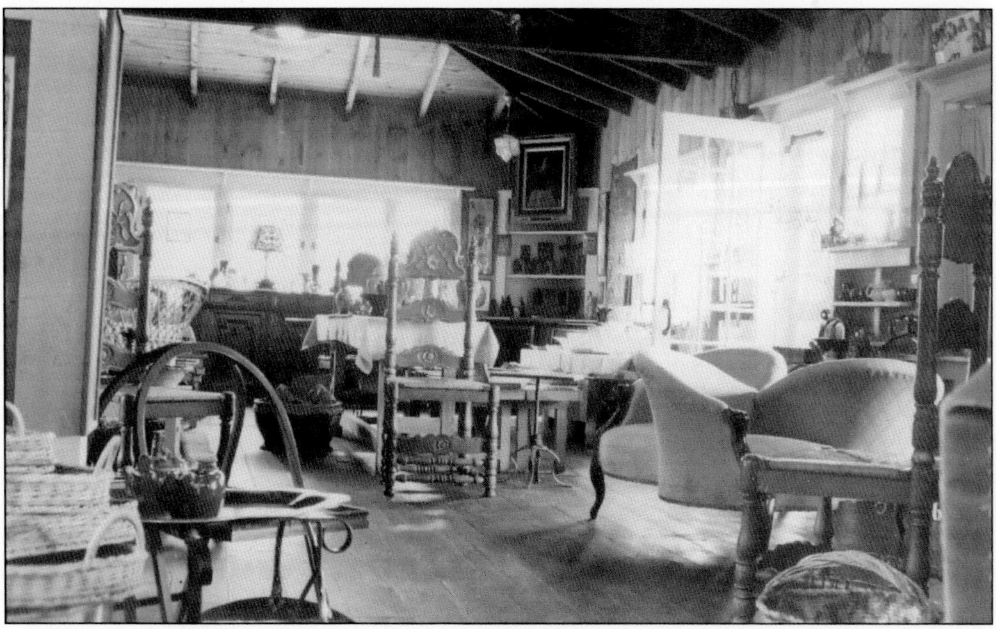

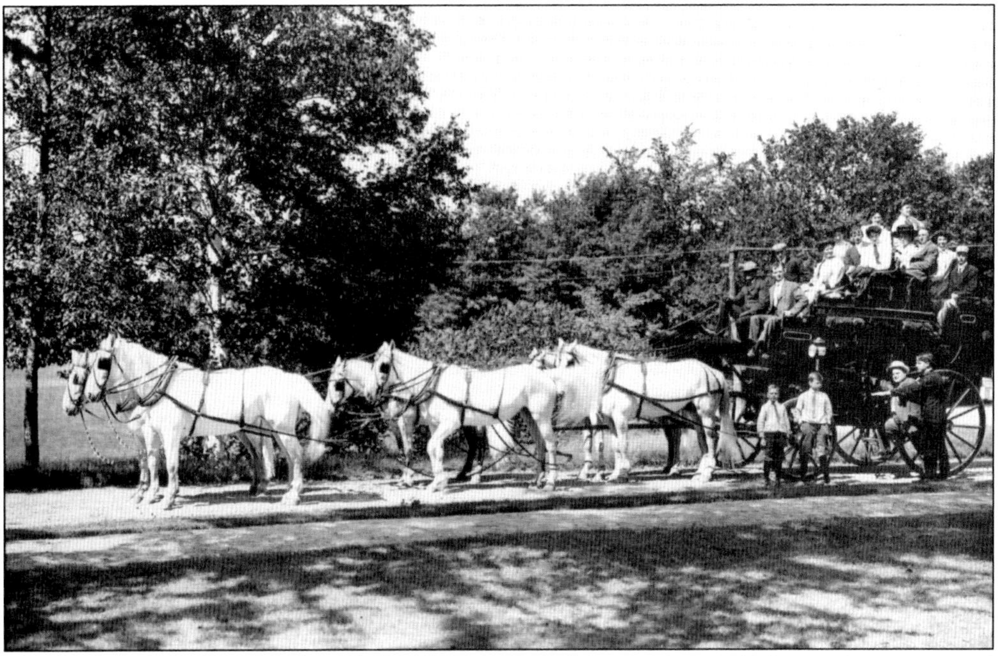

At the northernmost point of North Conway, a tourist district comprised of several inns sprouted up, including the Bellevue, Clarendon, Idlewild, Intervale House, Langdon House, and Pendexters. The area also had its own train depot and store. The above photograph is of the Bellevue House Concord coach. Each major inn had its own coach with the inn's name prominently displayed on it, and tourists explored the region in them during the day. The prized seats were on the roof of the coach. There was a fierce competition for business among the inns. Seen below, the Clarendon Inn, built in 1872, was later annexed as part of the Bellevue complex. By 1901, the Bellevue was specializing in winter entertainment like sleighing, snowshoeing, camping, coasting, and tobogganing. It was destroyed by fire in December 1962. (Both, Henney History Room, Conway Public Library.)

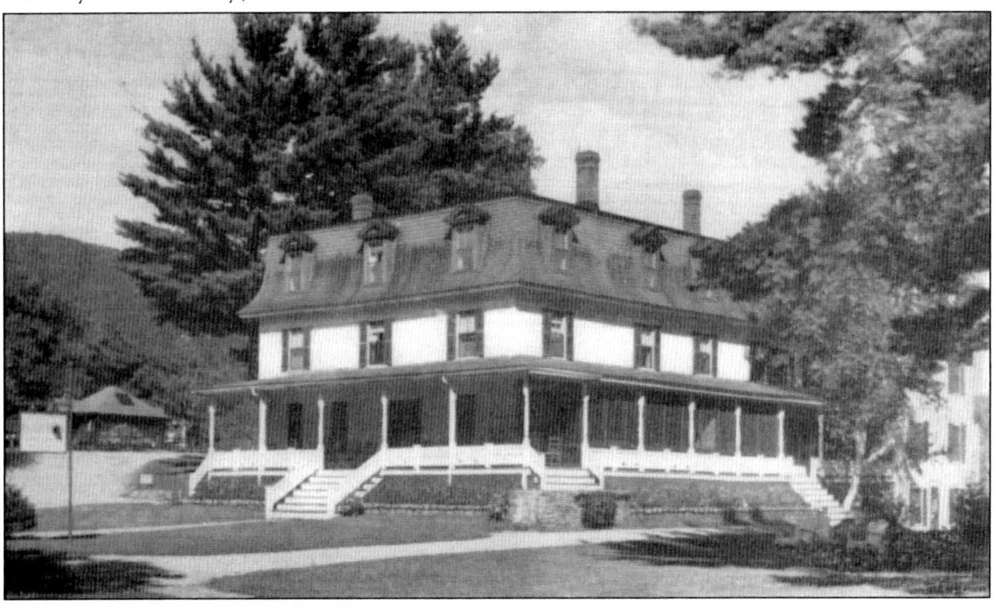

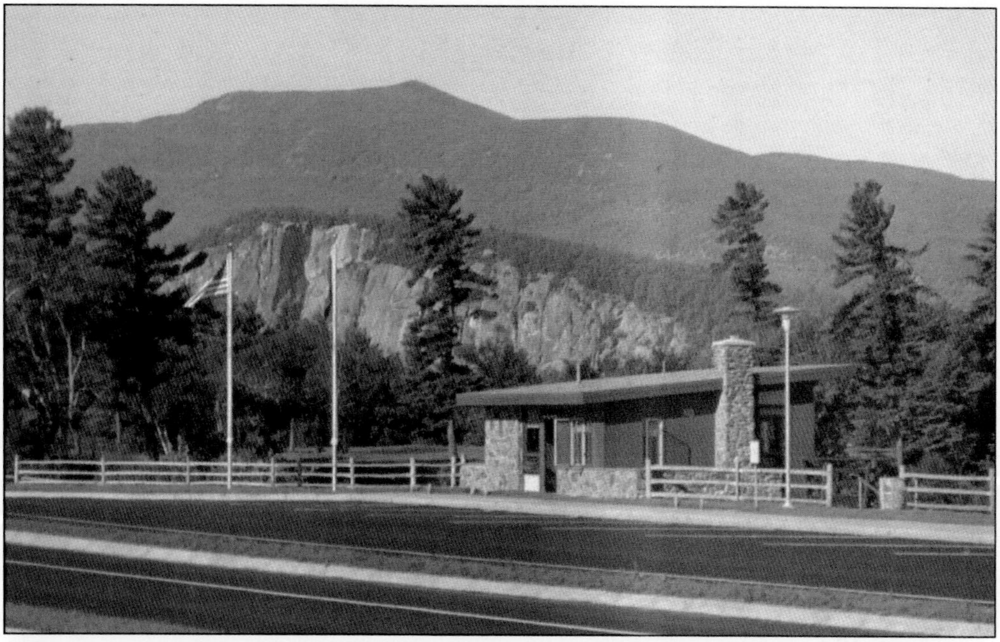

This view across the intervale of the Saco looking toward Cathedral Ledge and its distinctive rock face, or prow, was made famous in a painting by Albert Bierstadt of the White Mountain School of Art. For several generations, the Cannell family owned much of the land in this section of North Conway. They ran inns and shops for the tourist trade, although most of the inns have been lost to fire over the years. The Cannell's Old Fashioned Country Store is on the east side of the road. The family generously donated the land on the west side of Route 16 to the state in the early 1960s with the intention that it be preserved and used as a scenic overlook. A short time later, the state constructed the visitor center, parking lot, and picnic tables seen here. Recently, the original center was replaced with a more modern bunker-style structure. (Both, Henney History Room, Conway Public Library.)

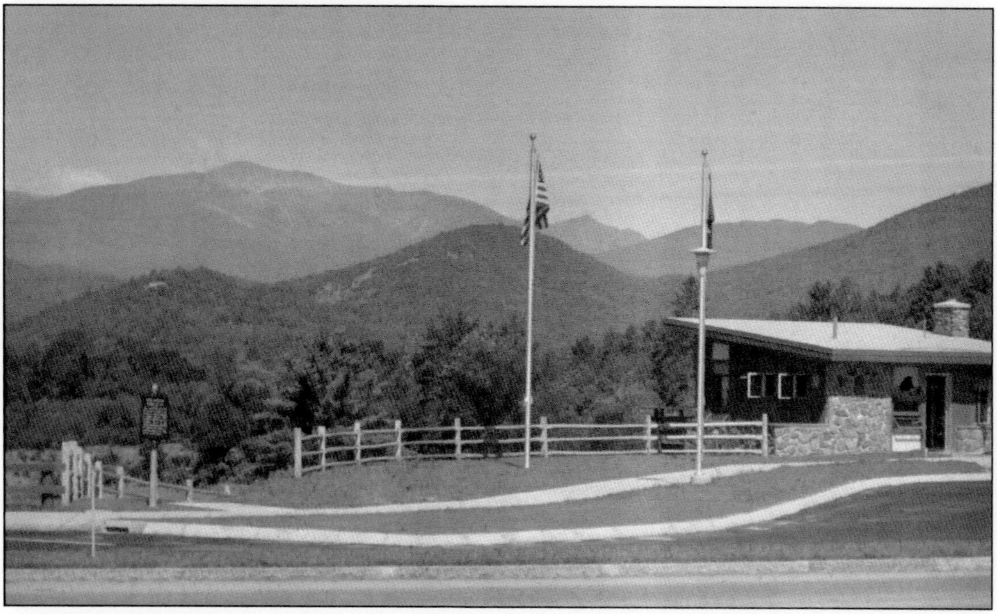

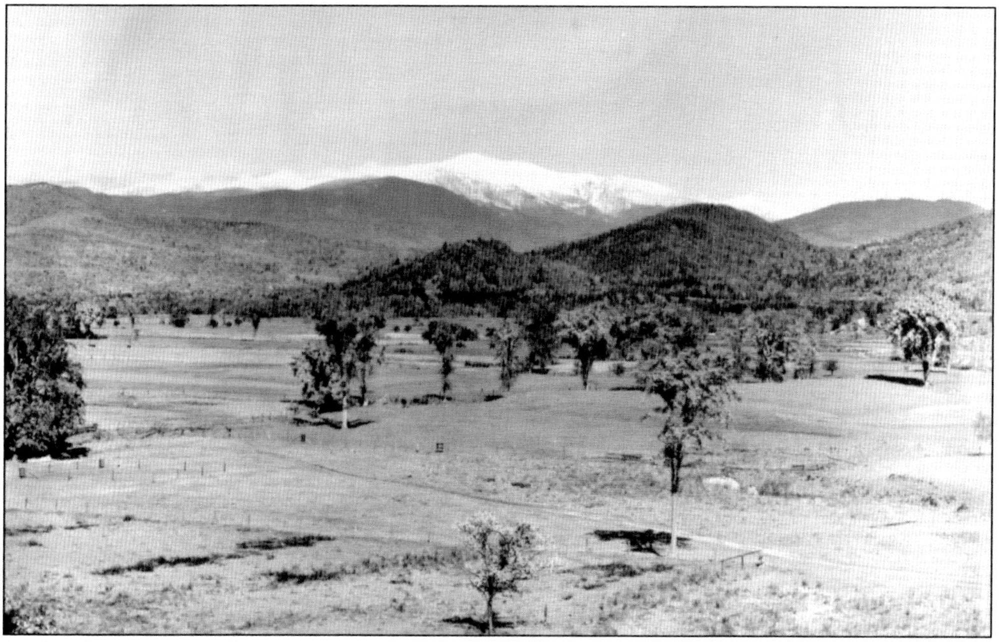

In the above view of the scenic vista, snow-covered Mount Washington is on the left, and the peak of Mount Adams is on the right. The vista serves as an object lesson in the history of White Mountain art. Below, a state historical marker proclaims the key role of the area in the White Mountain School of Art. Two of the school's most famous views came from this spot; the above view toward Mount Washington and Mount Adams was painted by dozens of artists, most notably Benjamin Champney. (Both, Henney History Room, Conway Public Library.)

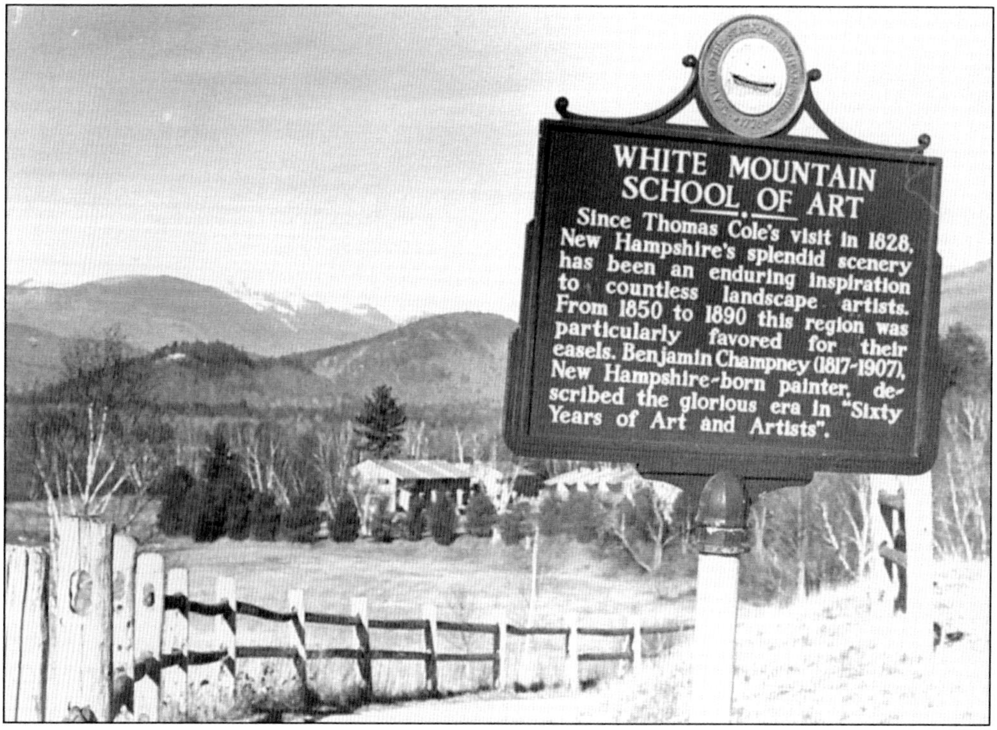

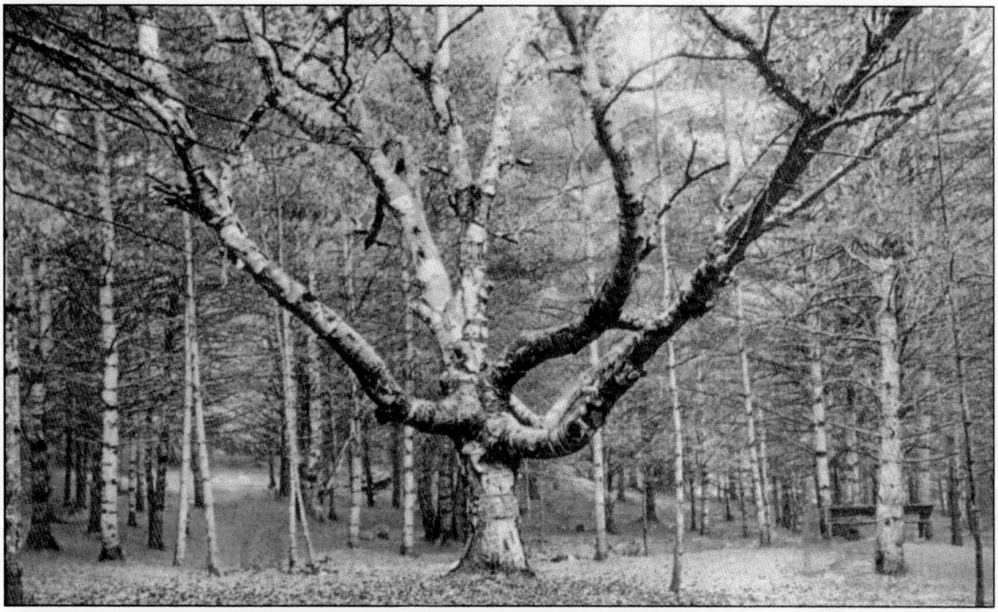

Several local groves, including Cathedral Woods and Enchanted Woods, became popular attractions because they reminded many of Gothic cathedrals in Europe and storybook legends. The massive gnarled birch above, which grew in Cathedral Woods, was known as the "Wizard." The Serpentine tree below was another famous tree; its curious shape was considered a wonder at the time and was written about in guidebooks. The appearance of these trees evoked the images of evil forest spirits—the devil and magic famous in legends and folktales. (Above, John Cannell collection; below, Henney History Room, Conway Public Library, photograph by Nathan W. Pease.)

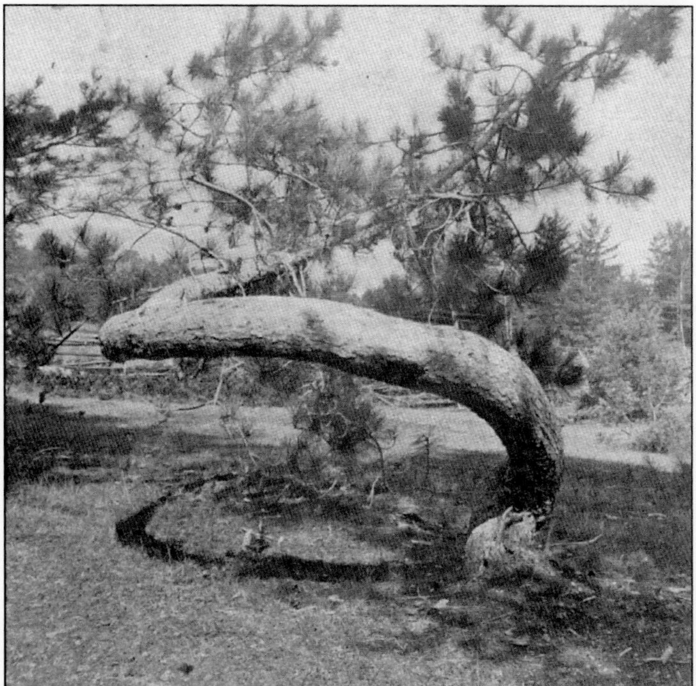

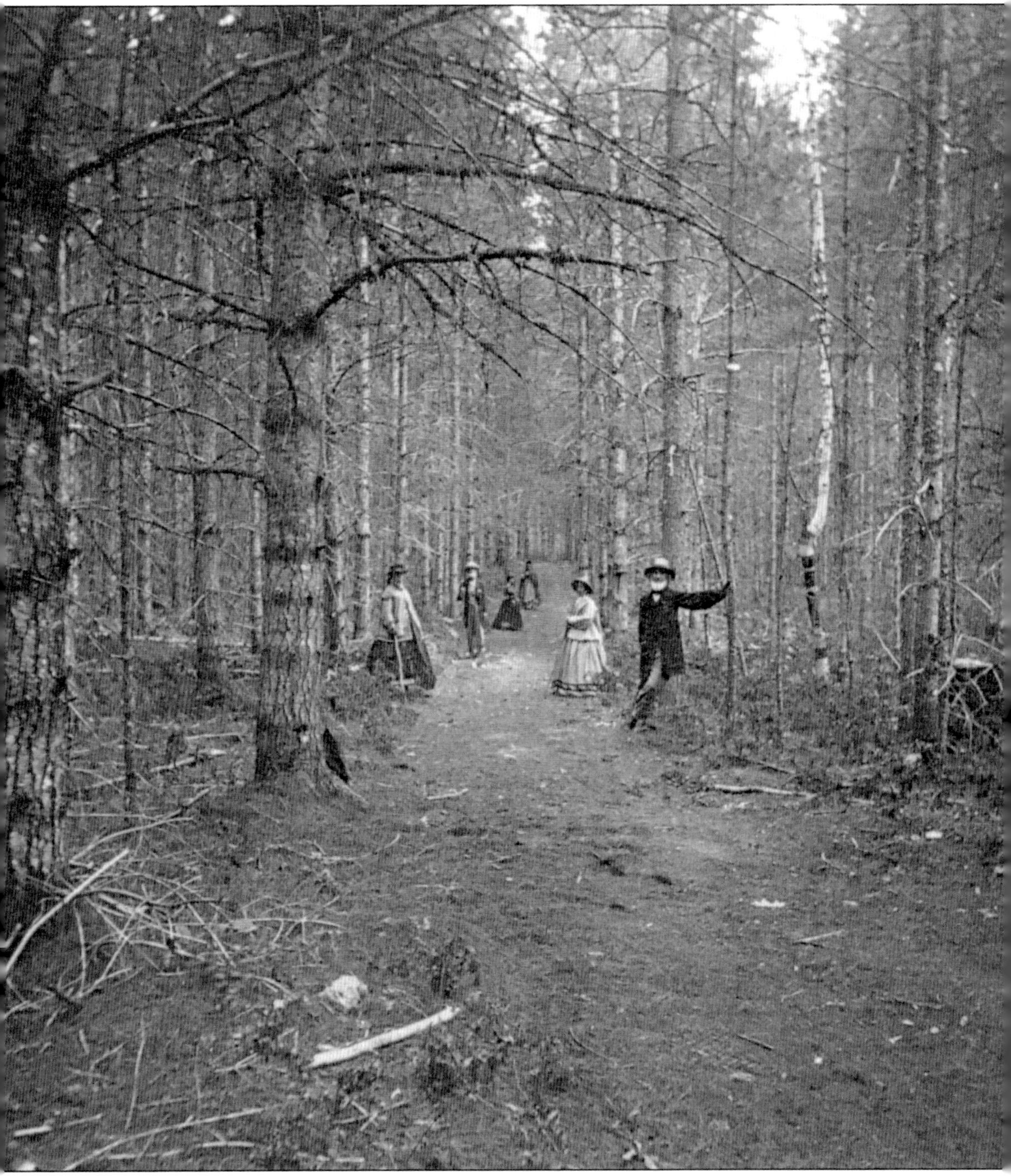

In the days before automobiles and air-conditioning, a cool, shaded wood close to a cluster of hotels near a train station provided relief from the summer's heat. Prior to the Weeks Act of 1911 and the movement to conserve and preserve forested lands, many forests had been clear-cut or severely altered by the logging industry. Large old trees were rare. Cathedral Woods was made up of old, tall, and straight trees, creating a cathedral-like atmosphere. The combination of the grandeur of the trees' stature, along with the cooling shade and welcome escape from hay fever, made these groves a popular tourist attraction. (Henney History Room, Conway Public Library.)

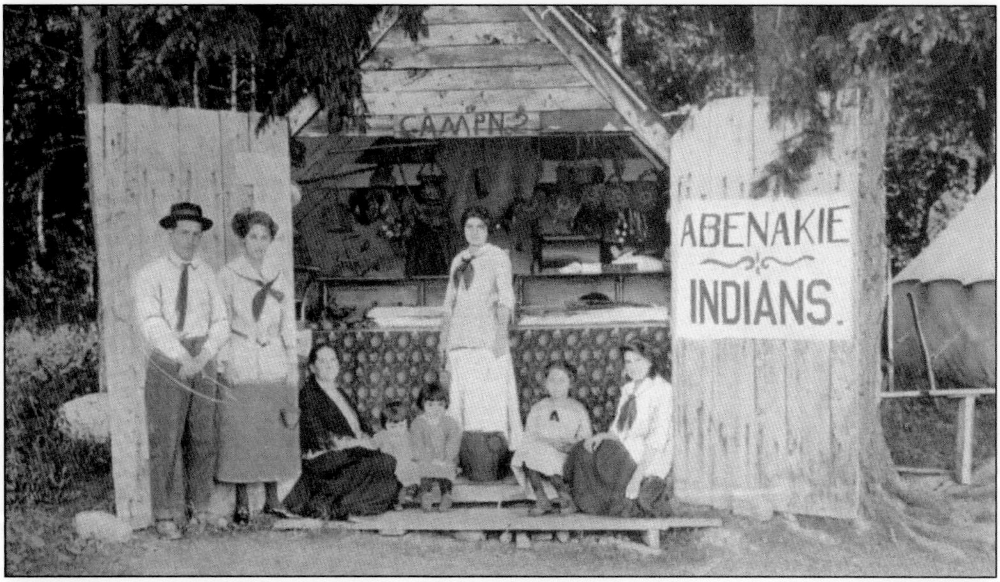

The Abenaki encampment was built in these woods near a freshwater spring in the late 1800s. The encampment included an Indian gift shop, five cabins, one wigwam, a flagpole standard, a totem-pole standard, and a monument to Chief Joseph Laurent. Laurent, a lifetime resident of the Saint Francis village in Canada and chief for 12 years, established the seasonal camp and trading post in 1884, the same year he published his Abenaki-English dictionary. The primary structure in the complex is the Abenaki Indian Shop. Originally owned and used by the railroad as a shed for a handcar and tools, it was purchased by Chief Laurent from a woman who had bought it from the railroad around 1900. The gift shop sold handmade splint ash and sweetgrass baskets, moccasins, miniature totem poles, and other Abenaki-inspired items. (Above, John Cannell collection; below, Henney History Room, Conway Public Library, photograph by Nathan W. Pease.)

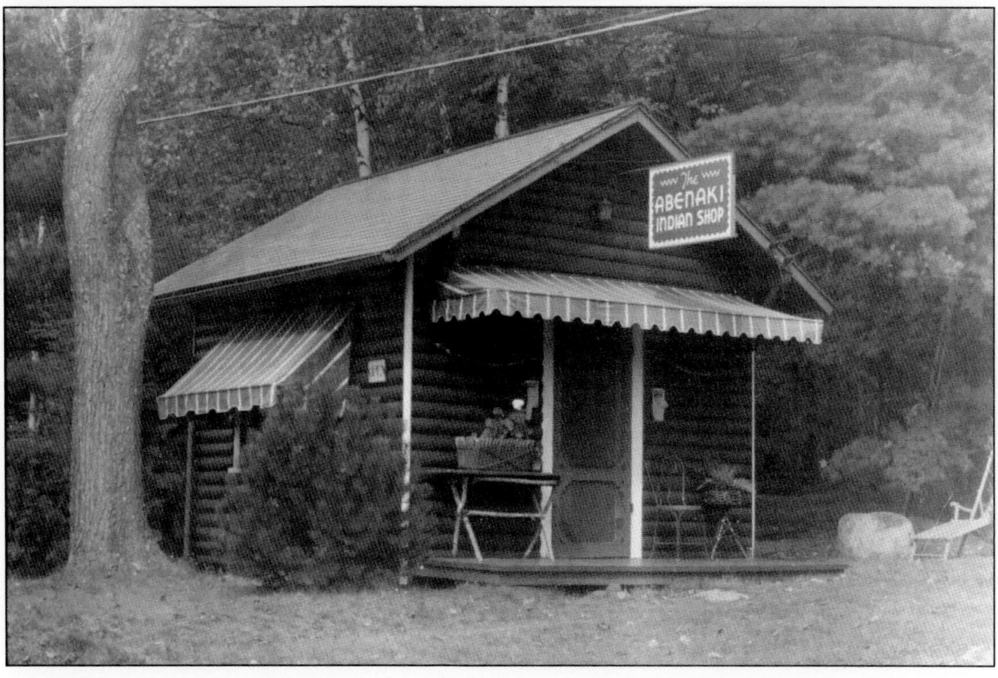

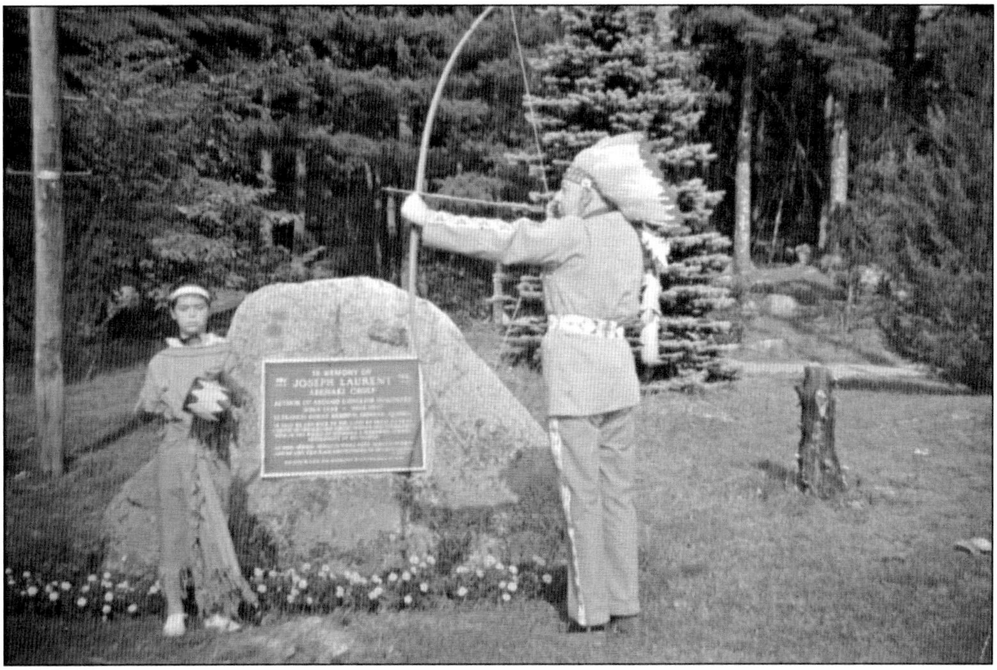

Local hotel guests liked to watch the Indians dance and demonstrate traditional activities, such as the use of the bow and arrow, and purchase their baskets. The monument to Chief Joseph Laurent was installed in 1959. The bronze plaque on the large granite boulder reads: "In Memory of Joseph Laurent/Abenaki Chief/Author of Abenake & English dialogues/Born 1839–Died 1917/ St. Francis Indian Reserve, Odanak, Quebec/In 1884 he led back to the land of their fathers a group of Abenaki and Sokoki Indians and established here in the woods of Intervale a perennial summer settlement of his people/*Ni odzi modzin nidali. Ta wdali paion agmatta wdakik*/And he left that place and returned to his country (St. Mark 6:1)/Erected in love and reverence by his children in 1959." (Both, John Cannell collection.)

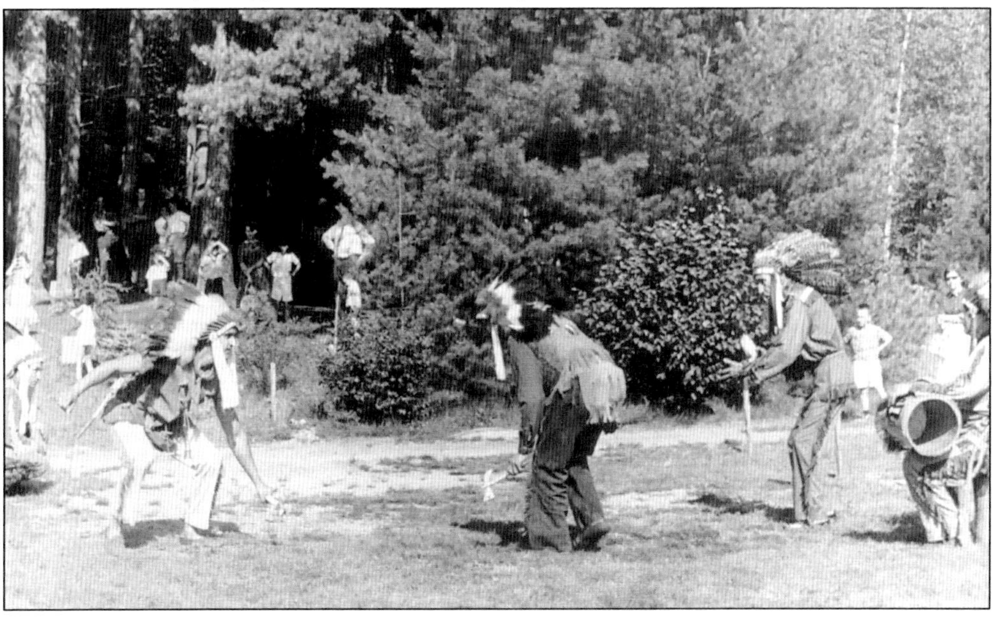

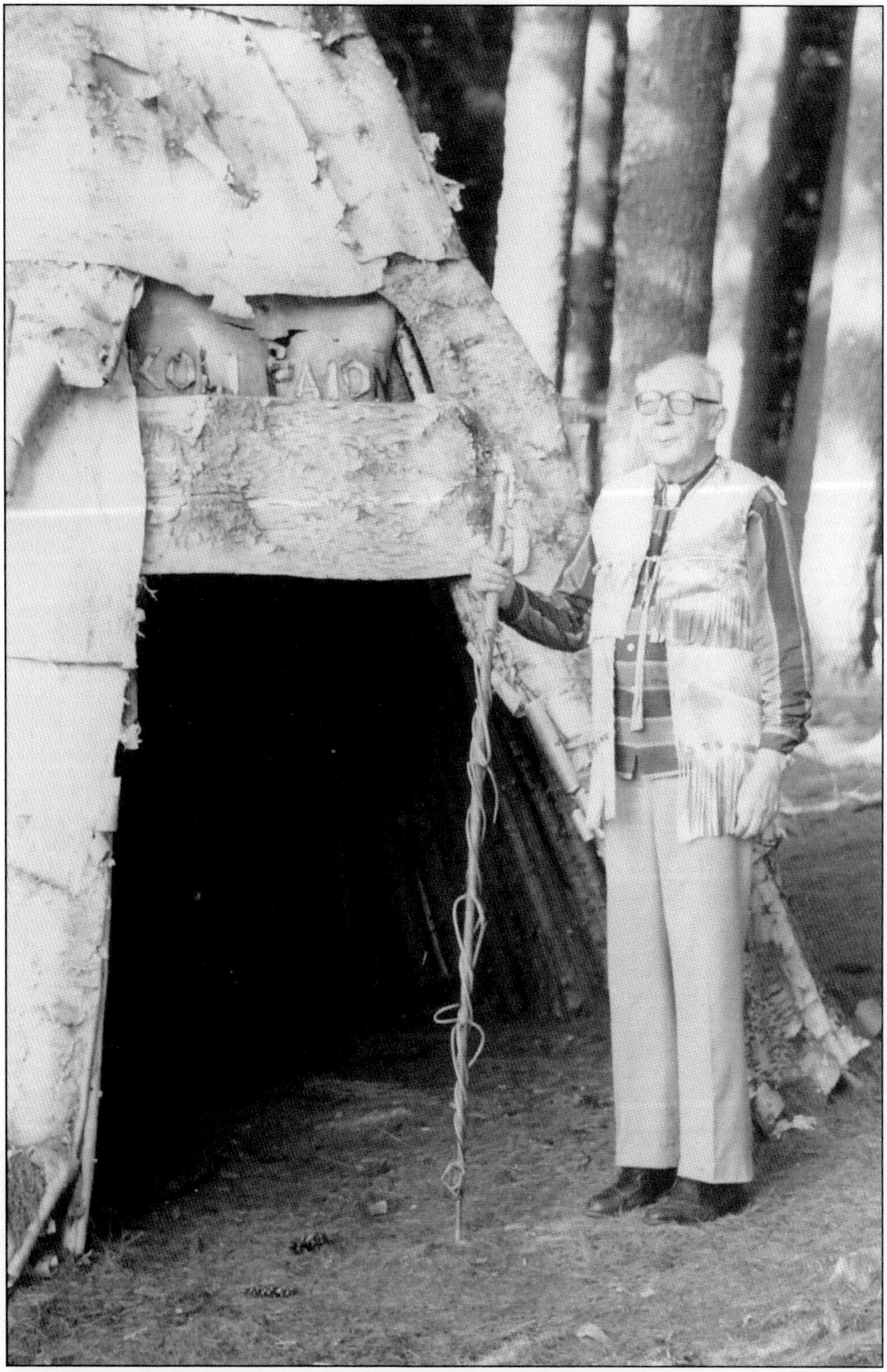

Stephen Laurent, builder of the model Indian village, stands in front of one of the last dwellings erected around 1970. In design and construction, it combined the traditional conical form with the traditional material of overlapped sheets of birch bark. It was formed by spruce logs two to three inches in diameter lashed together at the apex with alder sprouts and wire. The frame was then covered in sheets of birch bark. Over the door was a sign constructed of birch-bark letters reading "*Kolipaion*," or "Welcome." (Henney History Room, Conway Public Library.)

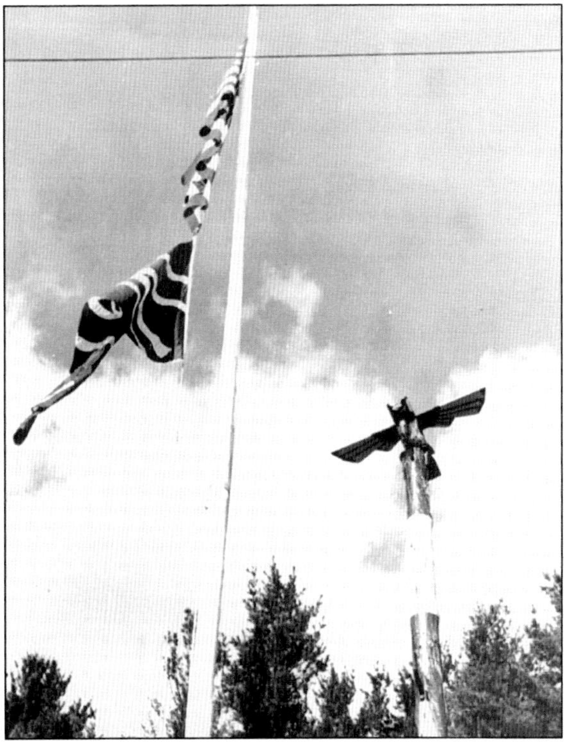

The totem pole was 40 feet high. Inscribed in the concrete footing is "Theo. Panadi Kisitok 1960," which literally translates from the Abenaki as, "Theophile Panadi made it in 1960." The first such modern ceremonial pole, carved by Adrian Panadis for a 1960 celebration, featured the turtle and bear motifs, symbols of the moieties of the Saint Francis Indians. The pole erected by the Laurents for their modern Indian village, carved by Theophile Panadis, also featured the bear totem. The totem was dismantled around 1982 for needed repairs. It has been carefully stored by a local resident and may be re-created in the future to celebrate the history of the Abenaki in the area. (Both, Henney History Room.)

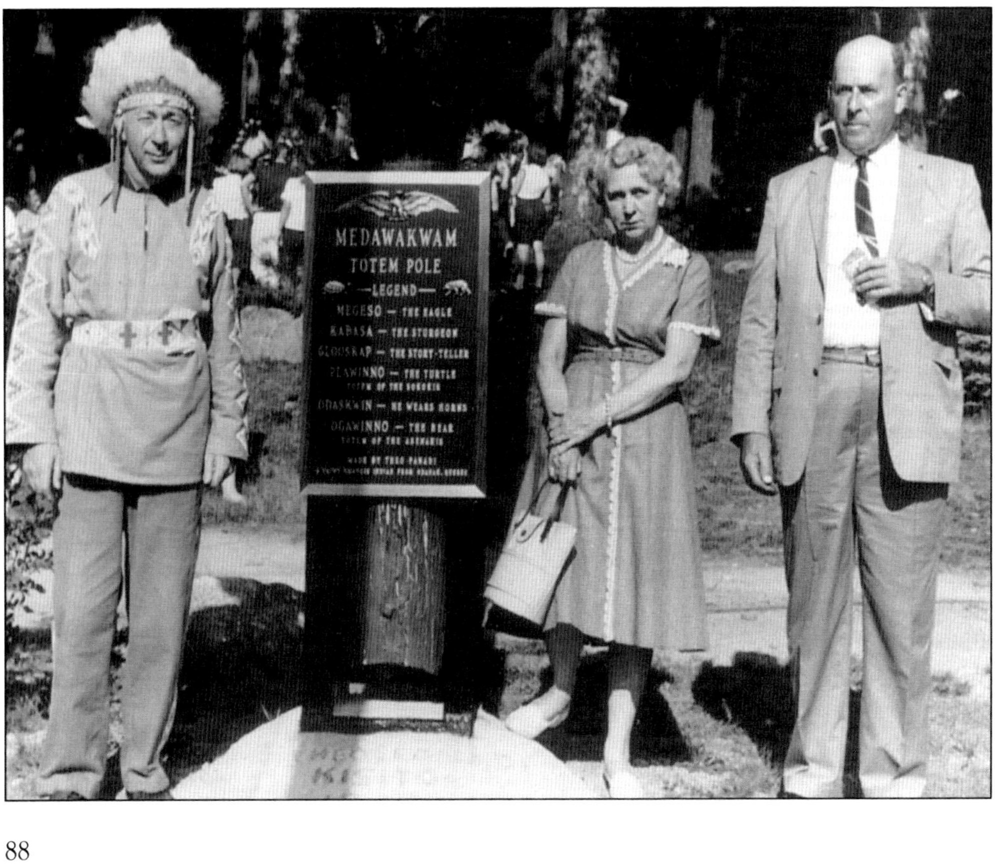

Four

WINTER PARADISE

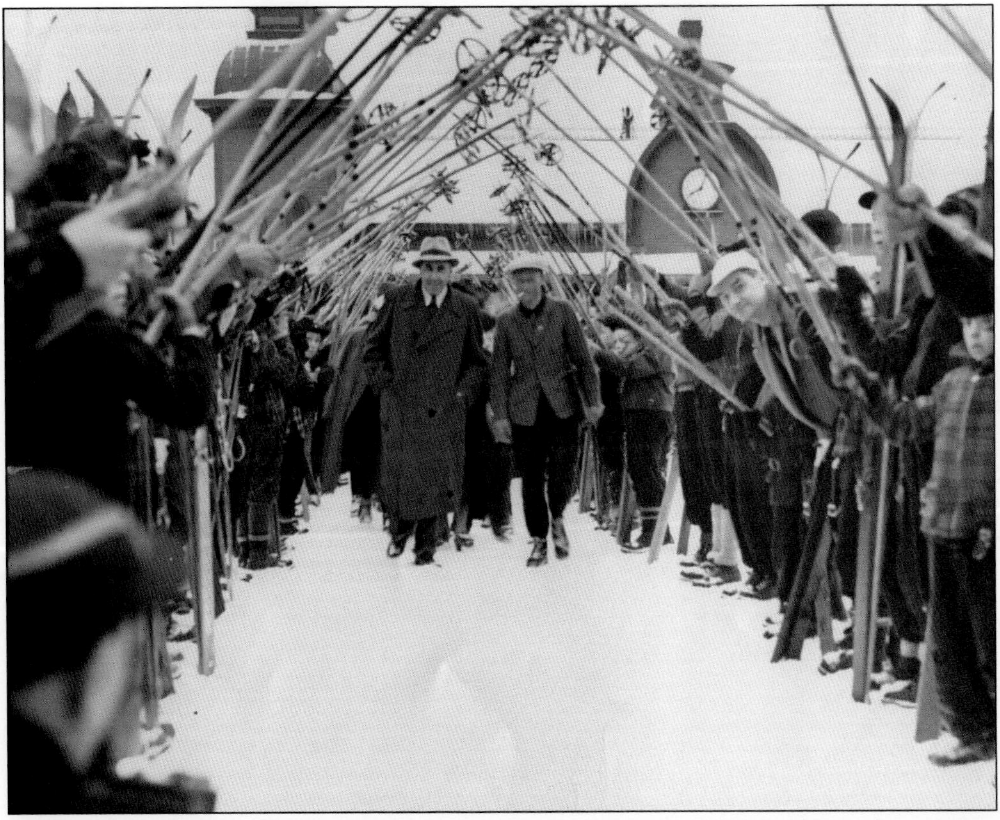

Skiing and winter sports have been a vital part of North Conway and the New Hampshire tourism industry since it blossomed in the 1930s with the famous Schneider School of Skiing, founded by Austrian skier Hannes Schneider. Here, Schneider (left) and Benno Rybizka walk in procession under an arch formed by fans holding ski poles at the train station on February 11, 1939. (North Conway Public Library, photograph by James M. Bray.)

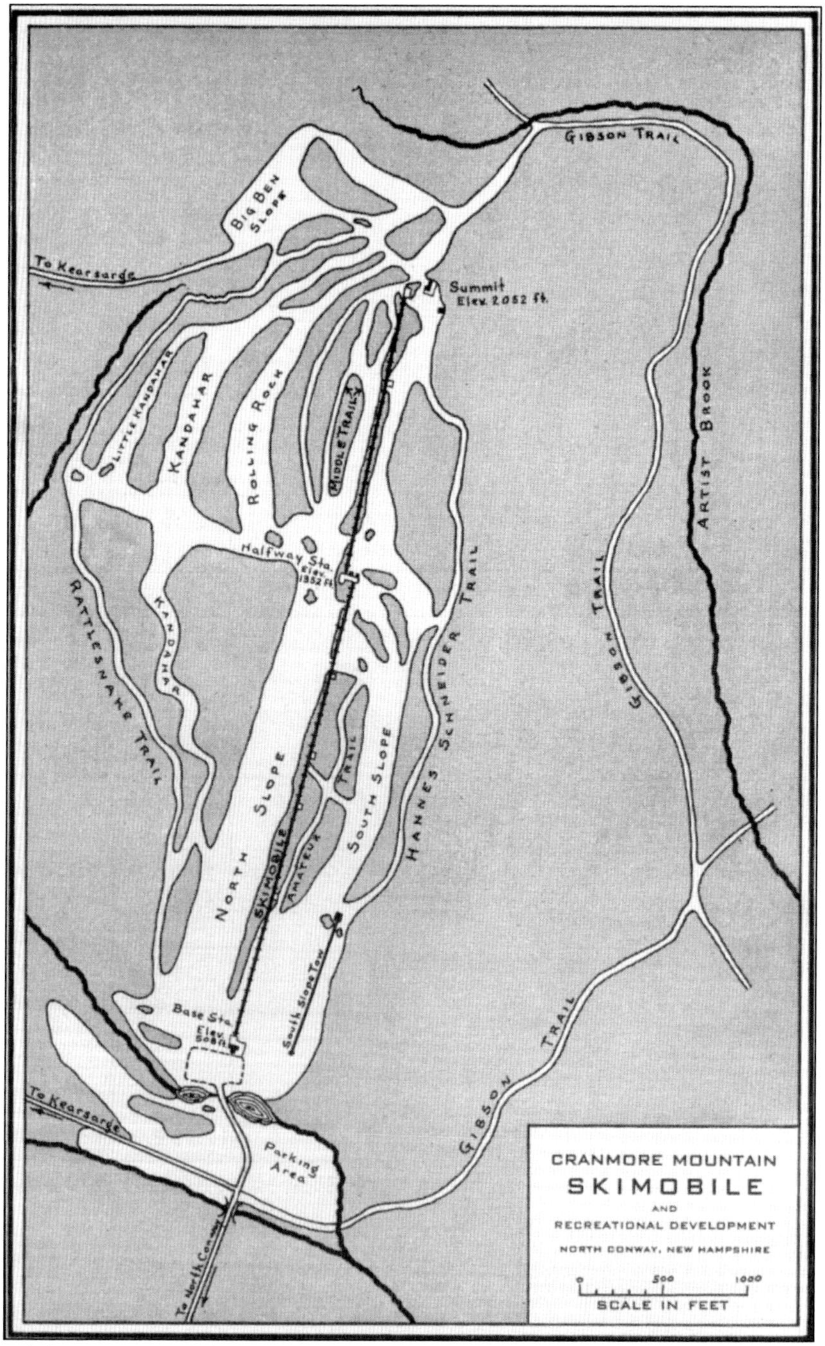

The skimobile transported skiers from the base station (elevation 508 feet) up to the halfway station (1,352 feet) and on to the summit (2,052 feet). Skiers descended from either the halfway or summit stations. The Eating House restaurant was located at the base station, and the Summit Chalet Restaurant was at the top. In 1937, Harvey Dow Gibson had secretly purchased most of the west side of Mount Cranmore with the intention of clearing ski trails. As an intriguing side note, according to historian Helen Nute, the Cranmore family name was pronounced as "Crammer" by locals early on. (Henney History Room, Conway Public Library.)

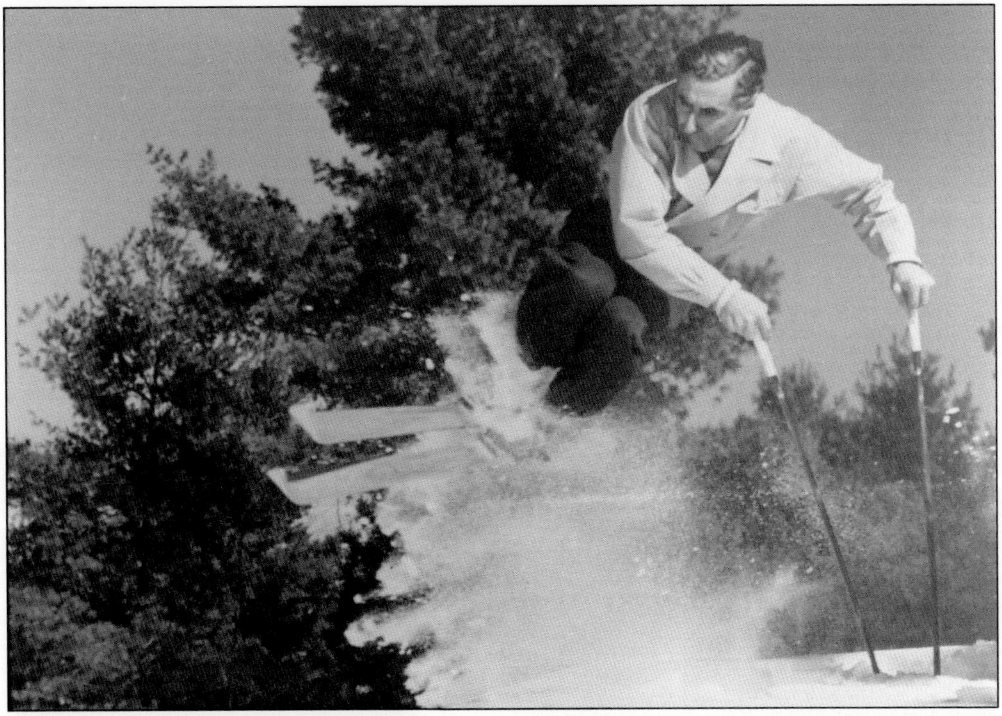

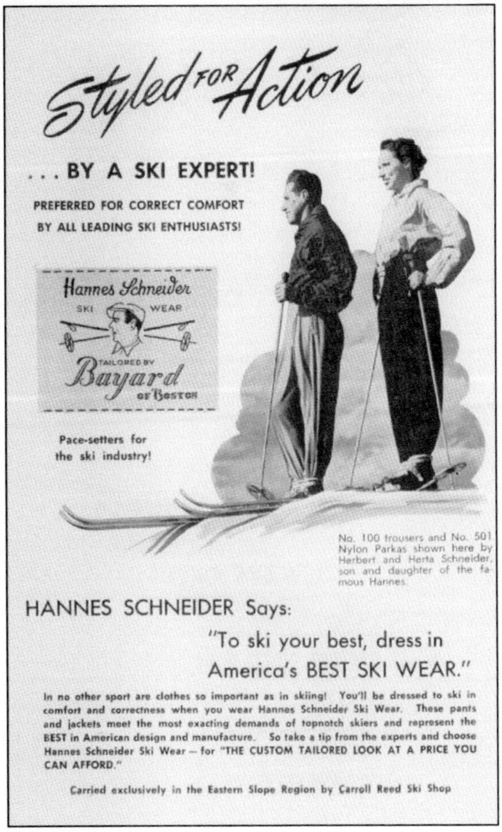

Here, Hannes Schneider demonstrates his famous jump turn. Schneider had already started a ski school in the Alberg Pass in the Alps when Carroll Reed skied the undeveloped Wildcat Mountain and was severely injured in an accident. While at Memorial Hospital, Reed talked with Dr. Harold Shedd, who suggested they should develop a ski area in North Conway. Harvey Dow Gibson was then approached about establishing the ski area and bringing in Hannes Schneider. Initially, Schneider's student Benno Rybizka was brought over to start a ski school. In 1939, after Gibson used his influence to get Schneider released from a Nazi prison and allowed to enter the United States, Schneider quickly became a celebrity, offering his own line of ski apparel and equipment, as seen in the advertisement. (Above, North Conway Public Library, photograph by James M. Bray; right, Henney History Room, Conway Public Library.)

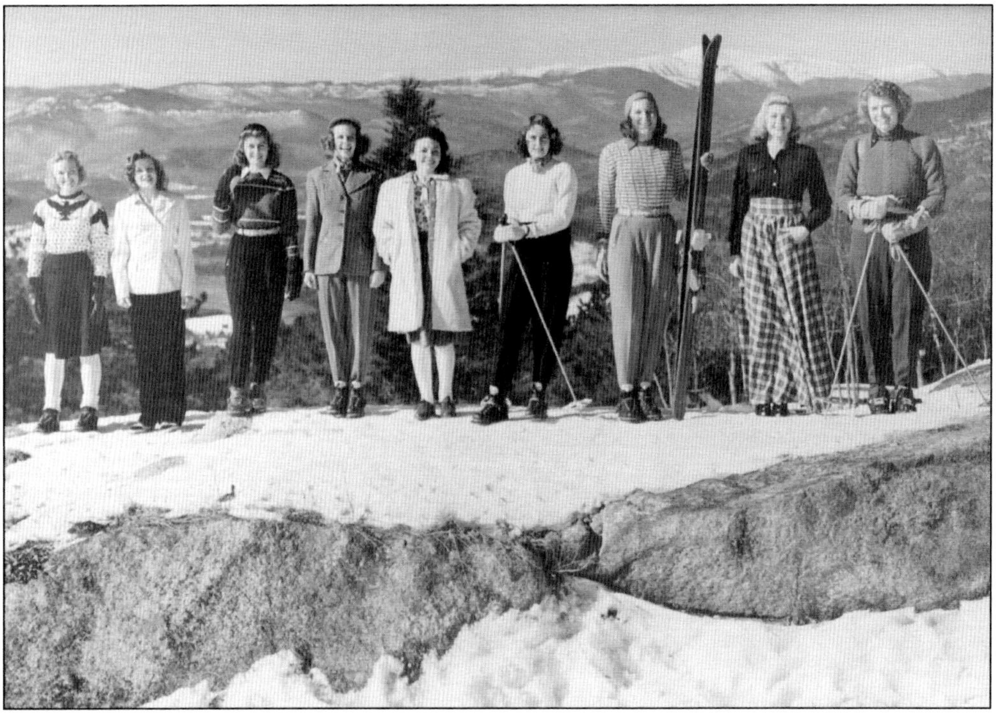

Harvey Dow Gibson created Cranmore Mountain Resort and promoted it using plenty of glamour and beauty. Here, he used picturesque Mount Washington as a backdrop for the second annual Ski Fashion Show atop Cranmore Mountain. The models wore fashion-smart ski and après ski outfits from the Carroll Reed shops, the Conway branch of Saks Fifth Avenue Shop, and Middlebrook & Boynton. (North Conway Public Library, photograph by James M. Bray.)

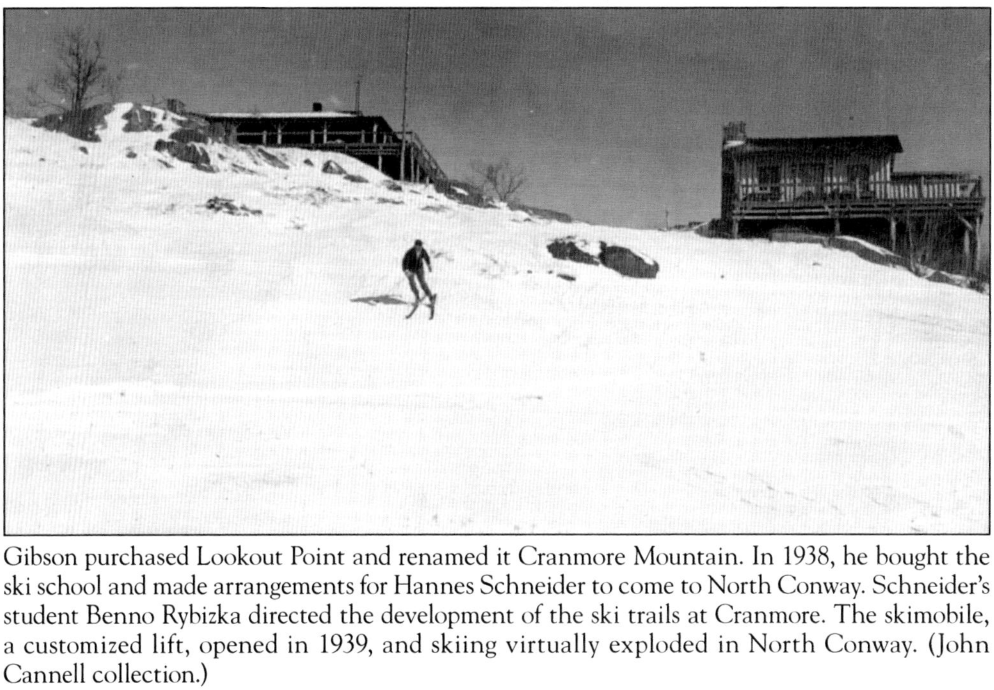

Gibson purchased Lookout Point and renamed it Cranmore Mountain. In 1938, he bought the ski school and made arrangements for Hannes Schneider to come to North Conway. Schneider's student Benno Rybizka directed the development of the ski trails at Cranmore. The skimobile, a customized lift, opened in 1939, and skiing virtually exploded in North Conway. (John Cannell collection.)

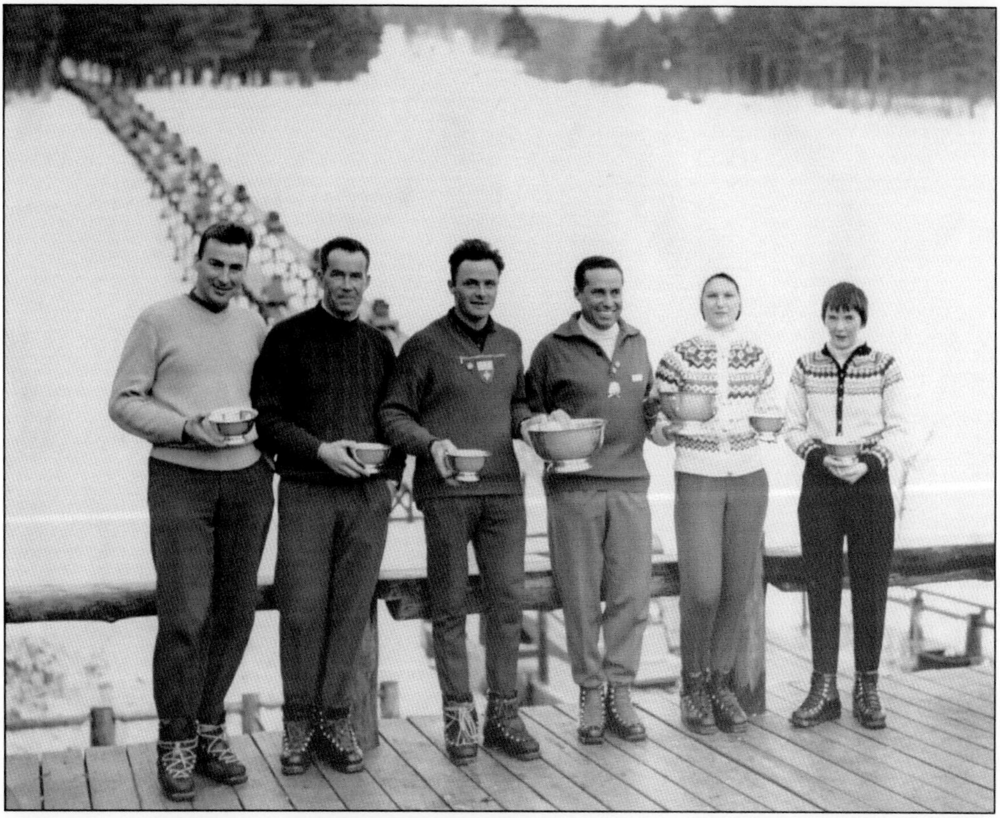

Racing became a popular activity with skiers. This photograph is from the Gibson Memorial Trophy Race on March 6, 1966. Hans Schneider's son Herbert is seen third from the right. (North Conway Public Library.)

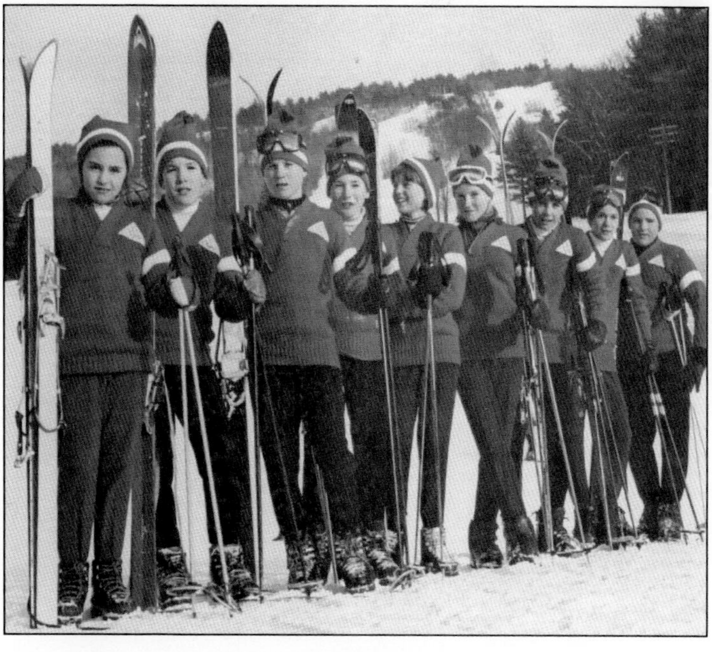

The Eastern Slope Ski Club was organized in Dr. Harold Shedd's rambling yellow house on Kearsarge Street in 1935. When it became affiliated with the US Eastern Amateur Ski Club in 1936, Dr. Shedd and Joe Dodge of the Appalachian Mountain Club's camp in Pinkham Notch were named delegates. The club's distinctive logo is seen on the triangular patches of these young students' matching sweaters. (Henney History Room, Conway Public Library.)

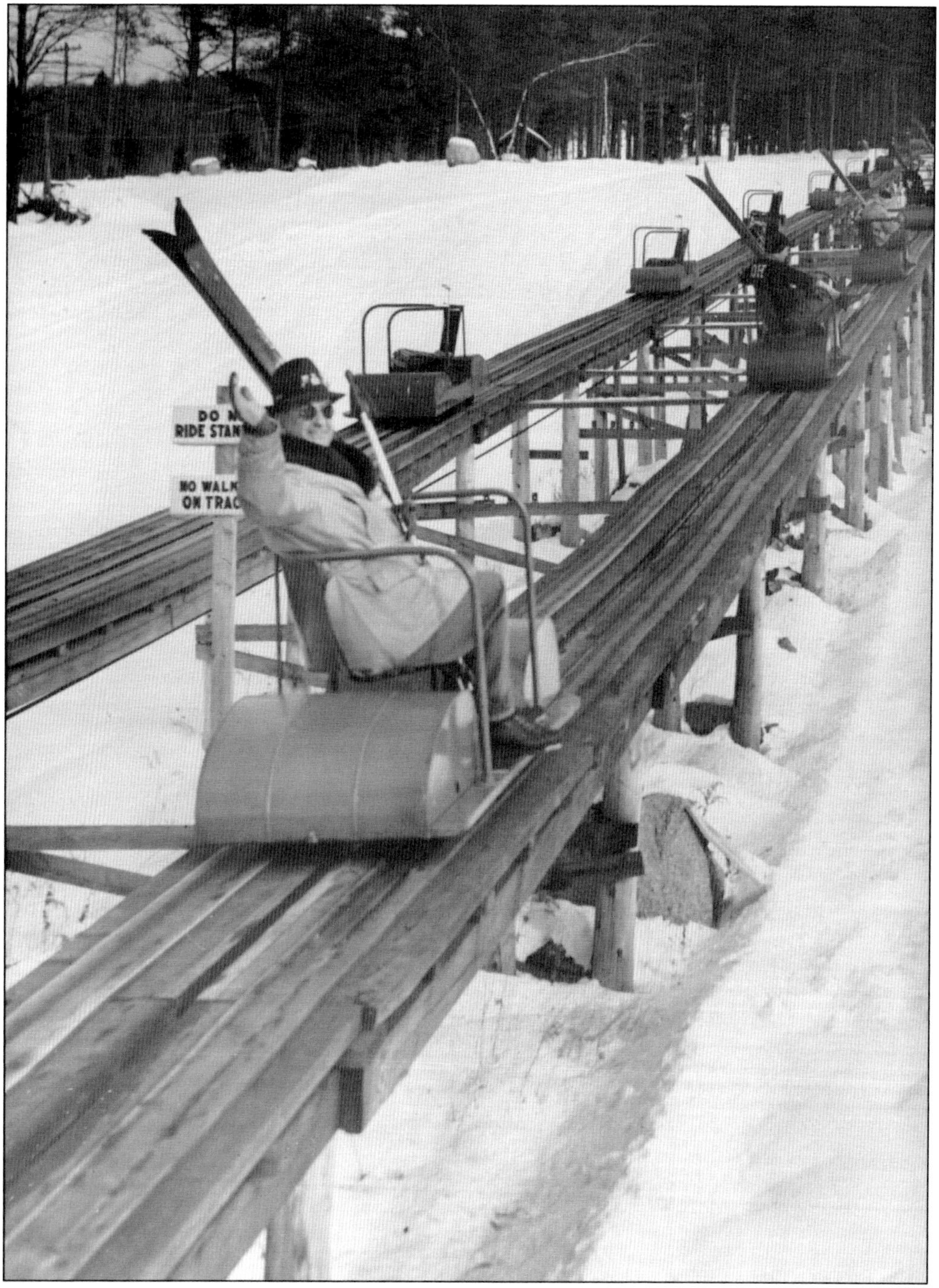

When the Swiss government refused to share its chairlift technology, Harvey Dow Gibson contracted a local mechanic, George Morton of Bartlett, and sent him cross-country to other ski areas to devise his own system for transporting skiers to the top of Cranmore. He returned to North Conway with the blueprints for the first modern-day skimobile, which has now been dismantled. A number of the skimobile cars are still displayed around North Conway. (North Conway Public Library.)

Five

Summer on the Slopes

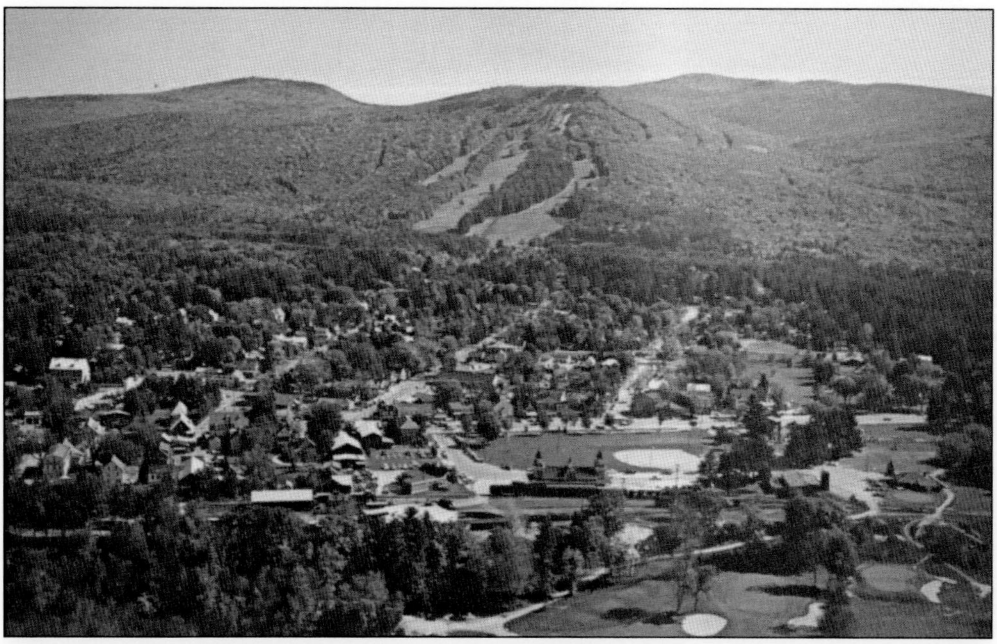

Summer has always been the premier tourist season for North Conway. Many attractions, recreations, and services were developed to entertain visitors, as well as new residents and businesses. This aerial view shows the golf course in the foreground and the train station in the center with the ski slopes of Cranmore Mountain Resort behind. (John Cannell collection.)

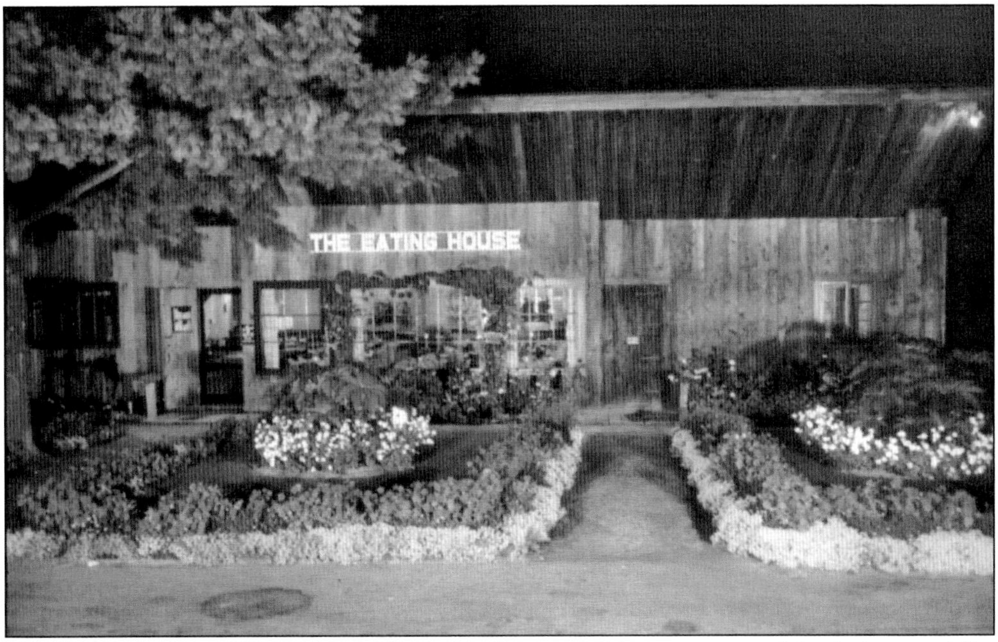

Cranmore Mountain Resort was the largest and most visible attraction in North Conway. The Eating House with its unique shape was located at the base station and served fine foods to hungry visitors in the summer and skiers in the winter. Diners could watch the Skimobile Tramway through large picture windows. (Mike Roberts, Conway Historical Society.)

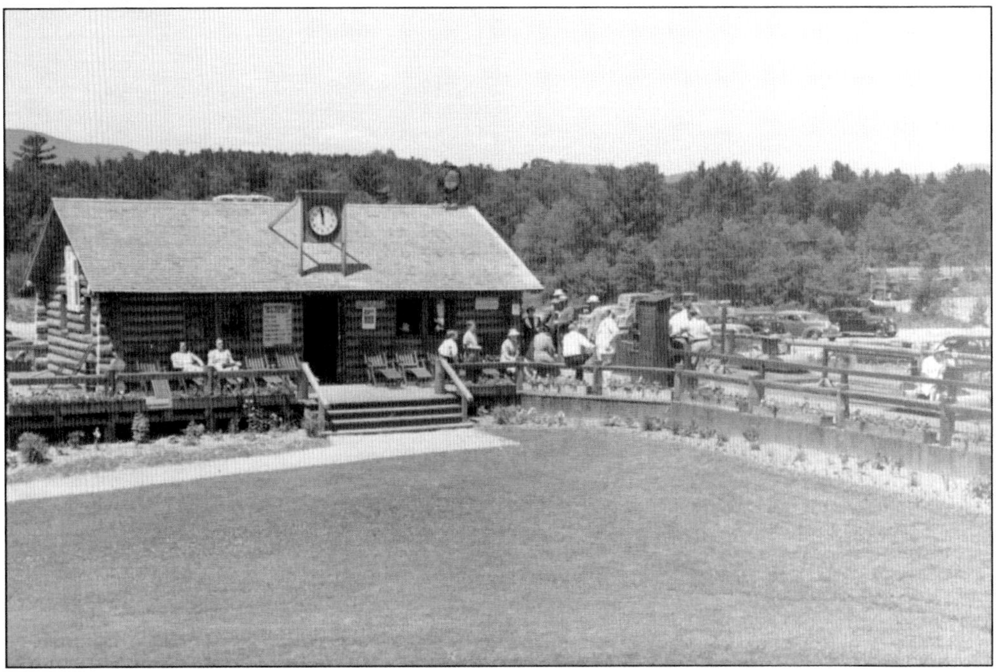

Cranmore was open during the summer, offering rides to the summit for viewing the scenic mountains and valley and hiking the many trails. The log cabin–style base for the skimobile was opened in 1940. Harvey Dow Gibson was fond of antiques and the rustic charm of historically stylish buildings, a taste that is reflected in this station. (North Conway Public Library.)

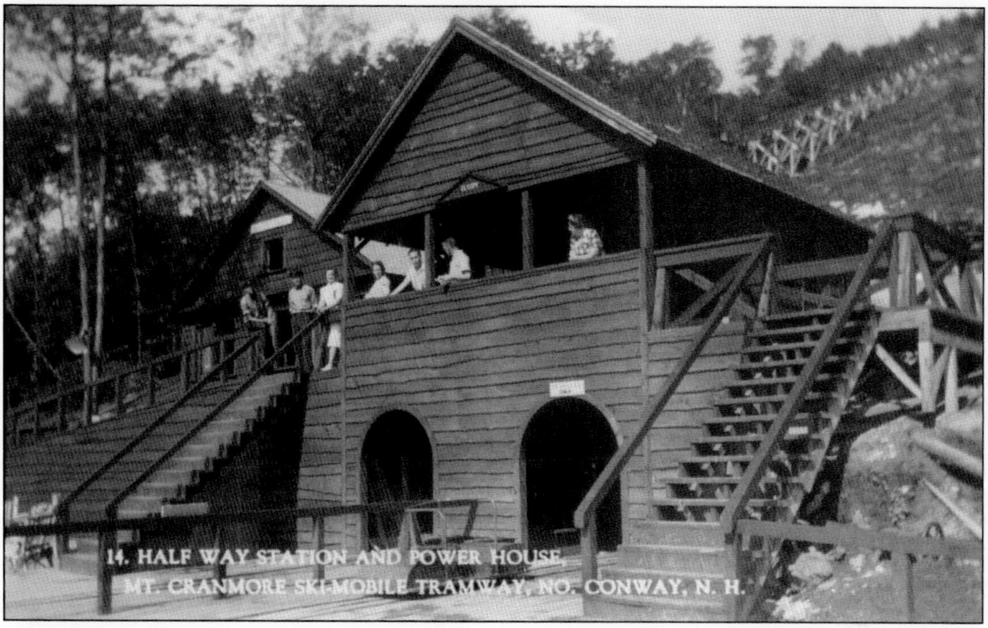

The halfway station and powerhouse, which mimicked the rustic style of the base station, served as an entrance to several hiking trails as well as a scenic viewing spot on its covered porch. The image below looks down on the halfway station. Each skimobile had a single seat and offered no restraints to secure riders. (Both, Henney History Room, Conway Public Library, photographs by Gordon Holland.)

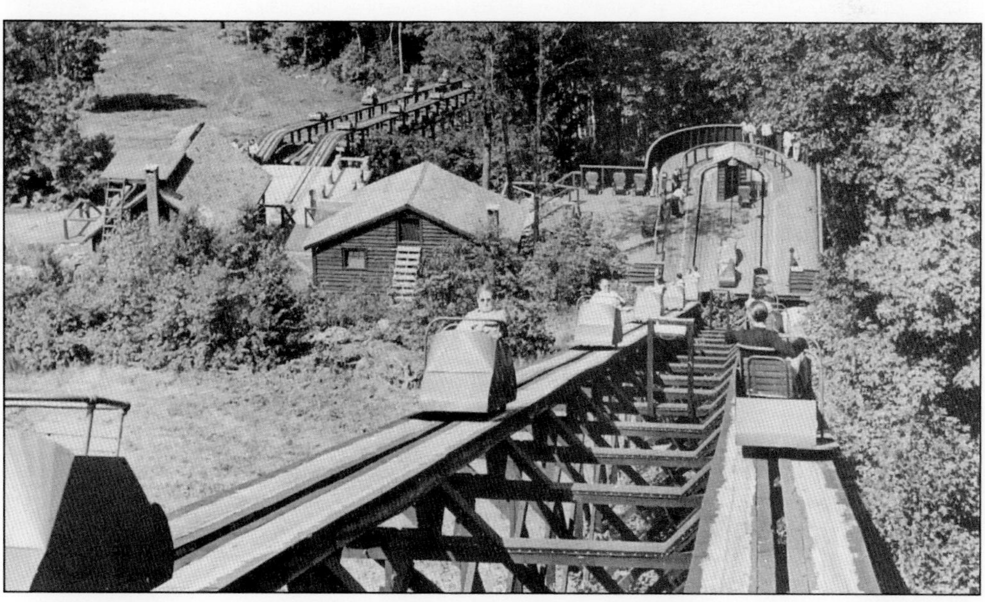

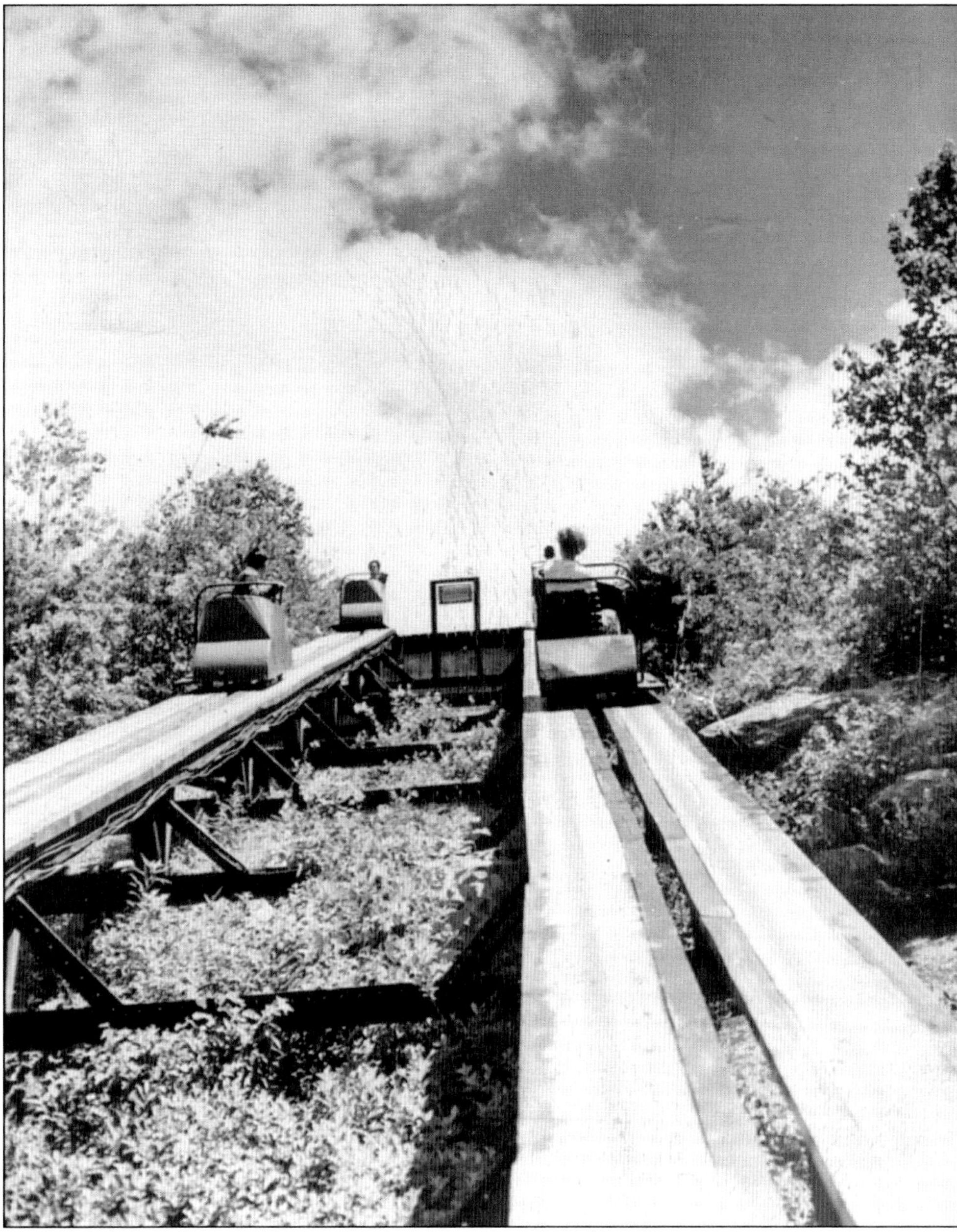

This photograph was taken from the halfway station looking up to the summit. The skimobile was invented by George Morton of nearby Bartlett, who Gibson sent out to study various systems around the country. After visiting the chairlift installed at Belknap Mountain in Gilford, New Hampshire, he realized he disliked his feet dangling in the air as he rode, so he created a semi-enclosed seated car that ran on tracks. Morton's son Parker had recently graduated from the Wentworth Institute in Boston with an engineering degree and played a major role in the lift's design. The cars were built in Massachusetts and shipped to Conway for painting by the Mortons. The skimobile opened in December 1938 with 150 cars painted red, white, and blue, carrying skiers halfway up Cranmore Mountain. The top half of the skimobile was completed the following year. (North Conway Public Library.)

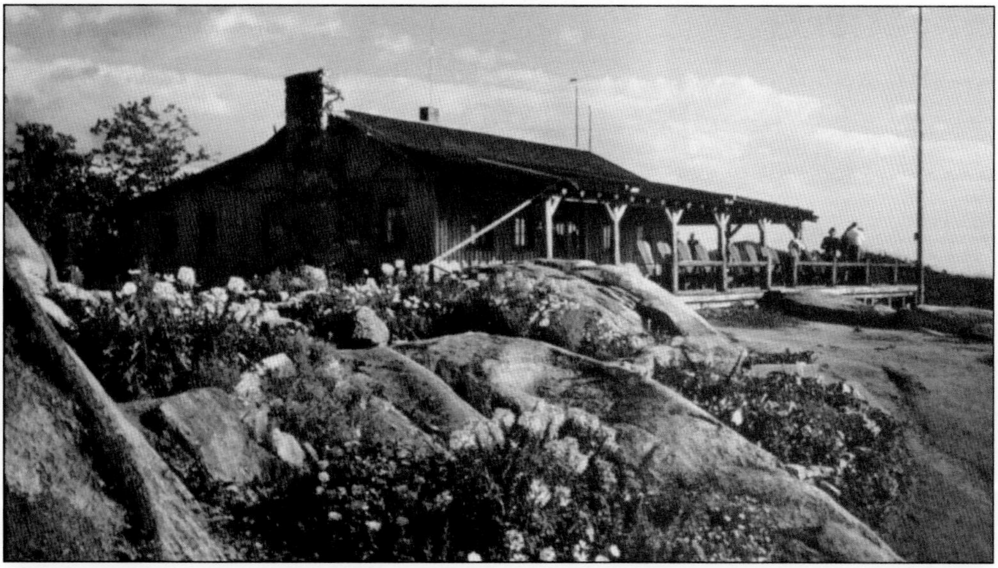

In the summer months, many people ventured to the top to take in the unforgettable majestic views, hike the summit trails, or eat delicious food at the Summer Chalet, a cafeteria-style restaurant. The summit was a particularly popular spot for photographers and artists of all skill levels. (Conway Historical Society.)

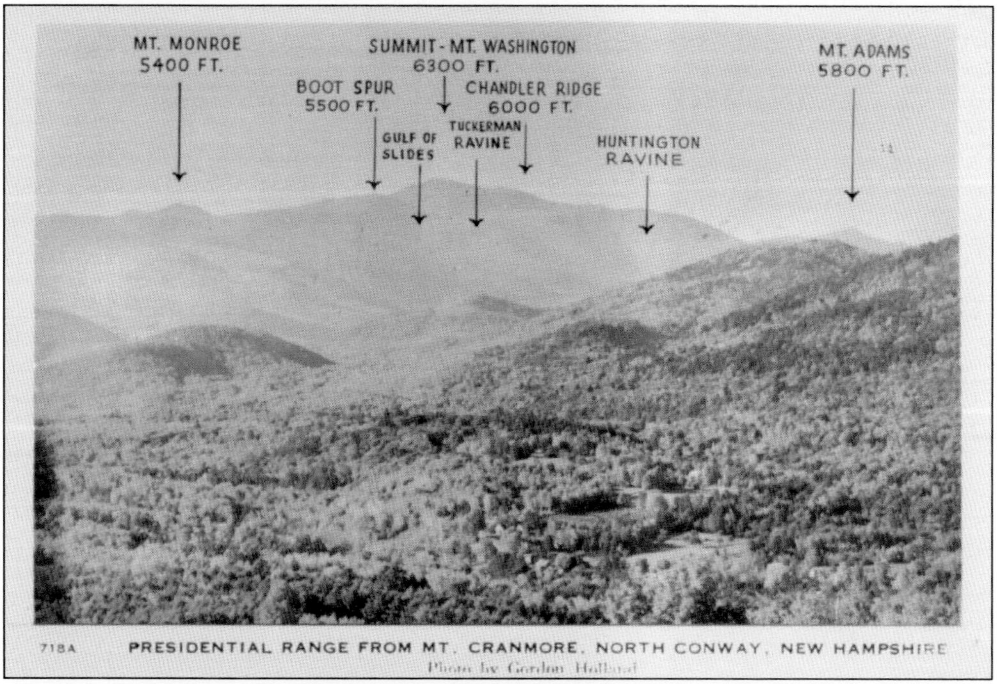

The views from the summit of Mount Cranmore were spectacular. On a clear day, the Presidential Range of the White Mountains was wonderful to behold. Seen here are Mount Monroe, Mount Washington, and Mount Adams. Several popular hiking locations on Mount Washington are also indicated, including the Boot Spur, Gulf of Slides, Chandler Ridge, Huntington Ravine, and the famous Tuckerman Ravine. (Henney History Room, Conway Public Library, photograph by Gordon Holland.)

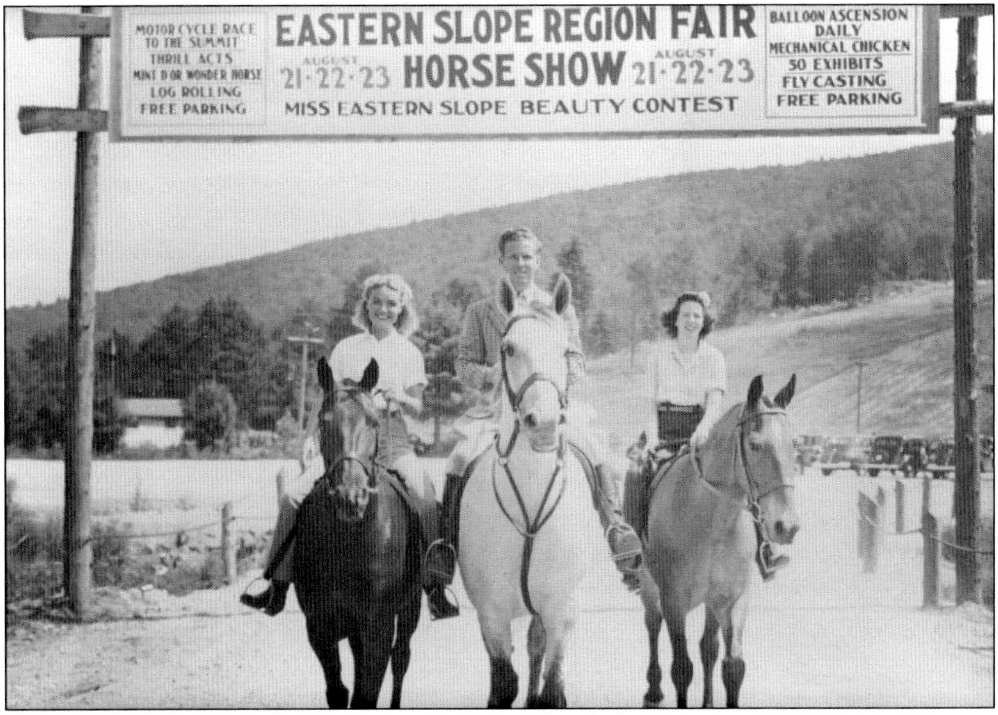

To capitalize on Cranmore's year-round appeal, events such as the Eastern Slope Region Fair were held. A wide variety of activities were advertised to attract locals and tourists; some of the specialty events included motorcycle races to the summit, logrolling and fly-casting demonstrations, hot-air balloon ascensions, and exhibits and oddities, such as the mechanical chicken. There was also the Miss Eastern Slope beauty contest. Gibson, who sponsored the fair, was an avid horseman and even wrote a book about the differences between American and British foxhunting practices; however, his interest in horses went beyond these refined types of horse events. During the fair, horses were regularly highlighted in thrilling displays like the one below, where a horse shows off its skill by jumping over an automobile as thrilled spectators look on. (Both, North Conway Public Library, photographs by James M. Bray.)

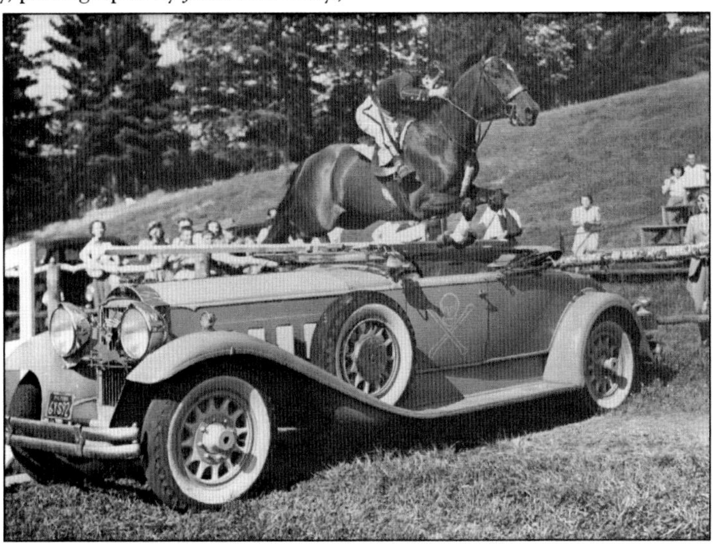

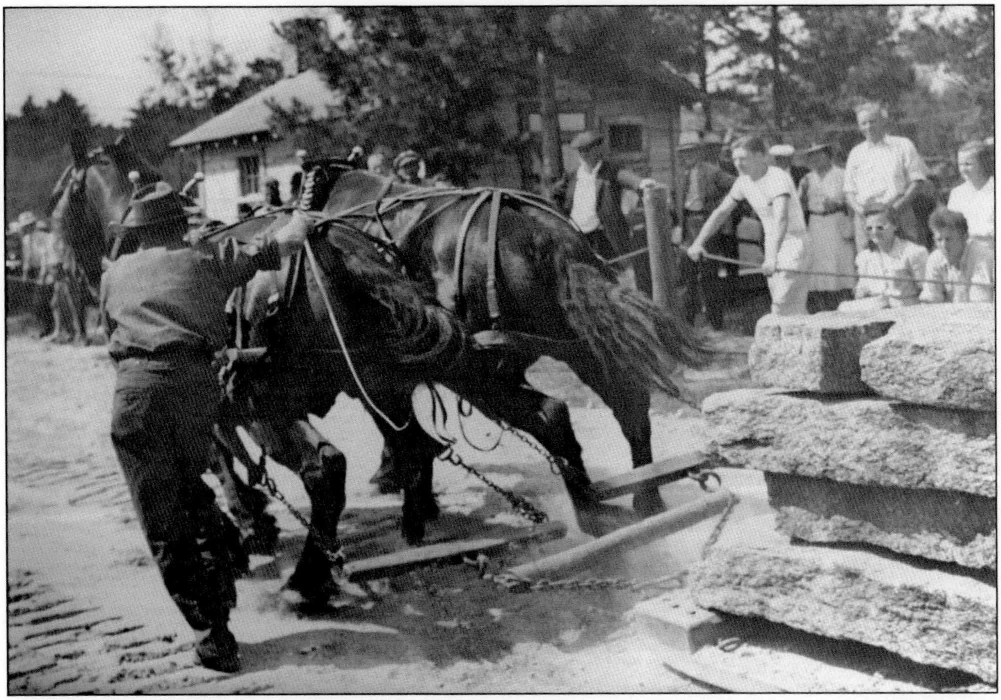

There was great debate in New England between "horse people" and "oxen people." Oxen are steers that have been trained to work in a head or horn yoke for three to five years. Any breed of cow can be used as oxen. Horse people cite the value of a horse's speed advantage over oxen, whereas oxen people proclaim their preference of the stability and calm nature of oxen over the more temperamental character of horses. Harvey Dow Gibson, being the savvy business and showman that he was, incorporated pulling competitions into the Eastern Slope Region Fairs. These images show the dramatic action of livestock pulling granite slabs at the fair in 1941. (Both, North Conway Public Library, photographs by James M. Bray.)

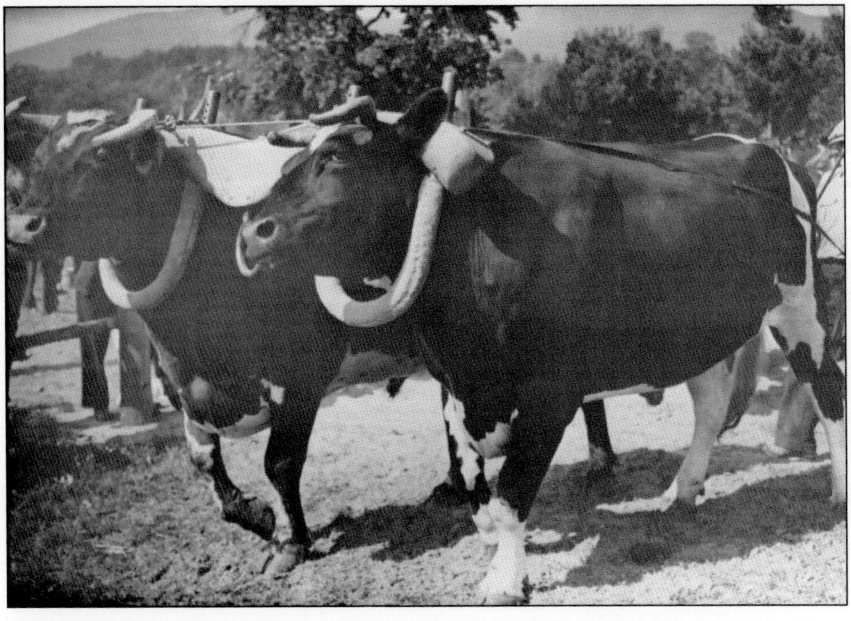

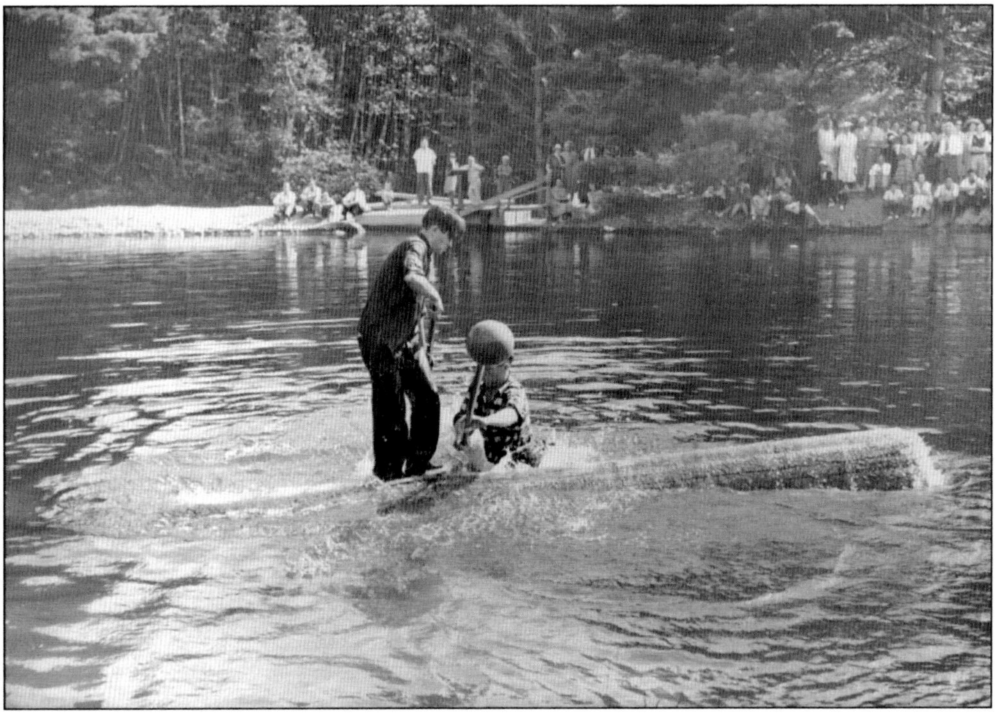

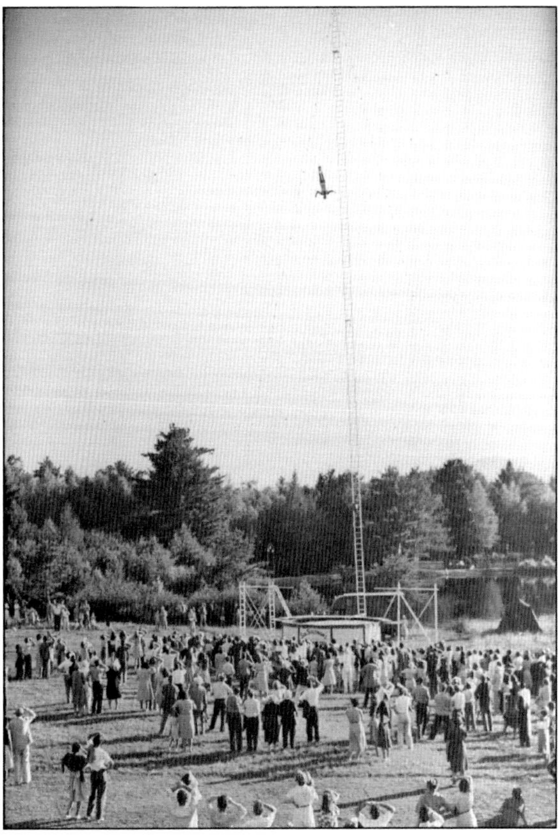

Timber has been an important industry in the region since colonial times. The British harvested mast poles for their naval ships from the New Hampshire forests. Since the state was heavily forested, wood became the primary material used for building houses, fences, roads, furniture, stuffing material (such as excelsior-shredded wood), tools, domestic equipment, shoe pegs, gun stocks, barrels, and wagons and carriages. In tribute to the many lumberjacks who worked the regional woods, woodsmen competitions and exhibitions developed at local fairs. The log-rolling competition above took place at the 1941 Eastern Slope Region Fair at Cranmore Mountain. More modern spectacles also took place at the fair, like the daring high-dive act of Sol Soloman, who always drew a crowd to see his daredevil skills. (Both, North Conway Public Library, photographs by James M. Bray.)

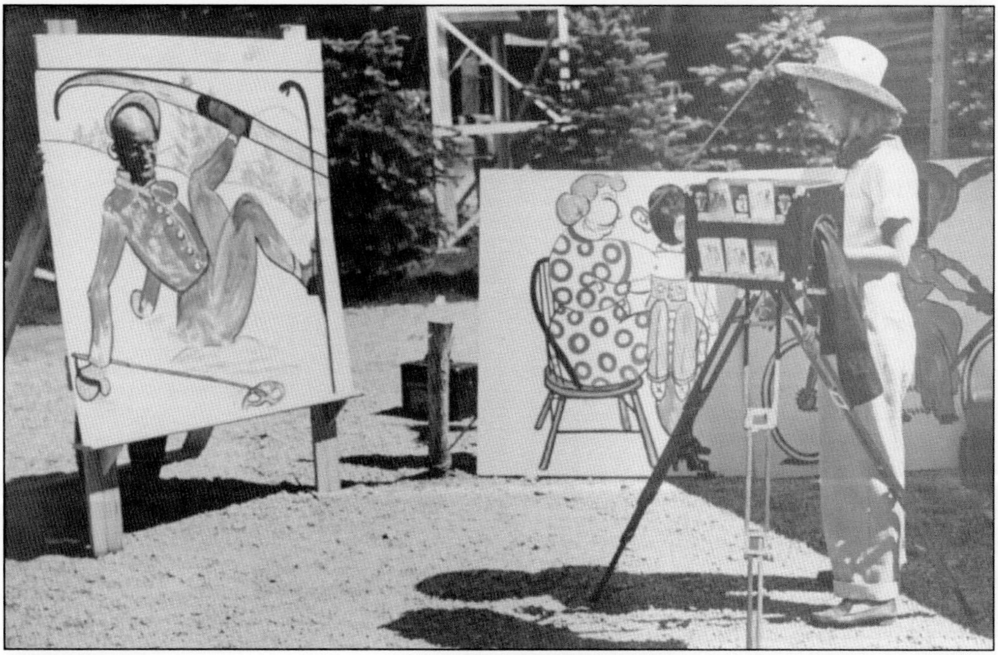

While the region was a focus for fine artists and craftsmen, simpler, more-humorous art forms were often practiced at the Eastern Slope Region Fair. Here, Gibson poses for a jokey photograph by Blanche Rybizka, wife of renowned ski instructor Benno Rybizka. (North Conway Public Library, photograph by James M. Bray.)

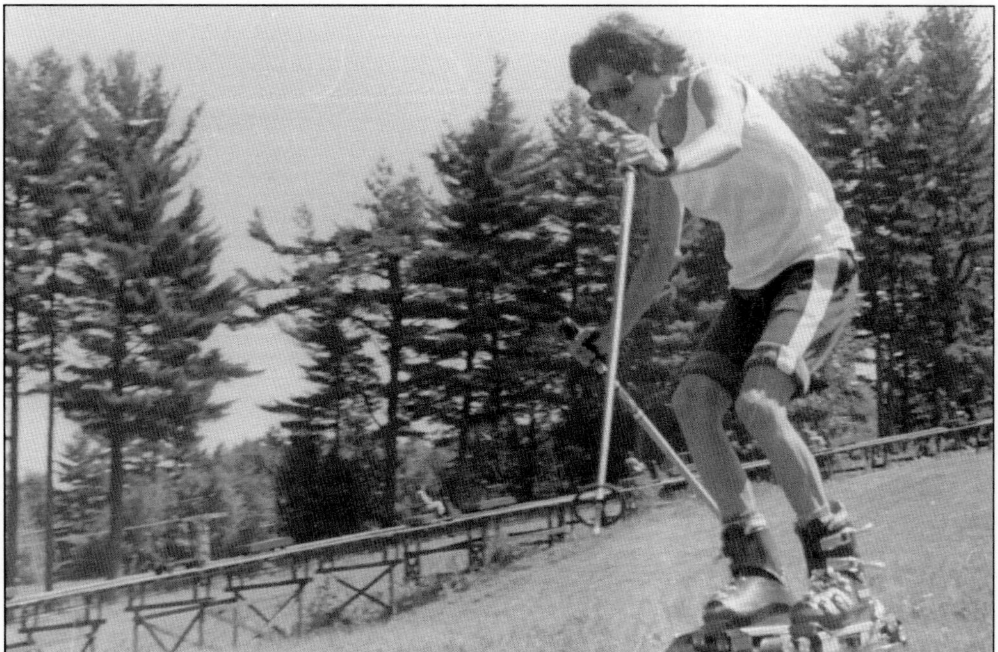

Dedicated, enthusiastic skiers want to keep in shape all year to be in top condition come ski season, and in-line skating often helped skiers maintain their muscle tone. Some diehard skiers even tried downhill inline skating. (Henney History Room, Conway Public Library.)

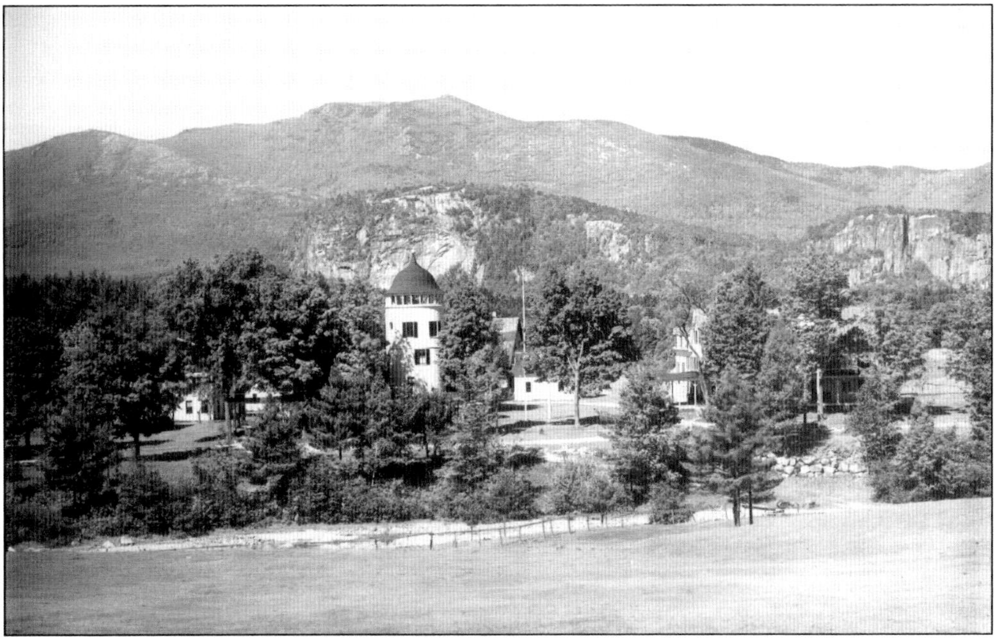

In 1863, Willard Russell and his son Frank started the Russell Cottages, offering less expensive, more rural options than the downtown hotels. The inn, easily recognizable by its distinctive tower, could accommodate 140 guests and was very popular. Its motto was, "The proof of the pudding is in the eating thereof." (Henney History Room, Conway Public Library.)

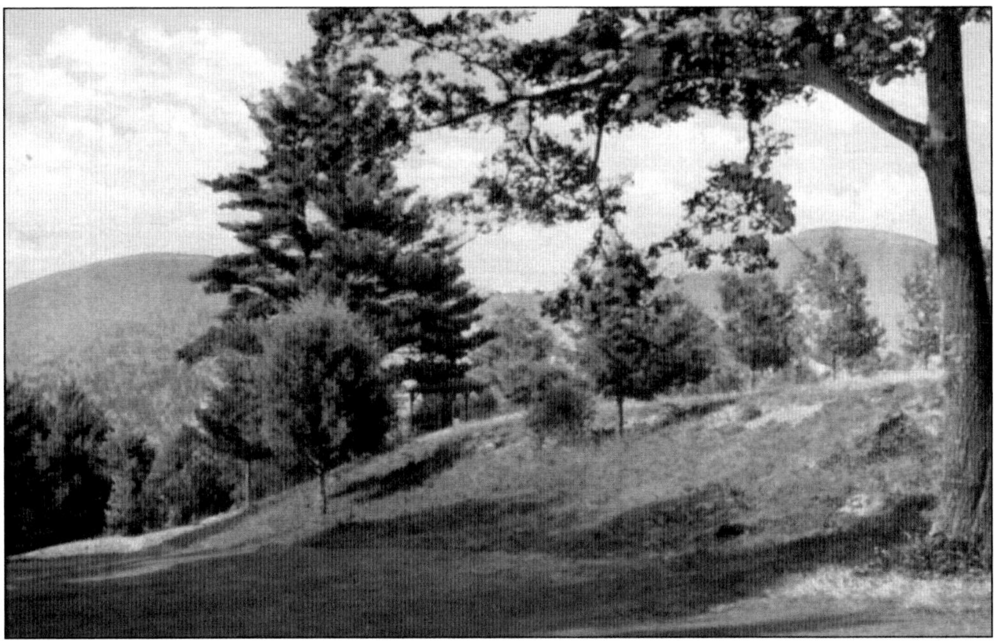

Golf has long been a popular pastime in North Conway, and the golf course near the Conway Scenic Railroad Station is well known to anyone visiting North Conway. The Kearsage Golf Course, seen here, was near the Russell Cottages, and the mountains give the slightly wooded course a beautiful backdrop. A rustic gazebo can be seen nestled in the pines. (Henney History Room, Conway Public Library.)

Six

The Western Edge of the Eastern Slope

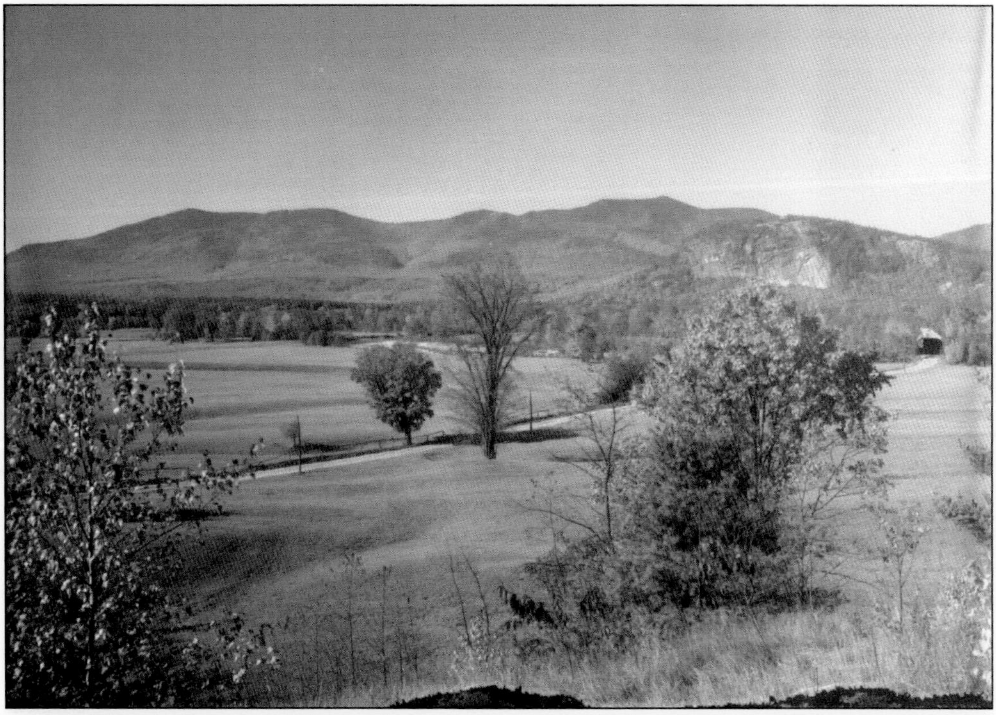

In the 1800s, the area was still considered exotic territory with a string of tourist attractions such as Cathedral and White Horse Ledge, Devil's Den, Diana's Baths, Pitman's Arch, and Echo Lake. Two miles from Route 16, entrance to North Conway was obtained through a covered bridge. From Intervale in the other direction, one entered over a unique floating bridge and through a tollgate. (Henney History Room, Conway Public Library.)

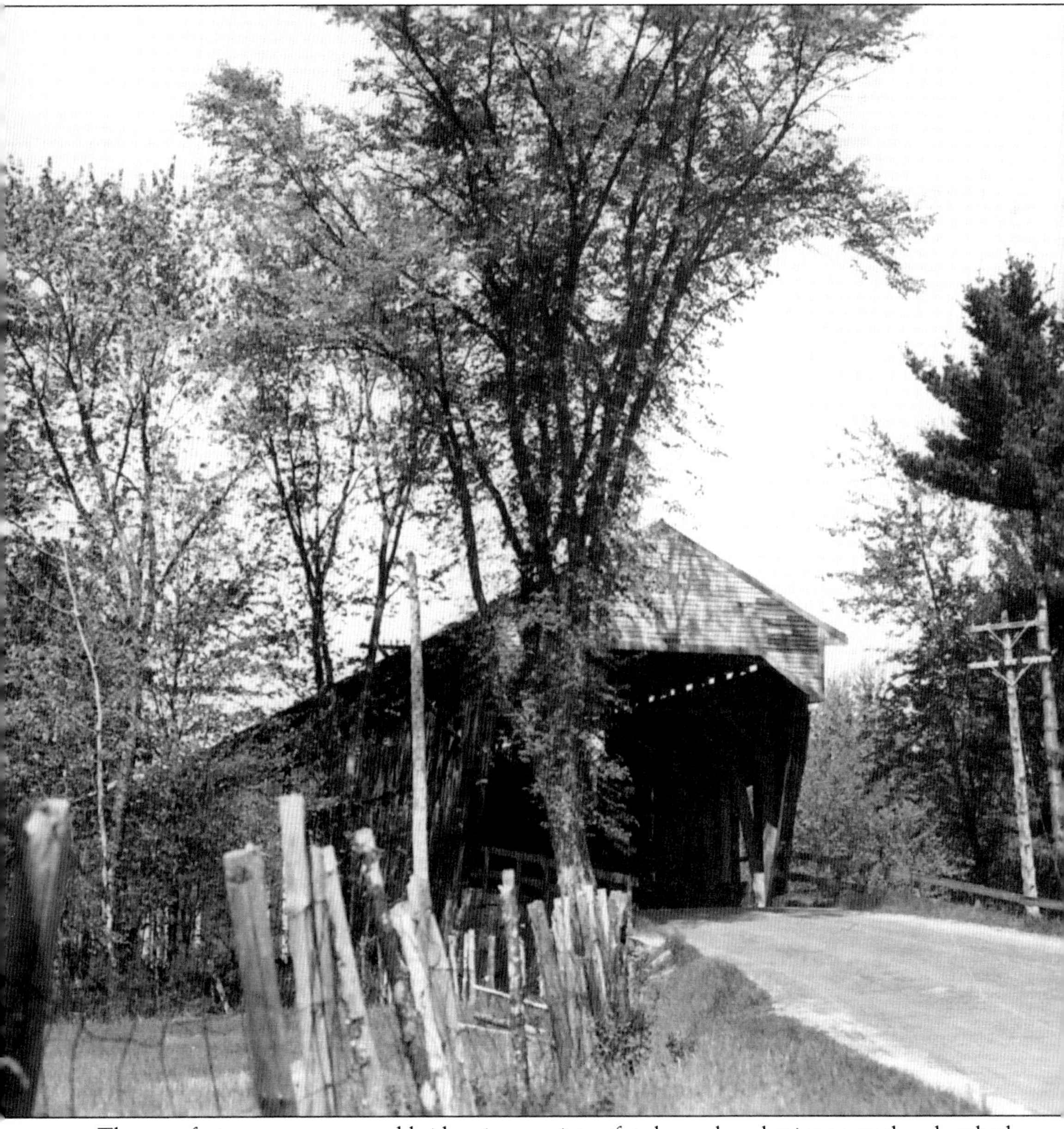

The area features many covered bridges in a variety of styles such as lattice trussed and arched trussed. The bridges were covered to protect the structure from the weather. Ironically, during the winter, snow was actually shoveled onto the bridges to allow sleds through. Most uncovered wooden bridges only lasted about nine years. Covered bridges, if maintained well, could easily last more than 80 years. Originally, these bridges only had to accommodate pedestrians, horse-drawn wagons, carriages, and later lightweight automobiles. (Henney History Room, Conway Public Library.)

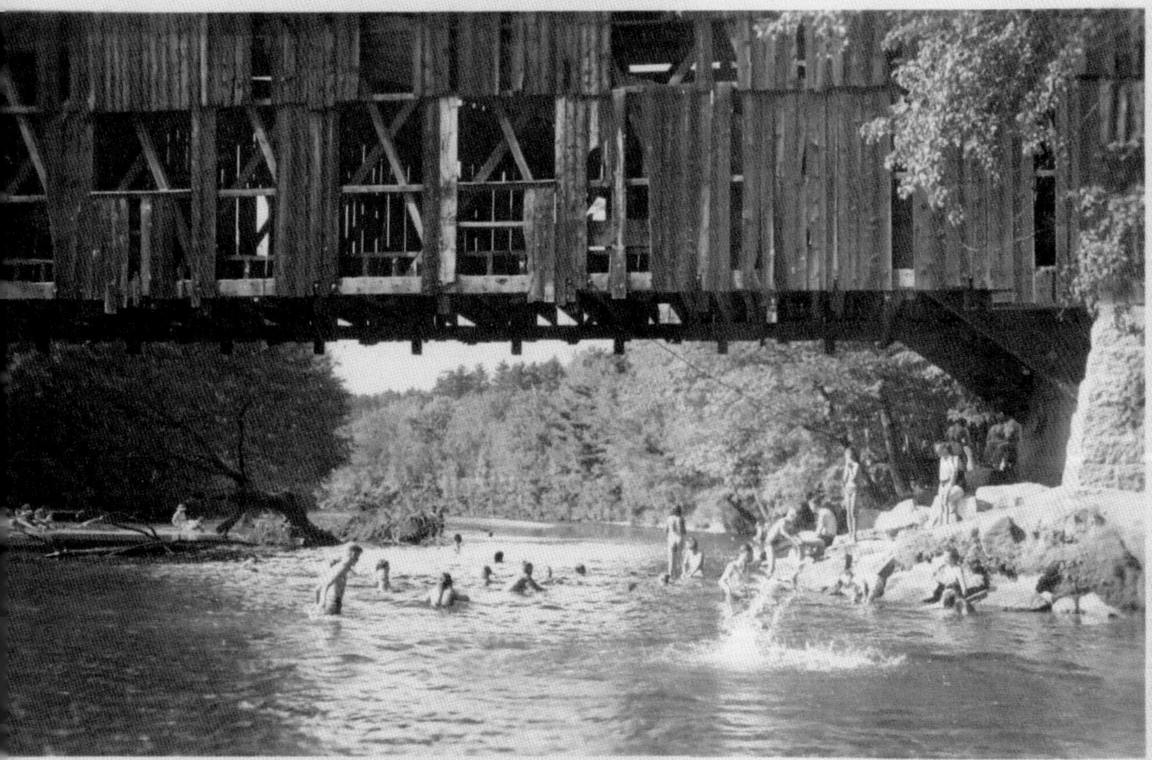

Saco River, North Conway, N. H.

The stone foundation supporting this bridge is made of granite from the Oak Street quarry, once owned by the Whitaker family, whose historic homestead is now Whitaker Woods Recreation Area. While red granite was quarried at the well-known Redstone quarry in nearby Redstone, most of the stone construction in North Conway was built with stone from the Whitaker quarry. Due to lack of maintenance, this bridge was missing boards from both sides, and eventually its upstream arch began to sag. In 1950, the town voted to replace it with a modern bridge. Many of the bridges around North Conway offer a swimming spot in the summer, and rope swings are often found nearby. (John Cannell collection.)

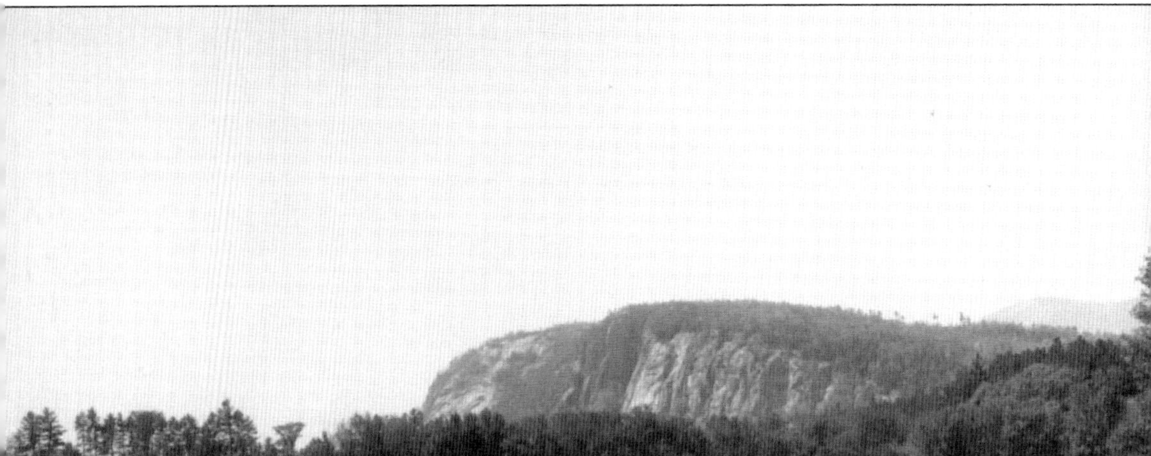

This floating footbridge was installed across the Saco River for the convenience of tourists wishing to walk to the ledges. The river, seen looking southwest toward Cathedral and White Horse Ledge, is rather wide at this section. If it were not for this simple pedestrian bridge, visits to the west side and its exotic features would have required a horse-drawn carriage, a horse itself, or lengthy hike. Covered bridges over the river were few and far between, and visitors would have had to cross using the North Conway covered bridge or travel even farther to cross in Conway to the south. This area offered a unique escape from the hustle and bustle of town. Natural attractions located off West Side Road include Cathedral and White Horse Ledge, Devil's Den, Diana's Baths, Pitman's Arch, and Echo Lake. (Henney History Room, Conway Public Library.)

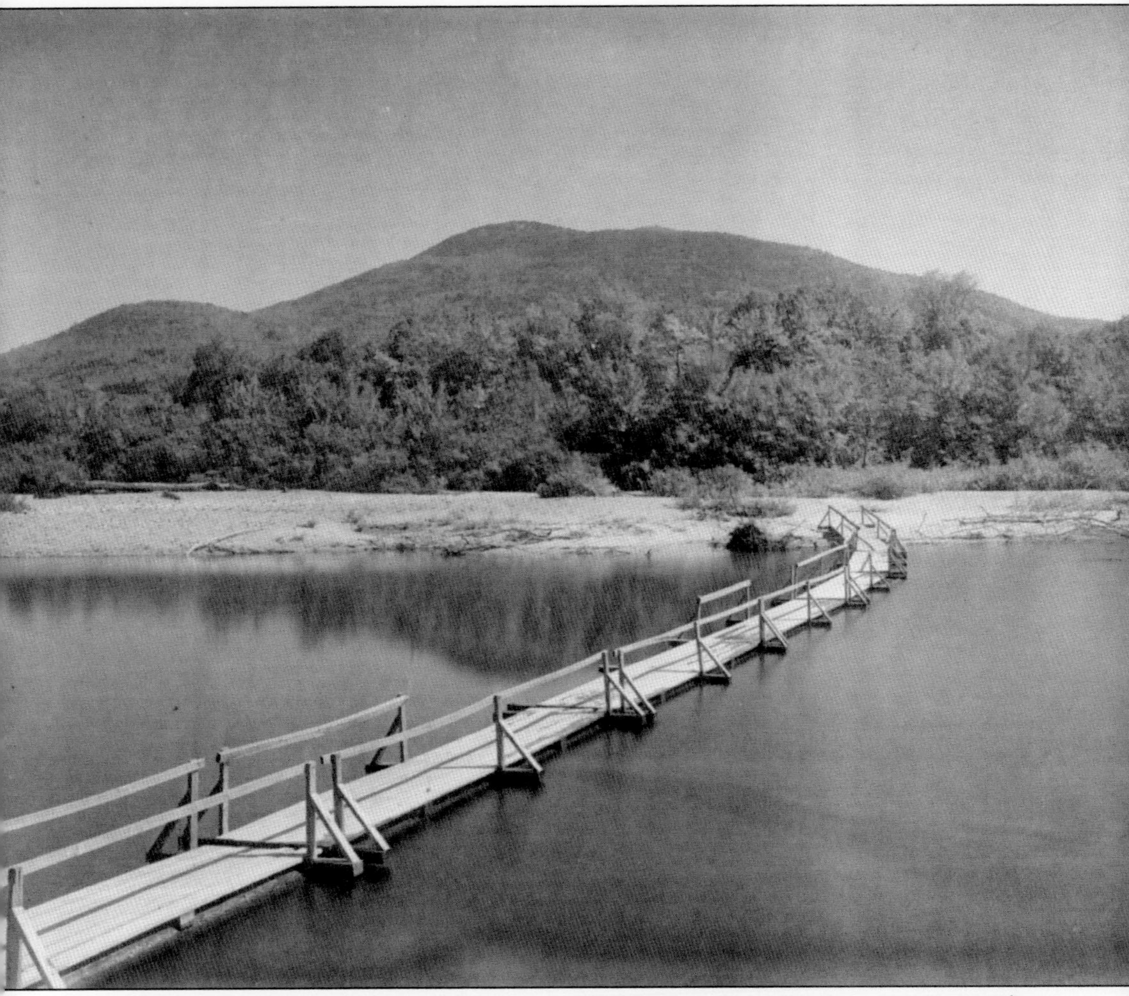

This bridge was an ingeniously designed, practical solution that allowed pedestrians to cross the river, combining dock, raft, and bridge construction techniques. The bridge is secured to the shore much like a boat dock or ramp. Underwater, logs spanned the length of each section and are covered with planks of wood to serve as the floor for each section. Angled braces extend off each side of the bridge section, providing stabilization for when the bridge was being traversed. A continuous handrail runs along the southern side of the bridge, while handrails are only intermittently placed on the northern side to allow access for swimming. No posts were sunk into the river bottom to secure the bridge into a stationary position, hence its name. (Henney History Room, Conway Public Library.)

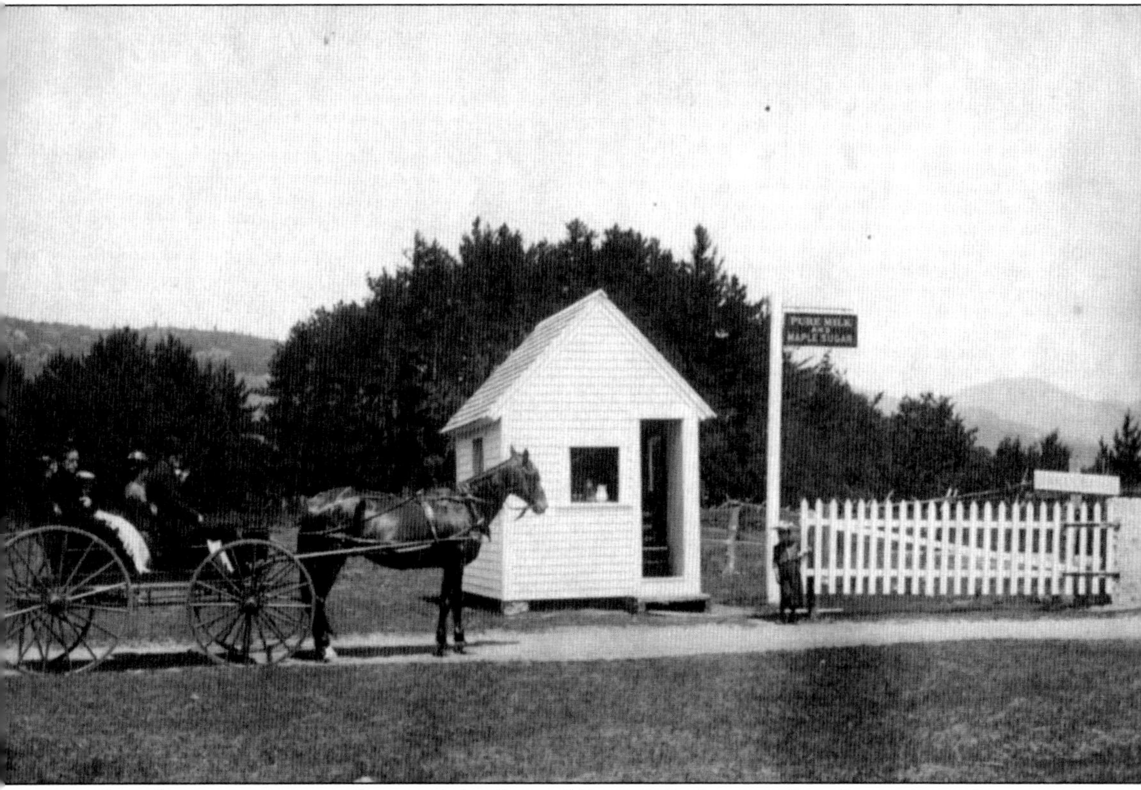

Local entrepreneurs made use of the draw of Diana's Baths to make a living. In order to visit, one had to pay a toll. Here, a young man guards the gate, opening it only to paying customers. The toll was collected in the small tollhouse, where visitors could also buy "Pure Milk and Maple Sugar" from the owner's farm. Diana's Baths is a beautiful natural feature with cascading falls and bathtub-shaped pools. (Conway Historical Society.)

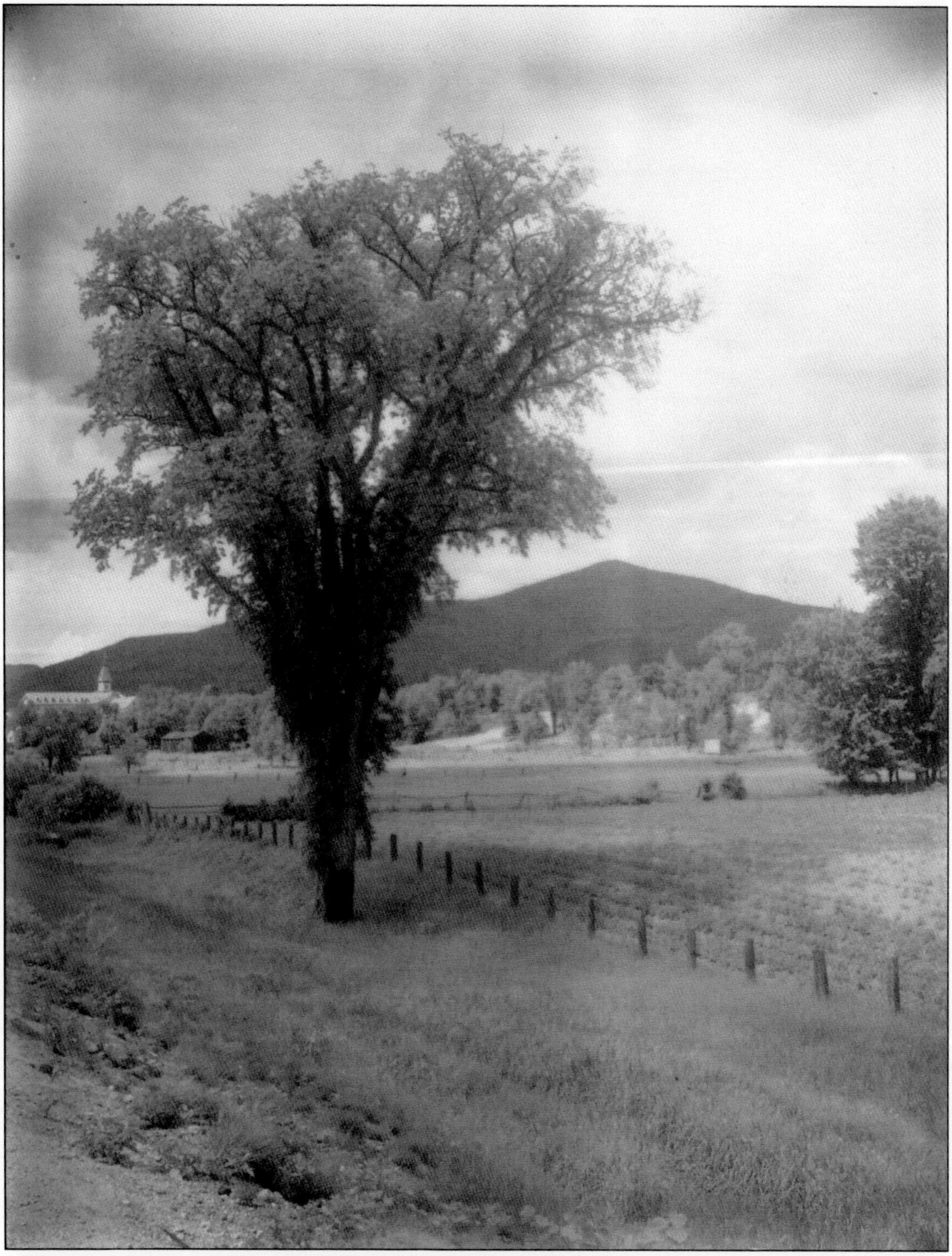

If North Conway village was not rural enough for folks, they could escape farther into the country by taking a small excursion to the west while still avoiding the truly wild mountains of the north. As visitors toured the farmlands, forests, caves, rivers, brooks, waterfalls, and other natural wonders off West Side Road, the town—civilization and safety—was still visible. The Kearsage House inn, located in downtown North Conway, is visible in the distance, and a barn, crops and a large sign are also seen in the photograph. Elms used to be seen all throughout the valley, but due to a blight that had to be eradicated, all the elms were destroyed. (Henney History Room, Conway Public Library.)

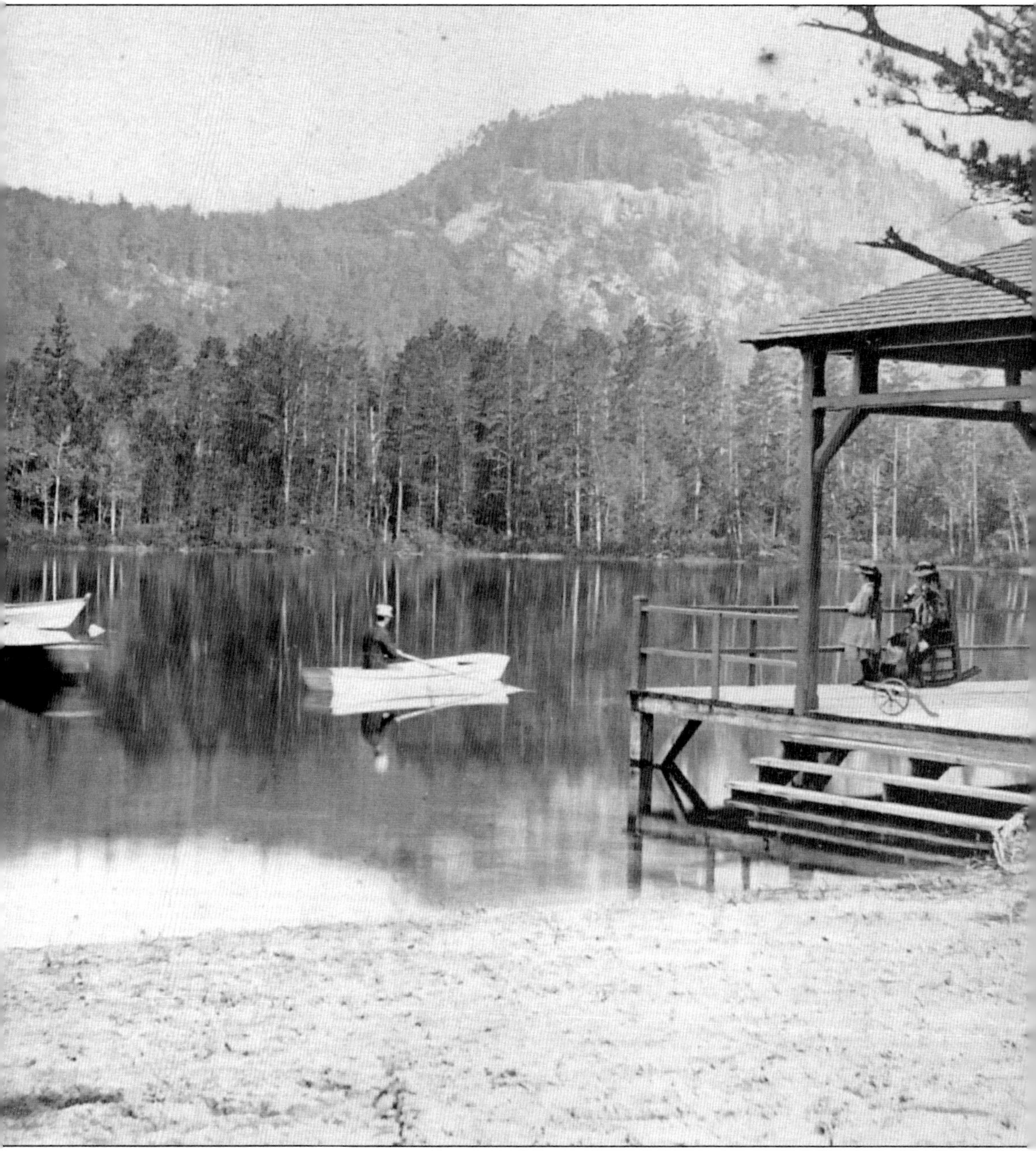

Echo Lake, located just a short distance from West Side Road, is only a few acres in size and offers a nice sandy shore. In the early days, boats were available to rent for pleasure cruising or fishing. A railroad guidebook published by the Boston and Maine Railroad in 1887 reported, "Just in front of these cliffs lies their mirror—Echo Lake. . . . The place seems dedicated to Silence itself. To destroy this illusion a man came out of a booth and touched off a small cannon. The effect was like knocking at half-a-dozen doors at once. And the silence which followed seemed all the deeper." This photograph shows a gazebo on shore with a group of finely dressed girls adorned with hats featuring flowing ribbons. A small cannon is also visible on the gazebo near the stairs, and several small boats are in use on the lake. (Henney History Room, Conway Public Library.)

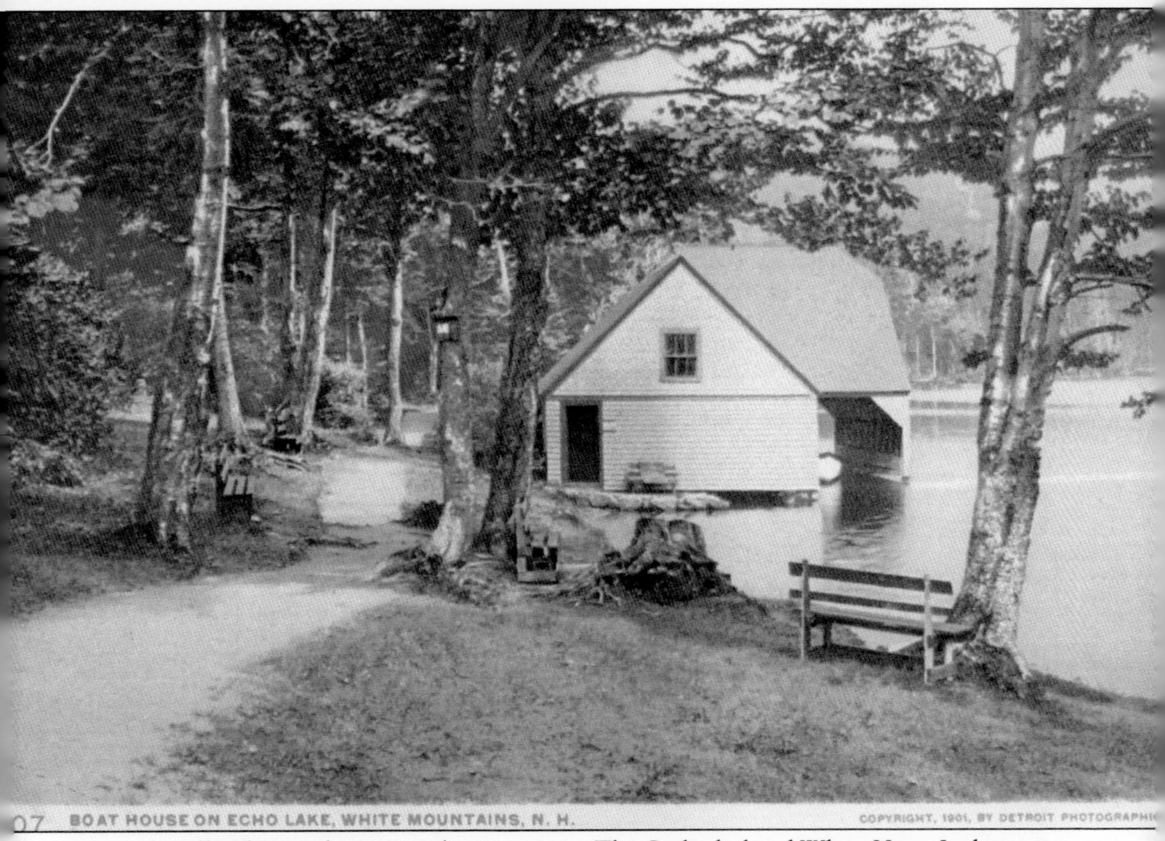

Echo Lake offered many fantastic sights to visitors. The Cathedral and White Horse Ledge were both visible from the shores of the lake, and a variety of rowboats were available to rent from the boathouse seen near the beach in this postcard. Guests could swim, boat, fish, and hike around the lake, as well as picnic, paint, take photographs, write, or simply rest and take in the fresh healing air and spring-fed waters. Echo Lake is now a state park, and the ledges are rock-climbing destinations. On any fair-weather day, climbers are on the face of Cathedral and White Horse Ledges. (John Cannell collection.)

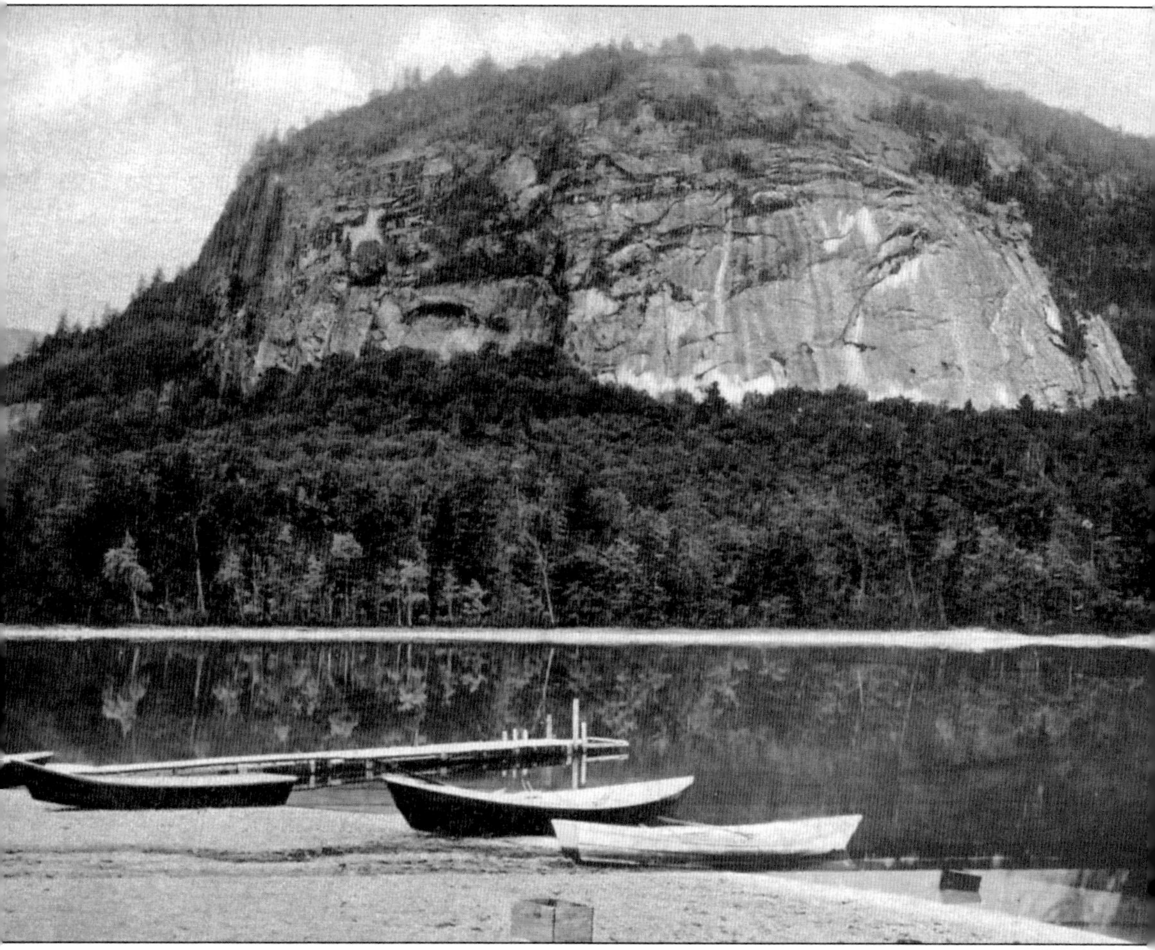

The "white horse," a patch of white quartz giving the illusion of a white horse ascending its side, is on the far left face of the ledge. An early guidebook explains that all marriageable ladies, maiden or widow, after running to see the white horse would count to 100, believing the next gentleman they meet will be their future husband. Today, White Horse Ledge is one of the major rock-climbing areas of New England. The cliff, more than 800 feet high, is divided into two sections: the Slabs area and the South Buttress area. (John Cannell collection.)

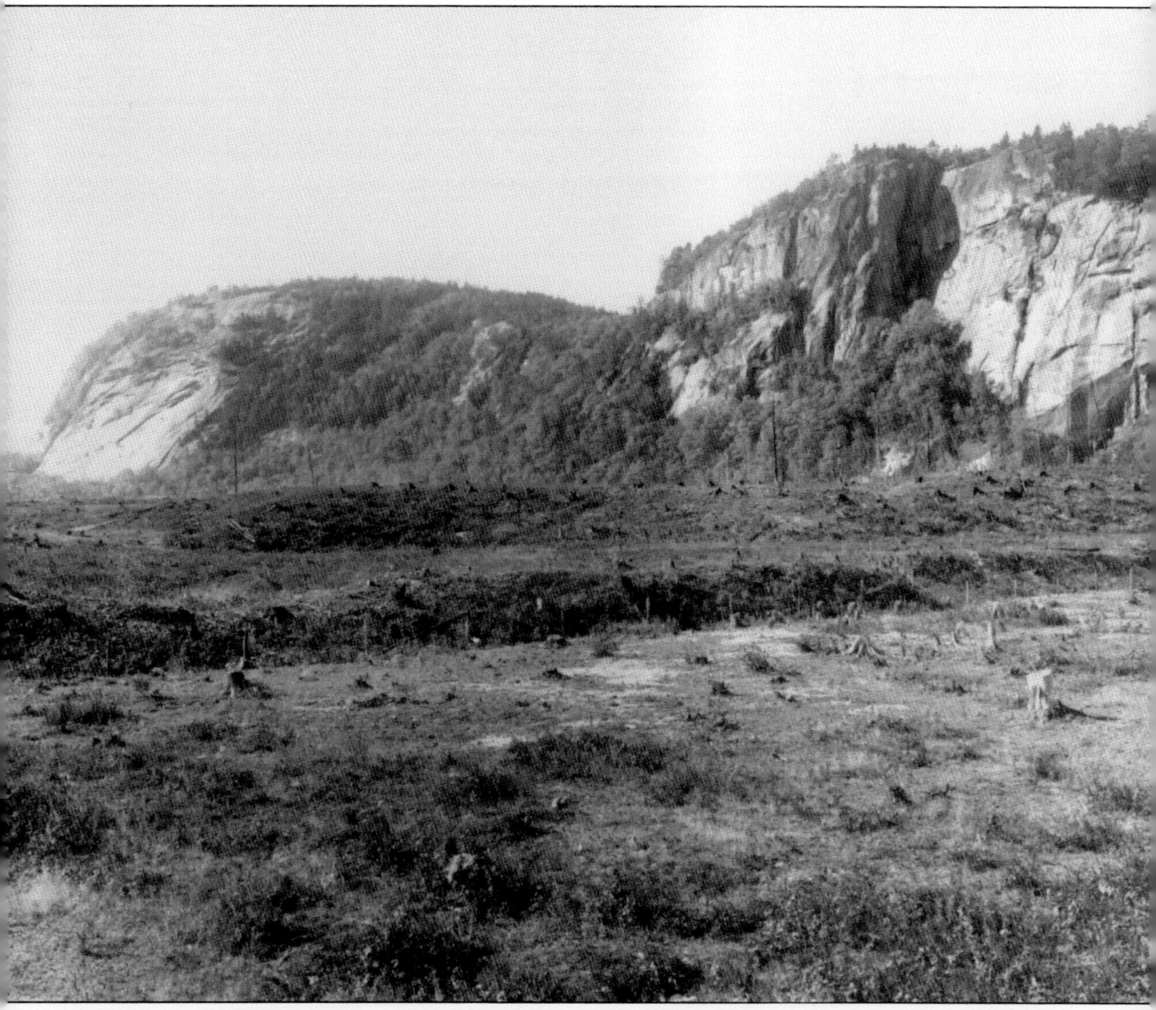

The trees in the foreground here have been clear-cut, providing an excellent view of the ledges, which are about seven-tenths of a mile apart. The forest has regrown and is called Cathedral Woods, not to be confused with the older Cathedral Woods across the Saco in Intervale. Until the forest preservation and restoration movement in the early 1900s and the corresponding Weeks Act of 1911, forests were seen as prime natural resources for lumber and, in many cases, were clear-cut. While this allowed for better views of some natural features, such as the ledges, it also caused great environmental stresses like the loss of wildlife, fires, and soil erosion. Thanks to legislation such as the Weeks Act, organizations such as the Society for the Preservation of New Hampshire Forests and the creation of the White Mountain National Forest, the land around the ledges has been reforested and is abundant with wildlife, artists, and recreation-seekers again. (Henney History Room, Conway Public Library.)

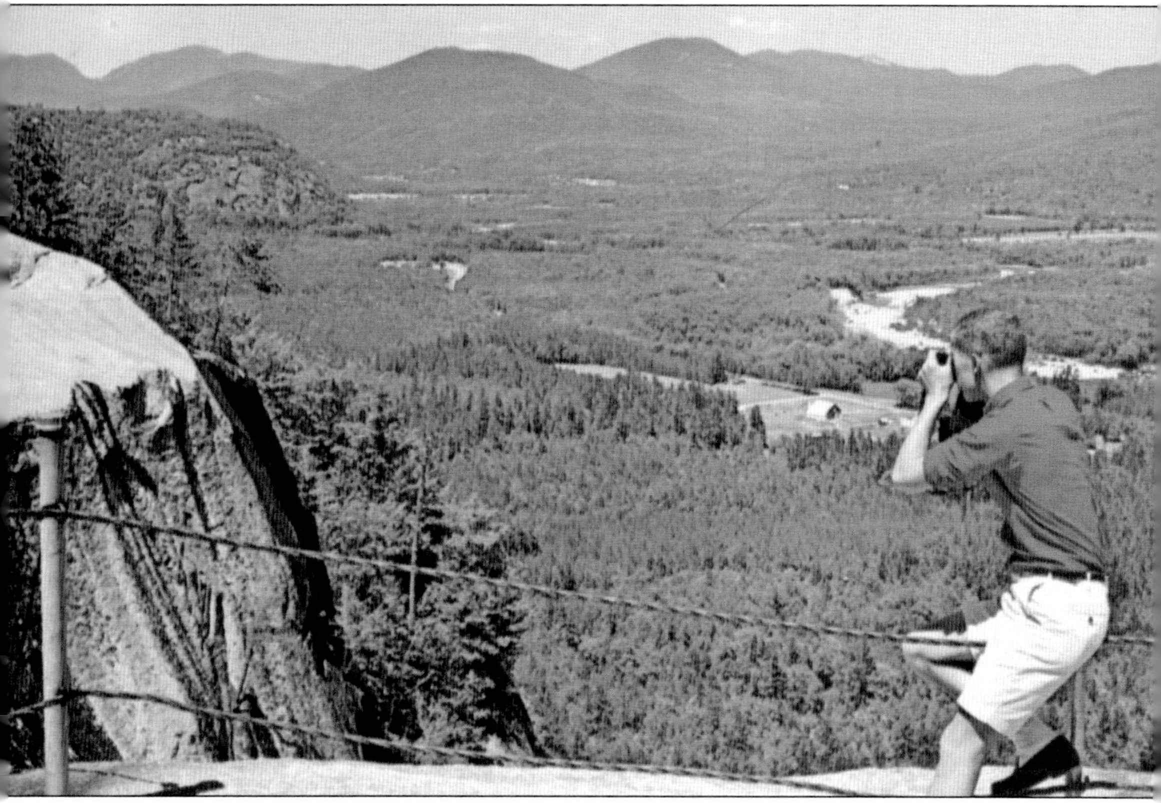

A road leads to the top of Cathedral Ledge, where a number of easily accessible hiking trails radiate out in several directions. With its 800-foot vertical wall, the ledge is very popular with rock climbers, and visitors are often surprised by a pair of hands and then the climber's head appearing up over the edge as they take in the sweeping views of the region. Part of Humphrey's Ledge and Carter Notch are visible beyond, and a farmer's fields and the winding Saco River are down in the valley below. This is one of the best locations in the area to enjoy a great view of the valley and surrounding mountains. The once-deforested slopes and valleys have again become lush woods, providing magnificent fall foliage in autumn. (Conway Historical Society.)

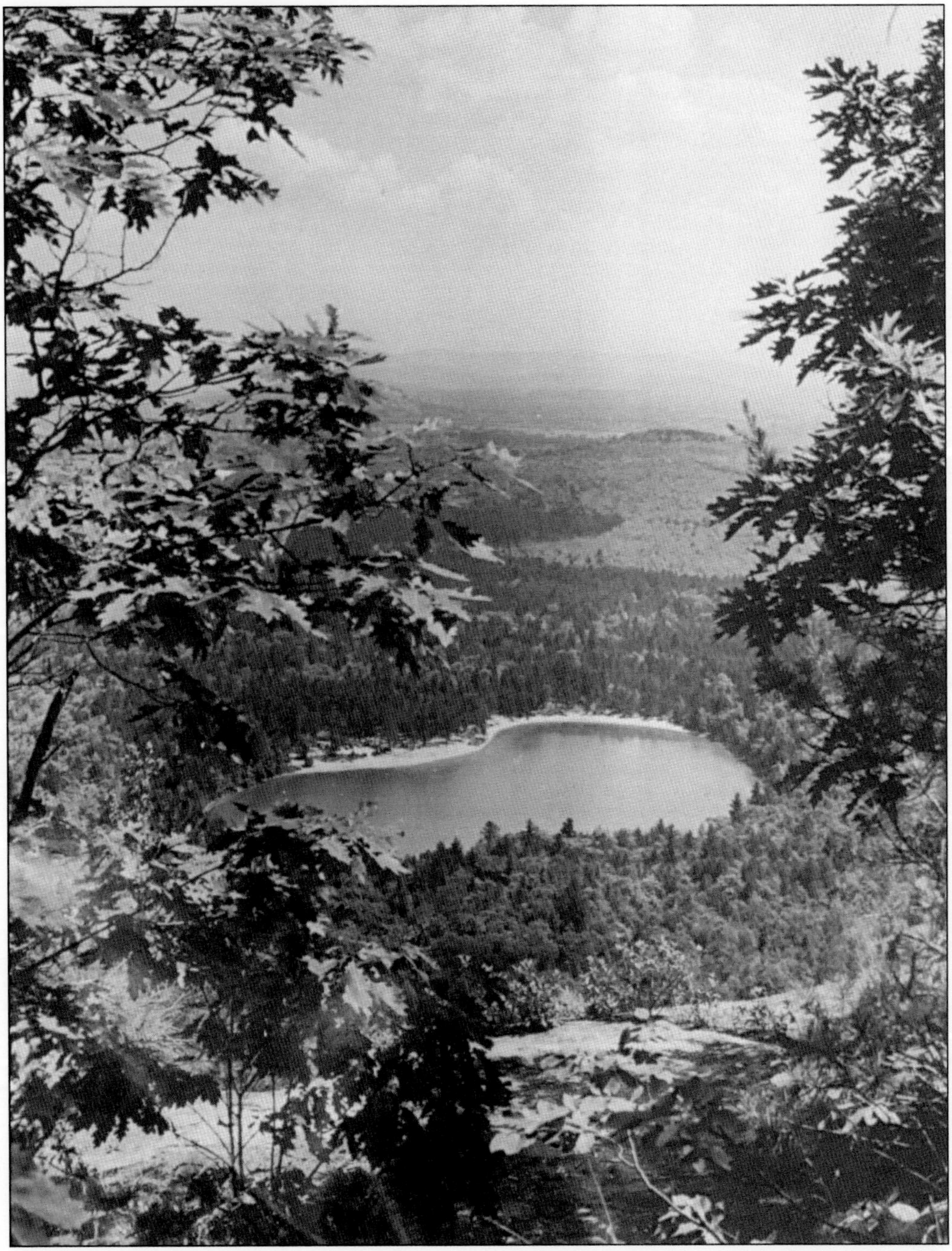

Around 12,000 years ago, New Hampshire was completely covered by a mile-thick glacier that gradually receded to the north. As it melted and moved, it reshaped the land beneath it, and boulders were slowly dragged across the land. Some were broken down into smaller rocks or into dirt, but some were stranded and are known today as glacier-era tics. Mountain faces were scraped, chipped, and shaped by moving rock, and rivers and brooks started to flow. In a process known as calving, blocks of ice fell off the glaciers as they moved, and melting ice created ponds and lakes. Echo Lake was formed when large blocks of ice calving from the front of a receding glacier became partially or wholly buried in sand and gravel. (Conway Historical Society.)

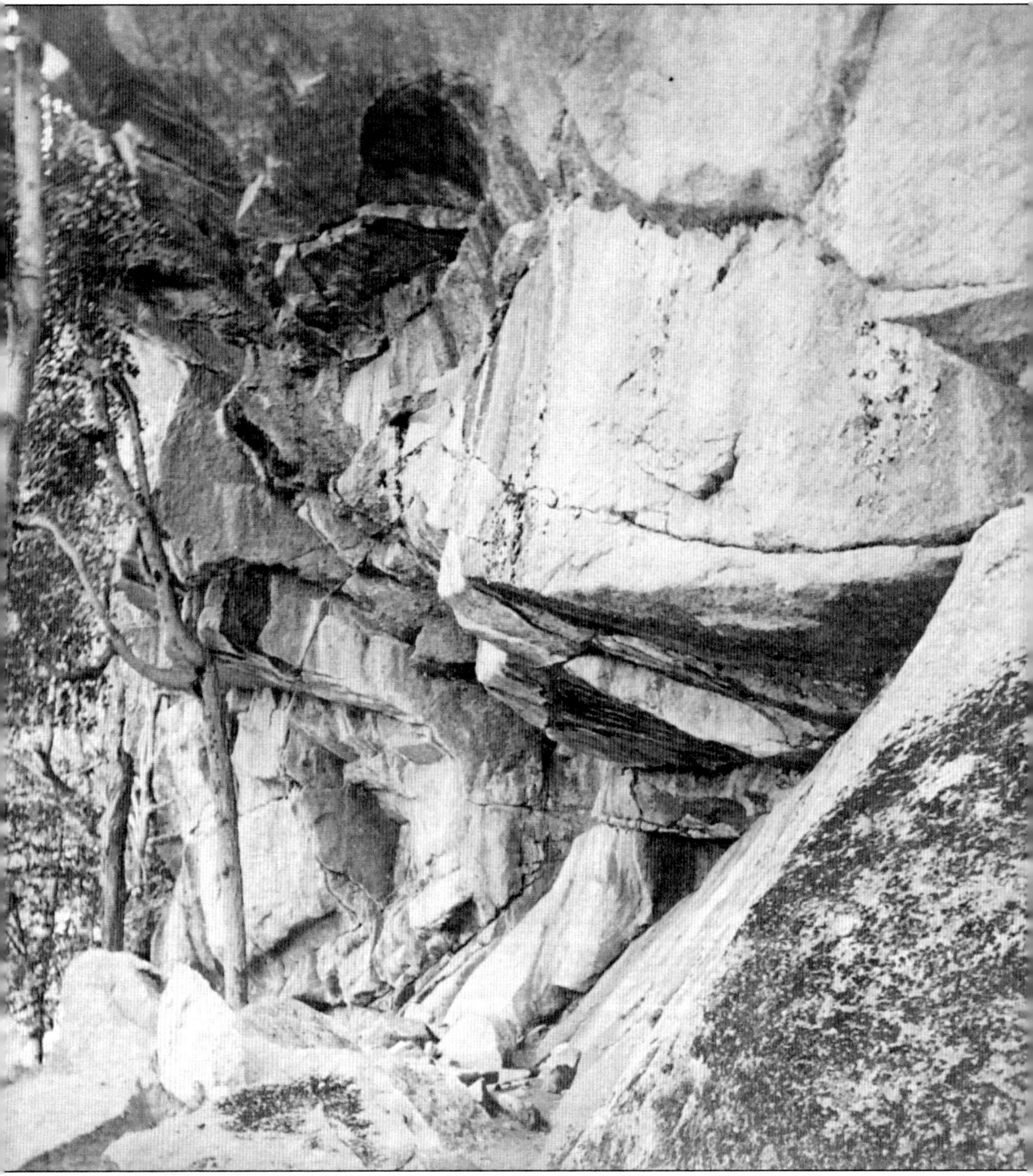

Long popular with area hikers, the Cathedral is an easy climb of 100 feet, carrying folks to a singular cavity in this ledge. Running waters, frosts, and storms have scooped and grooved its curves, and its appearance is similar to Gothic architecture. The cave is 40 feet deep and about 60 feet high, and the outermost rock of the roofing spans the entrance with an arch, half of which is as symmetrical as if an architect had planned it. The Cathedral seems to have been a common theme, as many local attractions share the name. The majestic, otherworldly appearance of these sites seems to evoke spiritual feelings and awe. Other examples are Cathedral Woods, Cathedral Ledge, and the Cathedral seen here. (Henney History Room, Conway Public Library.)

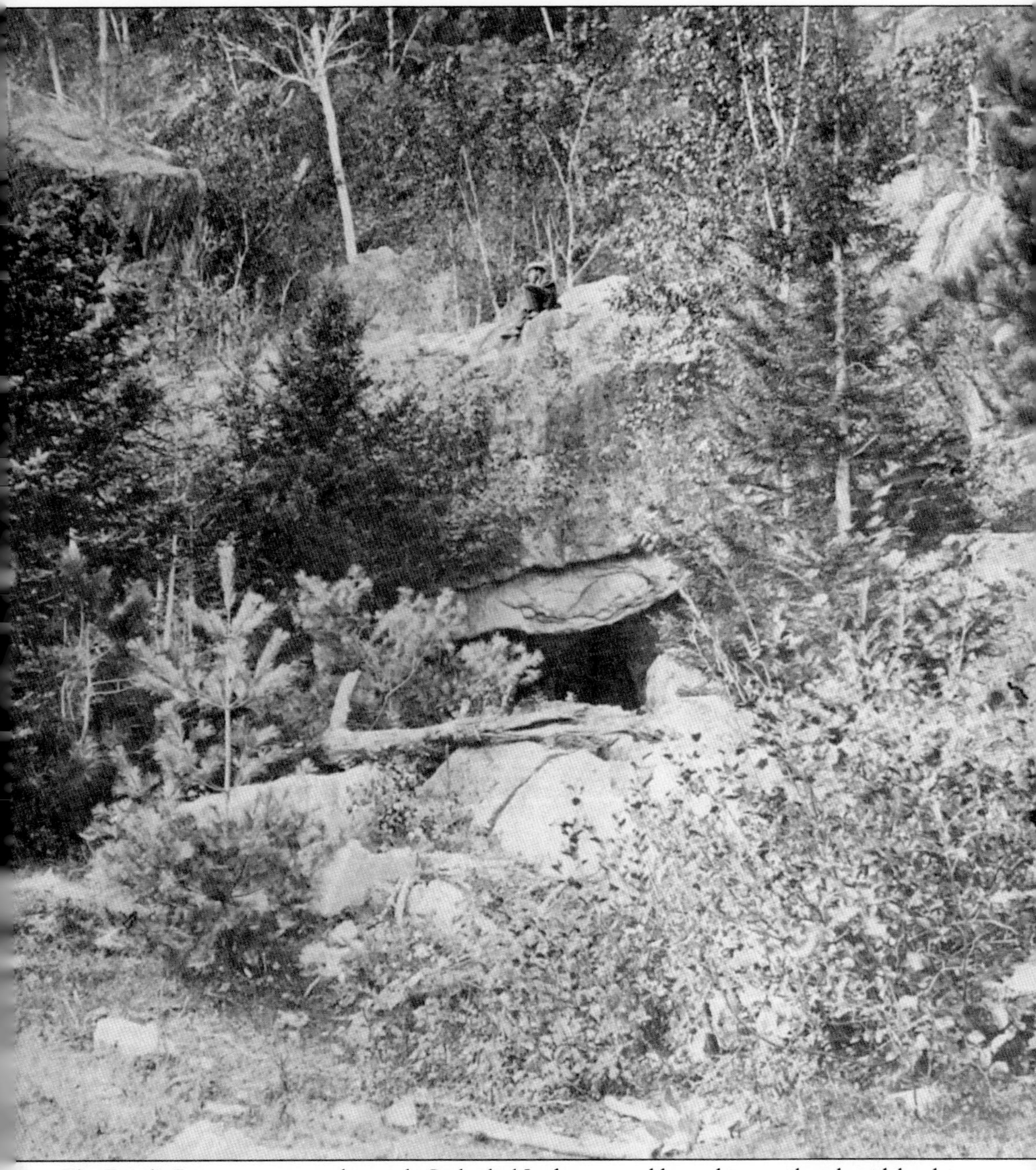

The Devil's Den, a cavern underneath Cathedral Ledge, was addressed in a railroad guidebook published by the Boston and Maine Railroad in 1887: "Go to the devil! To the Devil's Den we accordingly go. This abode of supposed evil is a cavern among fallen fragments underneath the Cathedral, reminding one of Herbert's remarks, No sooner is a temple built to God but the devil builds a chapel hard by." Although this is nothing more than a naturally created cavern, popular legends and folktales are full of stories of magical good and evil creatures or wild animals such as bears living in caves like the Devil's Den and the surrounding cliff area. These vivid images obviously made a lasting impression upon those who named the attractions. (Henney History Room, Conway Public Library.)

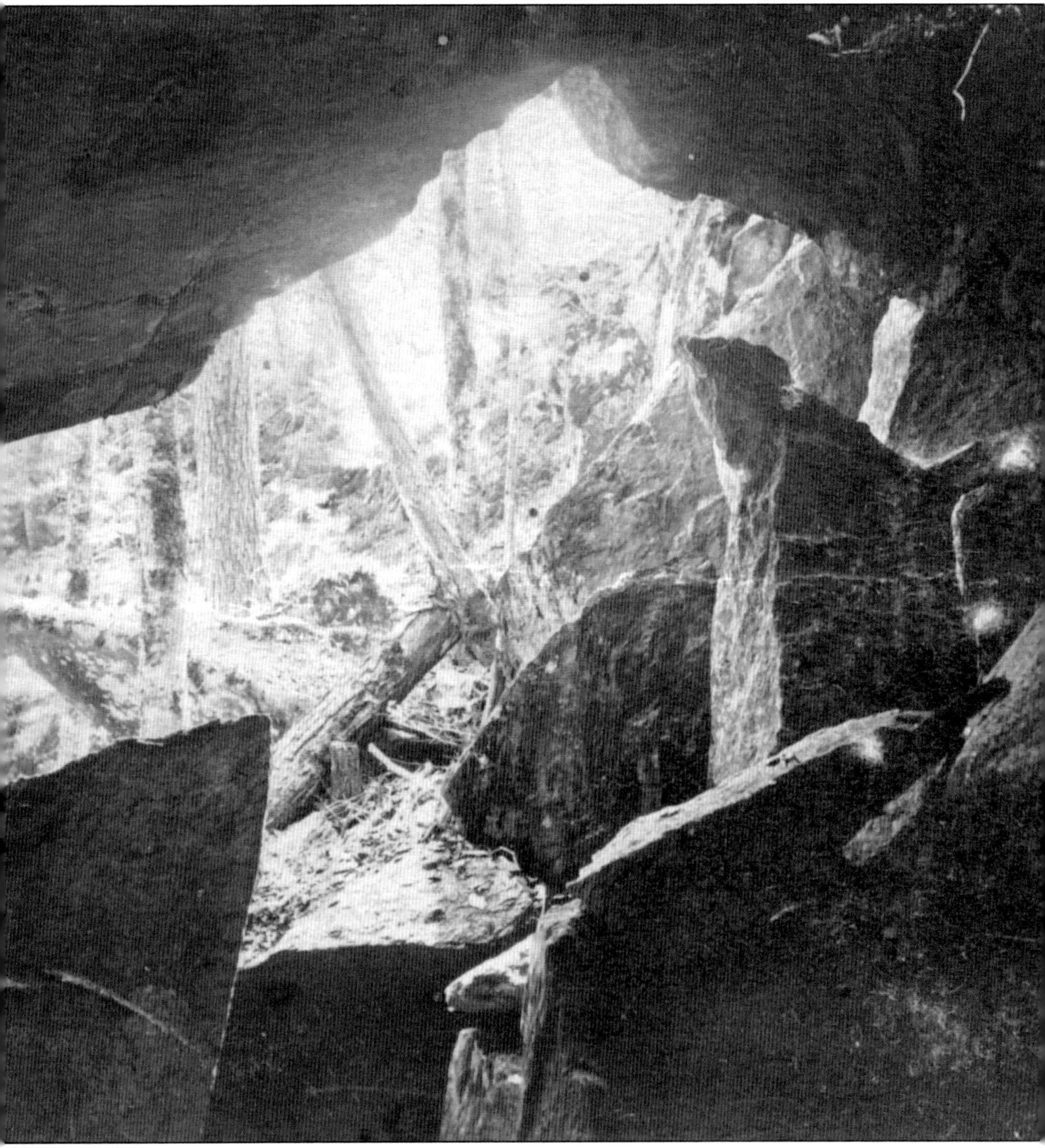

While the view of the Devil's Den was scary enough from the outside, a few brave souls ventured inside the den itself. This photograph shows the view from within the den looking out onto the ledge. Rocks that have fallen from the roof or walls lie scattered on the floor. Their jagged, foreboding appearance only enhanced the common belief that this place was evil, with its devil's mouth leading into the den or lair. Even if people did not actually believe these superstitions, it was fun to tell scary stories about it after a visit to the Devil's Den. When the area was clear-cut, the den was more easily seen from a distance, but as the forest returned, it has became more hidden from view. Finding the Devil's Den became more of an adventure, usually requiring the guidance of one who had already been there and lived to tell the tale. (Conway Historical Society, photograph by Nathan W. Pease.)

Until the late 1930s, skiing had been a sport for an adventurous few thrill-seekers in North Conway. Early skiers did not have the luxury of ski lifts, rope tows, groomed trails, base lodges, warming huts, or restrooms, so they would strap seal skin onto their skis and hike up the slope to the top or carry their skis and hike up in their boots. Once at the top, they removed the skins or adorned their skis and careened down the mountain on rough, un-groomed trails. If that was not difficult or thrilling enough, some chose to ski jump. The Cathedral Ledge area was a place of choice for such insanity, and these photographs show skiers coming down as throngs of spectators look on. (Both, Henney History Room, Conway Public Library.)

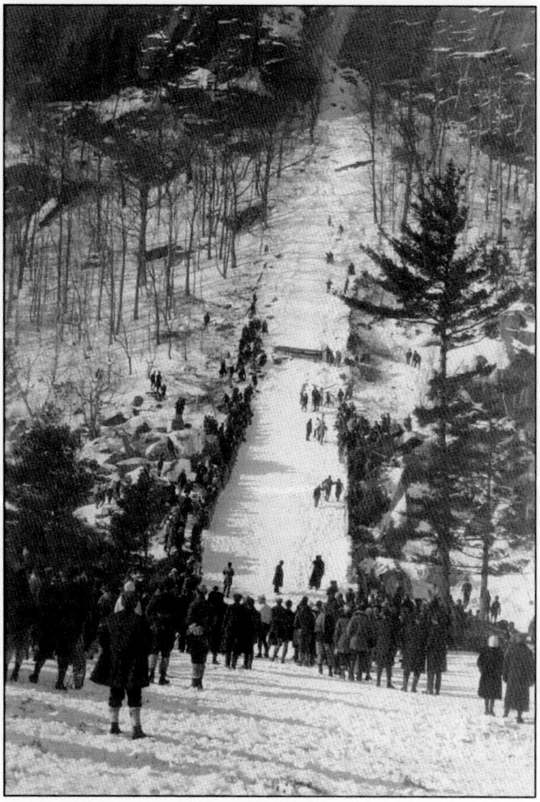

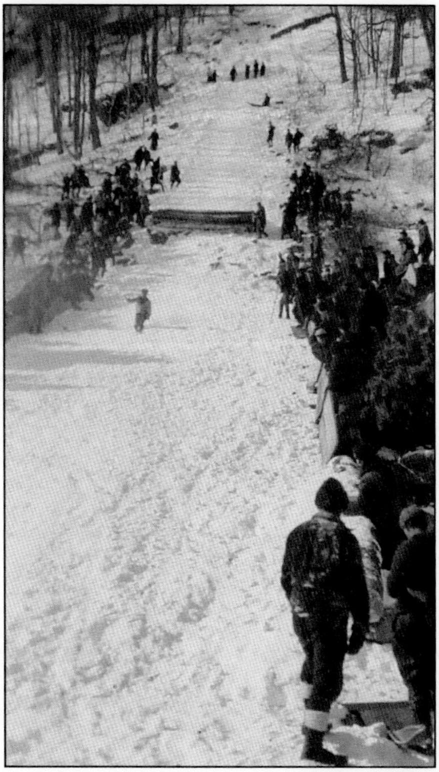

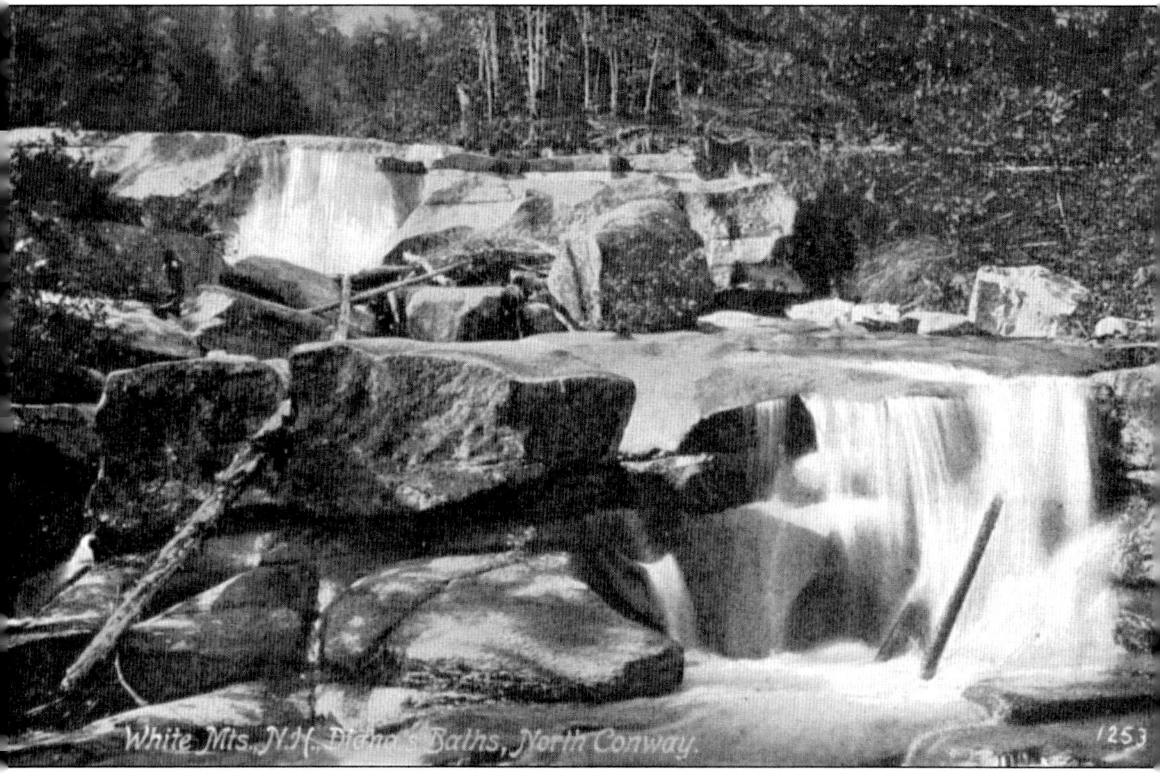

The trailhead for Diana's Baths is located about eight-tenths of a mile north of Cathedral Ledge, just south of the Bartlett town line. Glaciers and erosion have created a complex and interesting mix of angular and smooth sculptural shapes along Lucy Brook, and there is a long series of waterfalls and pools. All along the stream, numerous potholes, some as much as 10 feet in diameter and 10 feet deep, still contain the rounded stones that carved them out. The baths are still a popular sunbathing, swimming, picnicking, and hiking destination for locals and tourists alike, and the cool falling waters and deep bathtub-like pools provide much-needed respite from the summer heat and hay fever. (Henney History Room, Conway Public Library.)

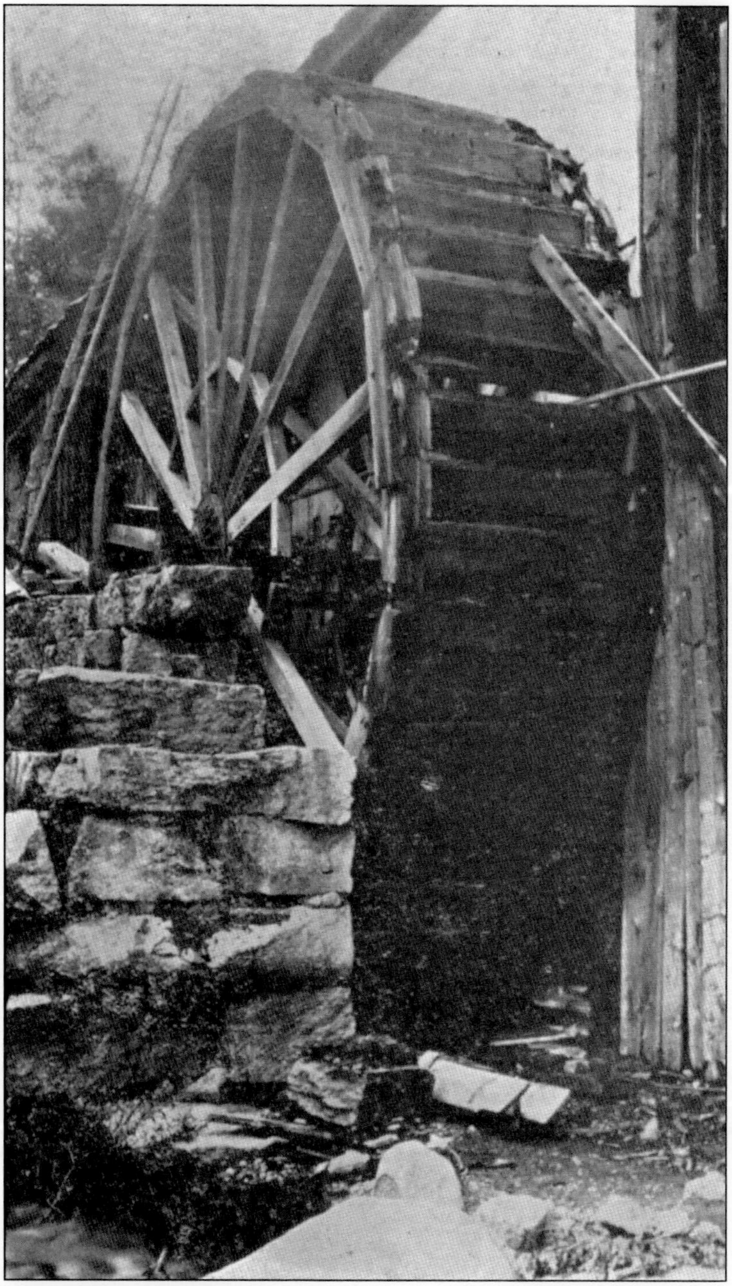

The area is blessed with numerous rivers that were necessary for powering the various mills early towns desired, such as gristmills for grain, lumber mills, textile mills, and later belt-driven machines for industry. The waterwheel at Lucy Mill, seen here, provided power for George Lucy's sawmill in the 1860s. In the 1890s, he built a 12-room boardinghouse for tourists to visit the site. In the 1930s, Chester Lucy built a concrete dam with a water feed and turbine system to replace the waterwheel and power the sawmill. Both the rooming house and sawmill were eventually sold to the US government and are now part of national forest land. Due to deterioration, the buildings were removed from the site in the 1960s, but remnants can still be seen today, including the old cellar holes and parts of the dam system, feed tube, and turbine gears. (Conway Historical Society.)

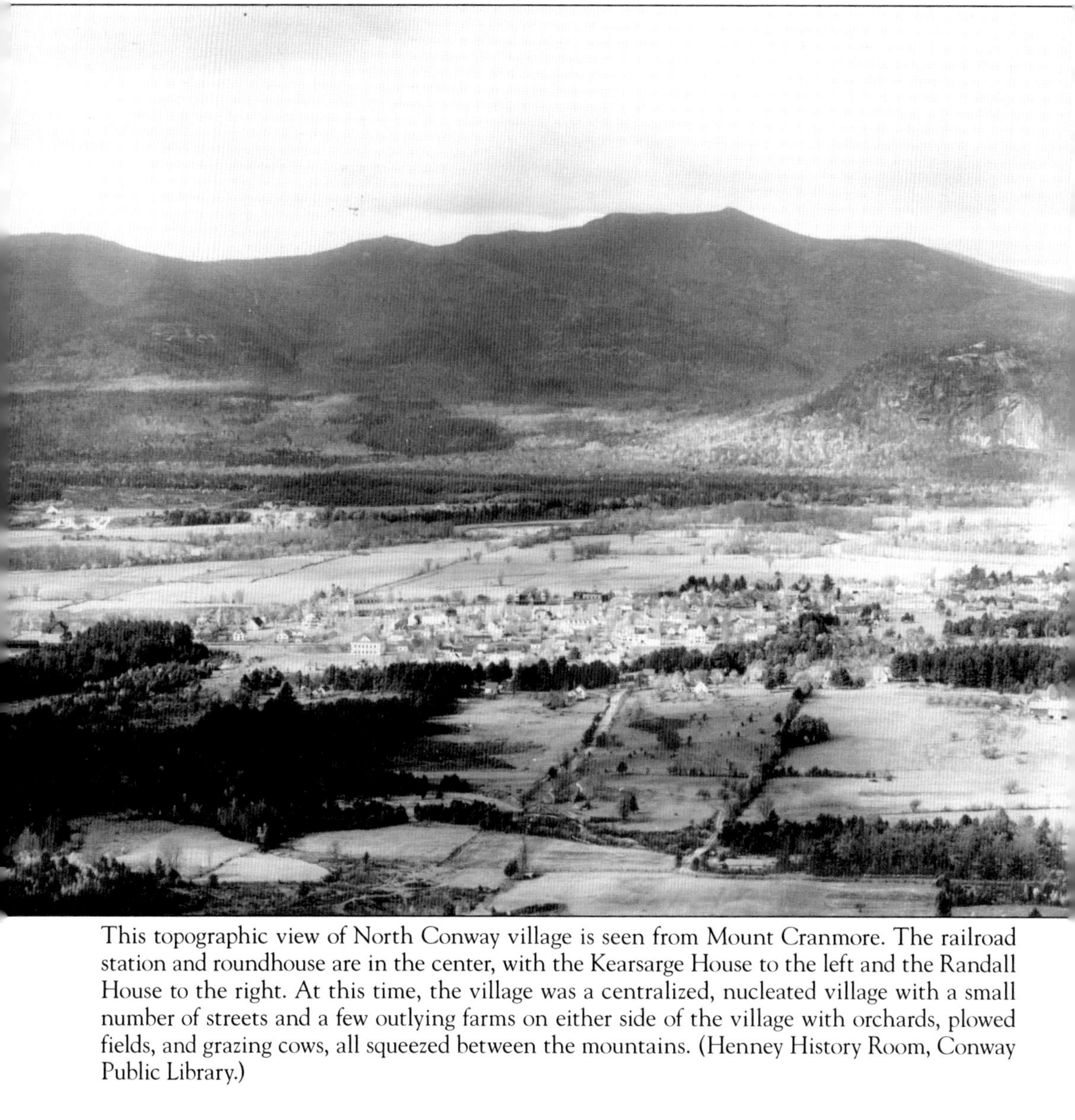

This topographic view of North Conway village is seen from Mount Cranmore. The railroad station and roundhouse are in the center, with the Kearsarge House to the left and the Randall House to the right. At this time, the village was a centralized, nucleated village with a small number of streets and a few outlying farms on either side of the village with orchards, plowed fields, and grazing cows, all squeezed between the mountains. (Henney History Room, Conway Public Library.)

Seven

Conclusion

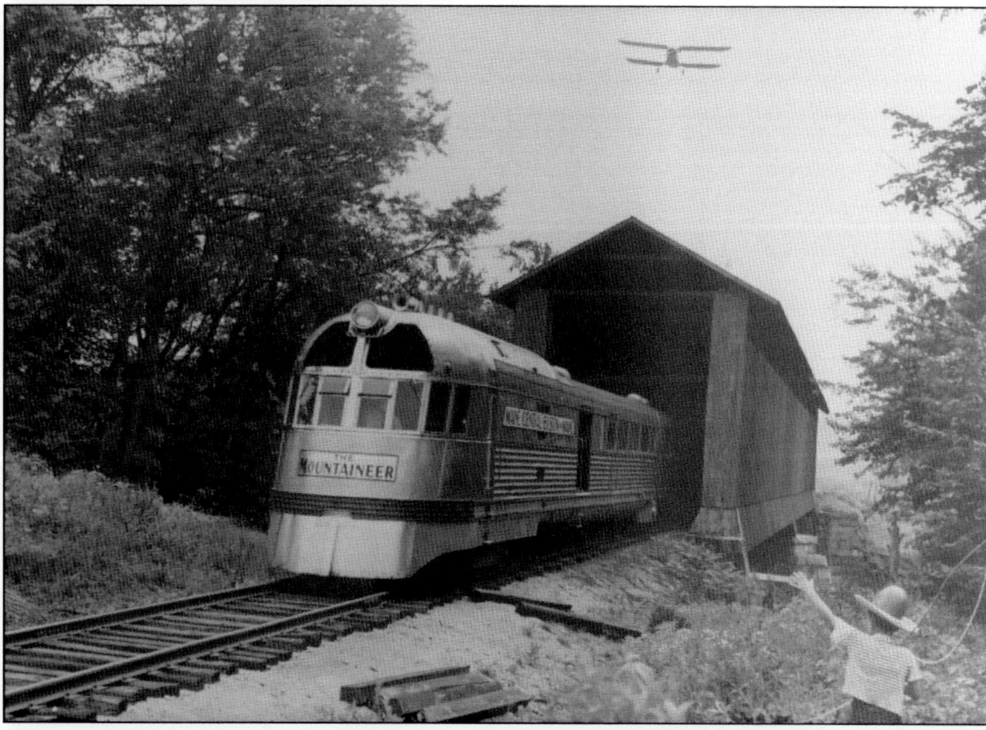

This photograph of the *Mountaineer*, belonging to the Boston & Maine/Maine Central Railroad, was carefully arranged, with its wooden covered bridge, the country boy fishing, and the biplane flying overhead, capturing the challenges and opportunities of balancing tradition and change in the Eastern Slope region. The streamlined, stainless-steel train seen here is currently being restored and also saw service under other names such as the *Flying Yankee*, the *Chesire*, and the *Minute Man*. (North Conway Public Library, photograph by James M. Bray.)

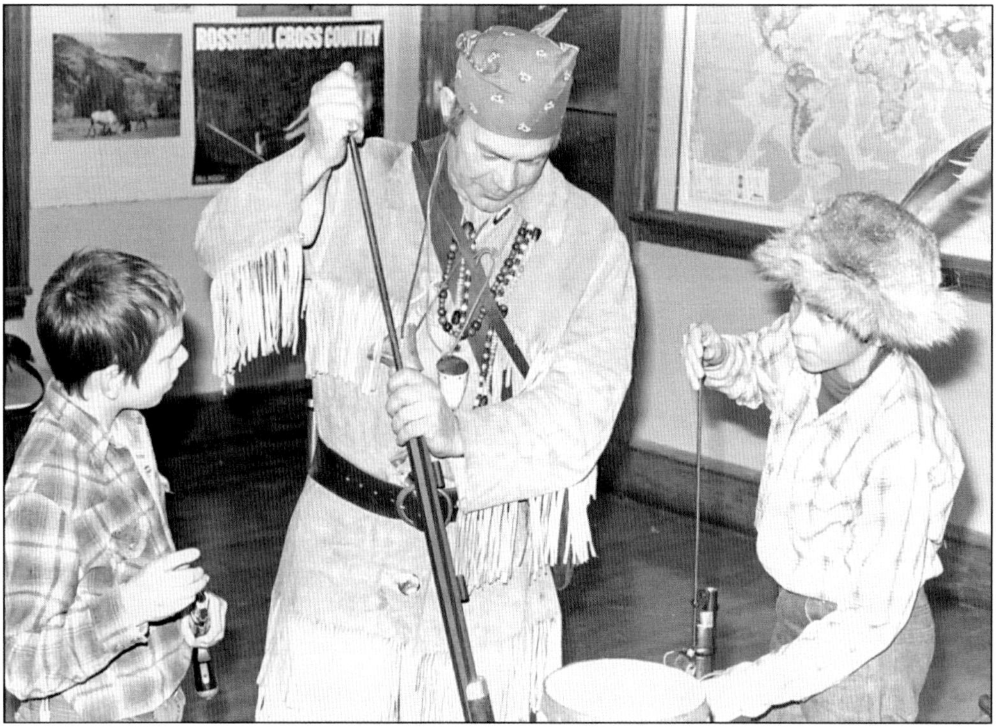

Conway was chartered in 1765 by colonial governor Benning Wentworth, and the town celebrated its bicentennial in 1965 with numerous living history programs and community events. Bob Duncan photographed the beard-growing contest and many of the town's business employees in historical costume in front of their patriotically decorated workplaces. There were exhibits of White Mountain art, quilt demonstrations, historic house tours, special historically themed church services, rock-climbing demonstrations, Abenaki Indian programs, old-time ball games, historical pageants, puppet shows, storytelling, firemen's musters, parades, antique auto shows, costume balls, special lectures and publications, commemorative plates and buttons, walking and driving tours, and much more. In 2015, the town will celebrate its 250th anniversary with these and similar events, including reenactments of early settler life where folks will learn about loading flintlock muskets, using powder horns, and cooking with cast iron. (Both, Henney History Room, Conway Public Library.)

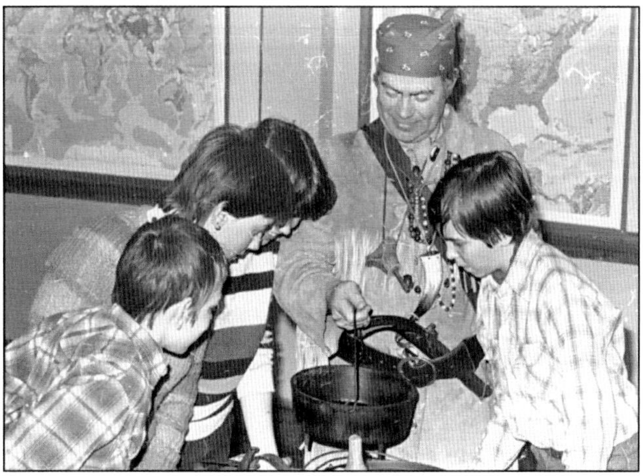

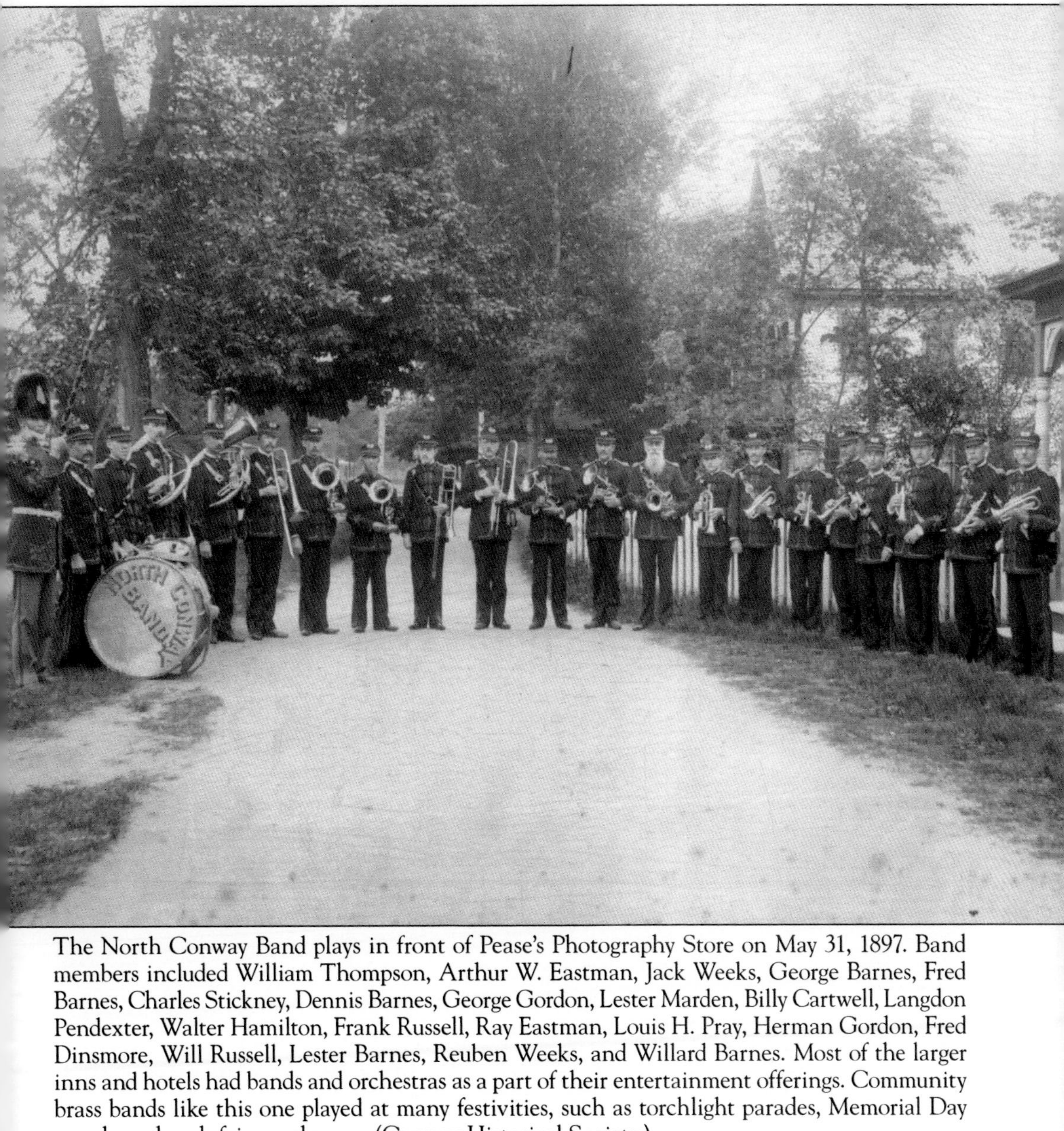

The North Conway Band plays in front of Pease's Photography Store on May 31, 1897. Band members included William Thompson, Arthur W. Eastman, Jack Weeks, George Barnes, Fred Barnes, Charles Stickney, Dennis Barnes, George Gordon, Lester Marden, Billy Cartwell, Langdon Pendexter, Walter Hamilton, Frank Russell, Ray Eastman, Louis H. Pray, Herman Gordon, Fred Dinsmore, Will Russell, Lester Barnes, Reuben Weeks, and Willard Barnes. Most of the larger inns and hotels had bands and orchestras as a part of their entertainment offerings. Community brass bands like this one played at many festivities, such as torchlight parades, Memorial Day marches, church fairs, and so on. (Conway Historical Society.)